W9-CXT-924

Nudes in Landscape (191)

Analysis, page 393

The Art of
CEZANNE

BY

ALBERT C. BARNES

&

VIOLETTE de MAZIA

WITH 171 ILLUSTRATIONS

Published by

THE BARNES FOUNDATION PRESS

MERION, PENNA.

PREFACE

This volume embodies a systematic study of the features of Cézanne's work that determine its characteristic form. The method employed in the study is that of science, and hence involves two aspects or phases. Objectively, scientific method is a record of actual physical characteristics, the qualities of whatever object or process is to be explained, and the record can be verified by any properly qualified observer. Subjectively, it is an intellectual process, a plan or program of experimentation, which depends for its success upon the endowment and training of the investigator, the sensitiveness of his perceptions, the acuteness of his intelligence, the accuracy of his discrimination between essential and accidental. These two phases, while distinguishable in the abstract, are actually co-implicated in every fruitful investigation. Without constant reference to objective fact, reflection sinks into reverie; without reference to general principles, to ideas or hypotheses suggested by the funded experience of the investigator, observation becomes mechanical registration, an inventory of meaningless detail. It is the interaction of the subjective and objective in a continuously unfolding process that constitutes experience: experience, in other words, is the perception of meanings in any field of human activity.

The essential identity of experience in all its forms points the way to a study of art by the same method that has proved so fruitful in the understanding of nature. A work of art is part of the material world, with its own components and a distinctive method of organization which endows it with characteristic identity or form. In a painting these components are color, light, line, and space, and their union constitutes what we have termed "plastic form." Plastic form embodies the artist's experience of a particular situation in life; it is the expression of his personality and is as distinctive, as individual to him, as his physical and mental make-up. Its value depends upon the depth and range of the experience expressed in it, upon the extent to which the painter has assimilated the traditions of art and made them instrumental to a penetrating and comprehensive vision of his own. As he develops in sensitivity and power of organization, his form incorporates in itself more and more of the universal values of experience, both human and plastic, and at the same time becomes more completely and significantly individual.

The problem of the observer is to recognize this individuality and to share the values communicated in and through it. He must be able to identify plastic form when he encounters it in a picture, that is, to distinguish between an organic union of insights won by personal experience, and plastic clichés assembled according to a stereotyped formula. He must, in brief, *learn to see,* and the process is long and arduous, involving as it does constant practice in the sharpening of perceptions of color, of the play of light and shadow, of the sequence and rhythm of line and mass, of the inter-relationships between these factors that endow each of them with meaning. It requires a knowledge of the traditions of painting and of the technical means by which the artist works. Competently applied, the process yields results inaccessible to casual or untrained observation, and when guided by scientific method it develops an objective criterion or standard of judgment of the same order of certitude as the findings of pure science.

Our efforts to apply the scientific method to a study of Cézanne's work has required a *detailed* examination of his technique and form, as they emerged throughout the course of his development. The investigation began twenty-five years ago, and by 1925 had reached a stage that seemed to warrant publication of a section, entitled "The Development of Cézanne's Technique," in the first edition of our book "The Art in Painting." [1] This chapter was omitted from subsequent editions because continued study of a steadily increasing number of Cézanne's pictures showed the data upon which it was based to have been inadequate. Our study, as presented herewith, amplifies the earlier investigation by including the significant findings of detailed analyses of practically all of Cézanne's important paintings, from the beginning to the end of his career.

The qualities that make Cézanne's work seem strange, baffling and often incomprehensible to the casual observer are the reflection of traits intrinsic to his extraordinary personality, traits which are the main source of his power and individuality as a painter. The connection between his distinctive achievements in art

[1] See Albert C. Barnes, "The Art in Painting" (first edition), pp. 484-498, Barnes Foundation Press, Merion, Pa., 1925.

and his personal eccentricities and limitations is the subject of the chapter on his life and psychology, and is further developed in the chapter entitled "Cézanne and Renoir."

Cézanne's rank as an artist can be judged adequately only in the light of a knowledge of how he used the accumulated capital of the great traditions of the past to achieve his own expression. And his importance as a stimulus to significant painting subsequent to his own is best revealed by a review of what phases or aspects of his form have been utilized creatively by contemporary artists. In order to show this continuity of tradition, we have traced Cézanne's derivations in antecedent painters, and have presented a brief account of some of the later artists who have drawn upon Cézanne's contributions in creating forms individual to themselves.

ALBERT C. BARNES
VIOLETTE DE MAZIA

Merion, Pa., January, 1939

CONTENTS

xi

CONTENTS

LIST OF ILLUSTRATIONS

CEZANNE

xiii

DELACROIX

THE ART OF CEZANNE

CHAPTER I

THE GENERAL CHARACTER
OF CEZANNE'S FORM

To the uninitiated, Cézanne's paintings seem strange to the point of bizarreness, alien to all the traditions of painting; but to the student who has grasped the essential nature of these traditions and observed their evolution, the novelty, the bizarreness in Cézanne's work are the identifying marks of a profoundly individual vision, in which the forms basic to some of the greatest works of art in history are re-created and revitalized.

The essential and fundamental effect of Cézanne's form, in its best estate, is the quality of power, rendered in legitimate painting terms. Perhaps no other painter has so successfully made power the keynote of his design; not even Michelangelo, whose means were partly sculptural, partly literary, and whose effects are in consequence largely vitiated by a confusion of values. Cézanne, taking the dynamic relation of planes and solid color-volumes in deep space as the principal theme of his paintings, does not duplicate sculpturesque surface-effects or devices, and the intensity of drama in which his power largely resides is practically independent of represented action. Except in the pictures of his apprenticeship, influenced by Tintoretto, the late Venetians, the Spaniards, Delacroix, Daumier, Courbet, and Manet, and painted before he had mastered the traditions and made them his own, the illustrative aspect of his work is relatively negligible. There is in his mature work abundance of movement, but it is plastic activity, that is, the result of the interplay of the essential components of the form, not depicted narrative. His figures are human beings only in broadest essentials: psychological characterization, as one finds it in Goya or Rembrandt or even Renoir, is absent, and little or no emphasis is put on the particular thing the subjects happen to be doing. Fundamentally, they are static: not inert or dead, but active as a tower, a pier or a buttress is active. The drama in which they take part is an interplay of ab-

3

stract tensions and forces, not one of human incident and personal emotion.

The term which most accurately describes Cézanne's form is architectonic. The characteristics which are absolutely indispensable in architecture—solidity, weight, equilibrium, the balance of forces—are those which are most in evidence in his work. In a good building there can be no mass which is not supported, no thrust not taken up by some counterthrust, no force exerted which is not planned and provided for: design is a practical as well as an esthetic necessity, and improvisation in essentials is an impossibility. The same is true of Cézanne's forms: they are designed and they are composed—composed not only in the usual sense of having their parts disposed in an orderly arrangement, but in the sense in which we speak of a person's "composure" as equivalent to his balance or poise. The exceedingly deliberate and purposeful character of Cézanne's pictures will be confirmed and illustrated by our study of his use of the plastic means; but even the first impression of his work, as received by a sensitive observer, is that of a systematically planned architectural structure.

Cézanne's form, however, is not merely architectonic, it is also monumental. Not in the representative sense, of course: no one ever employed more unpretentious subject-matter, or avoided more completely any associations of grandiosity. Even his landscapes do not directly convey, as do those of Claude le Lorrain, any convincing suggestion of illimitable space or towering natural majesty. They have rather the abstract feeling of a pyramid or a cathedral, an effect heightened by the clarity of their outlines, the absence of realistic detail of subject-matter. The departure from representative detail of figures and objects, necessary to obtain the basic architectonic character of Cézanne's design, is often so extreme that the inevitable result is the gross distortion of naturalistic appearances which shocks the uninitiated observer. The distortions, however, when studied in relation to the form, are perceived to be abstractions of the essentials of objects, ingeniously merged in a harmonious, highly individual total design. Cézanne's paintings are, in the best and most accurate sense of the term, abstract.

The architectural and monumental aspect of Cézanne's work appears even in his small still-lifes and figure-pieces, which are never conceived in terms that would emphasize the qualities of intimacy or charm; his figures, for example, have a sphinxlike fixity even when they are plastic constructions of the highest order. In this, Cézanne is somewhat akin to the Le Nains and is precisely the opposite of Chardin although there is a plastic resemblance with the latter: Chardin's warmth, intimacy and human appeal are almost wholly lacking in Cézanne. Unlike Renoir too, who could be epic and monumental when he wished, but who could also be spontaneously and unaffectedly charming, Cézanne always retains something forbidding and aloof.

This aloofness or austerity, inevitably a part of the monumental, appears also in the very restricted part which decoration plays in his work. His designs are always highly patterned, and at his best his color is deep, rich and glowing; these qualities give his form an inherent decorative appeal, but apart from them there is no added embellishment. Not only does he avoid recourse to specific ornamental detail such as we find in Matisse, but he seldom attains such intrinsically appealing natural qualities as the softness and warmth of flesh, the fleeciness of clouds, or the sparkle of light on water. In his designs, these qualities would be as incongruous as velvet upholstery on the columns of the Parthenon; his avoidance of them is therefore a sign of his single-mindedness, his resolute concentration of all his energies on what for him is essential; but it is also symptomatic of the limitations of his interest.

Cézanne, in other words, though a very great artist, was also exceedingly circumscribed in the range of his perceptions and of his effects. He was, in addition, limited also in his capacity for growth: he mastered his difficulties slowly and he seldom conquered all of them entirely. He did develop and modify his technique, but neither steadily nor consistently, and he constantly reverted to his earlier immature methods. His natural command of the medium of paint was not great, and in relatively few pictures did he attain to a uniformly high level of craftsmanship. The execution of his designs was always laborious; it was exceedingly imperfect in his early work, even in much of that painted after he had found his natural vein; and it remained of uneven quality all through his mature years. In this respect he was the antithesis of Renoir, who very quickly mastered the means of putting on canvas whatever he had in mind, and was able to explore new realms of tradition and experience, assimilating material from the most diverse sources, and thus broadening and deepening his own form. Cézanne, in contrast, found early in his career what was in essentials his own form of expression, and never thereafter introduced into it anything radically new; moreover, his efforts to realize it in paint frequently failed completely, were often only partially successful, and showed signs of characteristic awkwardness even in his latest work.[1] Indeed, very few of his pictures of the latest period are equal in expressive power and technical proficiency to a number of those painted during the late eighties and the nineties,[2] although he painted continuously up to the time of his death in 1906. This difficulty in execution circumscribed his energies and limited his scope; his designs were not stereotyped, but their general sameness in fundamental structure left room for variation in little except matters of detail. Nevertheless, the thoroughgoing integrity and originality of his vision was so complete and his expression of power so great that neither the defects of his craftsmanship nor his lack of versatility affect his high rank as an artist.

Cézanne's extreme single-mindedness appears not only in this concentration of his energies on a restricted range of effects, but in the very high degree of plastic integration of his forms. Just as it is impossible to point to one factor of his pictures as expressive, another as decorative, so it is impossible to separate in precise categories his means of modeling, drawing, placing in space, and composing: the means dovetail, they reënforce, supplement and become part of one another. In accordance with the architectonic character of his design, the linear aspects of his subject-matter are accentuated: they tend to play the part of piers and girders, which support and bind together the structure as a whole. But line in Cézanne is never the isolated, primarily decorative or illustrative element that it is in Raphael, Botticelli, Holbein, or Ingres. It is a part of modeling, a means of localiza-

---

[1] E.g., lumpy, grainy ridges of paint around contours of volumes—a result of repeated efforts to attain the desired color-values and relationships—appear in his "Man and Skull" (142) of c. 1892, "Old Woman with Rosary" (178) of c. 1900, "Three Skulls" (184) of the early 1900's, "Château Noir" (186) of c. 1904, and "Vallier" (188) of c. 1904-1905, in much the same manner as they had occurred many years earlier, as, e.g., in "Bathers at Rest" (63) of 1877.

Note: All numbers placed in parentheses after titles of pictures, as appear in the above footnote and hereafter throughout the book, are reference numbers used in the Catalogue Data listed in the Appendix, see p. 401.

[2] E.g., "Woman with Green Hat" (103); "Harlequin" (105); "Self-Portrait on Blue Background" (108); "Valley of the Arc" (109); "Madame Cézanne in Red, Holding Handkerchief" (133); "Woman and Coffee Pot" (140); "Oranges and Bottle" (148); "Bibemus Quarry" (155).

tion in space and of composition; its function is organic, neither imitative nor ornamental. As Cézanne gradually improved his command of pigment, compelling it to function as color, and at the same time infused with color the light-and-dark effects of his early period, his dynamic space-composition came to be fully integrated with the pattern of his brushstrokes, out of which his line itself is largely fashioned. In his best work, the unity of means becomes so organic that the separate means can be distinguished in function but not actually identified as separately existing factors, and even when halting execution leaves particular areas·of the canvas imperfectly realized, the unity of conception is not materially impaired.[3]

In subsequent chapters, we shall seek Cézanne's sources in antecedent traditions, study in detail the construction of his individual form, and discuss his specific adaptation of it to landscape, still-life and figure-painting. His color, light and drawing, while of fundamental importance, do not lend themselves to independent detailed consideration, because all of them, and especially color and drawing, are inseparably connected with his technique, pattern, line, space, and composition; and these latter topics will be treated separately. We shall then discuss his influence on contemporary art, an influence which has been of great importance both for good and, unfortunately, for evil. In the Appendix many of his important paintings will be analyzed, and the technical means of many of his effects described more exhaustively than is possible in the text.

[3] This, of course, does not apply to paintings which he abandoned in an unfinished state.

CHAPTER II

CEZANNE'S ORIGINS IN THE TRADITIONS

CEZANNE'S earliest painting, done in the 1860's before he made
the acquaintance of the impressionists, reflects strongly the influence of the Venetians (especially Tintoretto), Caravaggio, Ribera,
Zurbarán, Rembrandt, the brothers Le Nain, the seventeenth century Dutch painters, and Delacroix, Daumier, Courbet, and Manet;
but it already shows significant departures from its sources, and in
a direction which suggests the individuality and power characteristic of his mature form. Most of the basic essentials of these
early influences persist in generalized form in the work of his
maturity, but are individualized by Cézanne's own devices of
color, drawing, technique, and composition.

His early painting is for the most part the work of a beginner
handicapped by unskilled craftsmanship but feeling his way toward a personal form of expression. The outstanding characteristic of most of these early efforts may be said to be a feeling of
melodrama and literary romanticism, which is the antithesis of
the balance, the composure, of Cézanne's mature painting. The
drama results from the accentuated contrast between light and
dark areas, together with a general quality of swirl to which the
abruptly projecting parts of figures and objects contribute. The
romanticism arises both from the type of subject-matter and from
its illustrative treatment, which emphasizes such adventitious features as facial expression and represented behavior. Some of these
early narratives [1] have the exaggerated romanticism of Caravaggio
and the other Italian rhetorical painters of the sixteenth century;
others [2] are more akin to the work of Tintoretto, Rubens, Delacroix, Courbet, or Daumier; and practically all of them put the
emphasis upon a definite narrative and are thus clearly distinguished from the work of Cézanne's prime. Even at its worst,
however, the drama in the narrative is given a measure of con-

[1] E.g., "Murder" (20) ; "Reading at Zola's" (23).
[2] E.g., "Abduction" (8) ; "Alexis and Zola" (12) ; "Donkey Thieves" (18).

viction by its plastic embodiment in a distinctive form. This form is characterized by heavy impasto, sharp contrasts of light and dark, very emphatic rhythms extending in varying directions throughout the picture, alternation of patterned and unpatterned areas of canvas, and bizarre and picturesque distribution of subject-matter.

The color-scheme of these early pictures is for the most part dark, with pure blacks, greenish blacks, deep grayish-greens, and occasional deep reds, related to whites tinged with gray. Sometimes the blacks are replaced by deep blues and mahogany-browns which, when related to the grayish tan of the flesh, relieve the general somberness of the color-scheme and increase its richness, without, however, dissipating the general light-and-dark effect of the color-scheme as a whole.[3] Most of the pictures of this period reveal, in the color-scheme and the use of brushwork, in the swirling linear effects and the overaccentuated drama, the influences of one or more of the earlier painters mentioned.

Light at this period is present mainly as chiaroscuro, but with a stronger emphasis upon the pattern of light and dark areas than is to be found in the work of the old masters whom Cézanne followed. His use of this pattern is superior to that of the Spaniards, Zurbarán and Ribera, in that the light usually has greater internal luminosity; in his successful pictures it functions as a set of positive compositional color-areas and contributes to an authentic plastic expression of drama.[4] When, in contrast, plastic integration is unsuccessful and the effect secured is largely one of specious melodrama, the chief responsibility lies with mechanical, overaccentuated light-dark contrasts.[5] In general, the sharp contact of these light and dark areas, which are more definitely distinguished from one another than in the old masters, constitutes a first step toward Cézanne's later manner of construction in terms of color-contrast and -rhythm of dynamic planes.

Conjoined with the overdramatization of light in this early work is the feeling of active movement given to the pattern by

[3] Cézanne's "Judgment of Paris" (2), supposedly painted in the early sixties, is a notable exception to this rule: instead of somber colors, bright orange-rose alternates with areas of blue in the sky, and the nudes are of light-toned flesh modeled with brown shadows.
[4] Compare, e.g., Cézanne's "Autopsy" (15) with Ribera's "Entombment" (250), "Martyrdom of St. Bartholomew" (251) or "Dead Christ" (252).
[5] E.g., "Idyl" (26).

the sweeps, swirls, thrusts and counterthrusts of the light and dark areas. The movement arises from a type of drawing in which the linear effects of these sweeps and swirls are accentuated, very often by curvilinear, individual strokes of either brush or palette knife—a technique which harks back to Tintoretto through Delacroix and Rubens.[6] In short, drawing is characterized by abrupt changes and contrasts in linear direction that reenforce the contrasts of light and dark; and the striking appearance of the technique is often speciously emphasized by excessive use of the palette knife.[7] An actual contour-line or band of shadow occasionally separates the volume from the surrounding space [8]—a device to be found in Tintoretto, Delacroix and Daumier, which recurs more constantly and characteristically in Cézanne's later work. Both line and light are as yet inadequately supported by color, and the general composition is baroque, and much less coherent and closely knit than it is later to become. However, Cézanne's own intensity and power are already clearly in evidence, and his distinctive form takes shape as these personal characteristics find embodiment in inherent plastic structure rather than in illustrative incidentals.

We may now examine Cézanne's early work for the beginnings of the distinguishing marks which identify his mature form, and see how these were evolved by his creative use of features and methods to be found in earlier painters. First of all, from this standpoint, is the matter of technique. Mention has already been made of his application of paint in strokes of the brush and palette knife in such a manner as to accentuate the individual dabs and strokes, and make them play a prominent part in the pattern and intensify the drama of contrast between light and dark areas. The individual strokes resemble, at different times, those of Rembrandt, Hals, Velásquez, Delacroix, Courbet, Daumier, and Manet, but they assume new and distinctive functions in drawing, modeling, pattern-formation, and composition. In general they are broad, flat and loaded with pigment, and their abrupt contact with each other, corresponding to the sudden change from light to dark color, imparts a rugged, sometimes mosaic- or ceramic-

[6] E.g., Cézanne's "Abduction" (8); "Donkey Thieves" (18); "Scipio" (24).
[7] E.g., "Artist's Sister" (3); "Head of Man" (6).
[8] E.g., "Autopsy" (15); "Donkey Thieves" (18).

like surface to the objects depicted, together with the appearance of a series of facets which tend to function diversely as planes.[9] At this stage the strokes or planes are often swirling, so that the form exhibits the familiar movement common to Tintoretto, Rubens and Delacroix.[10] It is seldom, however, that the planes take on definite organization in the drawing, modeling or composition; hence none of these features has the firmness and fulness which more adequately controlled technique and more tightly knit organization confer upon his mature work. His unskilled craftsmanship at this early stage caused him to employ repeated coats of pigment, a thick piling-up of impasto, to obtain surface-quality and sculpturesque volumes which he was subsequently able to achieve by a greater mastery of technique and better and more immediately rendered relationships of color.[11] His own consciousness of the nature of his difficulty appears in his avowal, made years later, that it had taken him "twenty years to learn that painting is not sculpture."

The contrasting areas of light and dark are more definitely shaped in Cézanne's early work than in the painters from whom he derived them—Tintoretto, Rembrandt, Ribera, Zurbarán, Daumier, and Manet—and hence yield a more pronounced pattern.[12] They also tend to be used specifically as planes, defining and bounding volumes; but because of Cézanne's defective ability to control paint and coördinate color-relationships, the volumes are often broken up into a series of color-patches that appear either to sink into or rise above the surface.[13] The broken continuity of surface imparts a sense of movement to the composition, but the unity of the volumes is lost and the form as a whole is then reduced to a succession of unrelated units. With the gradual increase in Cézanne's sensitivity and skill, this in-and-out movement of the pattern of patches loses its disjointed character, and in the form which it finally assumes, with organically fused technique, drawing, modeling, and spacing, it conveys legitimately Cézanne's

[9] E.g., "Uncle Dominique" (5); "Head of Man" (6); "Artist's Father" (7); "Achille Emperaire" (9).
[10] E.g., Cézanne's "Banquet" (4); "Scipio" (24); "Idyl" (26); "Head of Emperaire" (28).
[11] Compare, e.g., "Artist's Sister" (3) with "Woman with Green Hat" (103); or "Head of Man" (6) with "Self-Portrait on Blue Background" (108).
[12] E.g., "Head of Man" (6); "Autopsy" (15); "Idyl" (26).
[13] E.g., "Uncle Dominique" (5); "Antony Valabrègue" (10).

characteristic effect of dynamism.[14] These finely adjusted relationships constitute composition in its highest estate.

Cézanne's progress is further illustrated by the gradually increasing effectiveness and individuality of his brushwork. Aside from the large and frequently swirling strokes, or blobs of thick paint in his earliest pictures, there appear also, though only occasionally, units which owe their distinctive character to an organization of hatchings, that is, overlapping parallel strokes that function as constructive planes,[15] and thus forecast his typical later drawing and modeling. Noticeable also in the early stage is the intermittent appearance of a device which he used consistently in the work of his maturity: the single, narrow, curvilinear brushstrokes, which by their sequence form a scalloped edge around volumes, especially masses of foliage,[16] much like the broken curves in his linear pencil drawings.[17] The germ of this practice may be in Rubens' familiar curvilinear contour-strokes or streaks,[18] but Cézanne's modification, simplification and more purposeful and comprehensive use of the device make it in his hands an instrument essentially new.

The color in Cézanne's earliest work repays careful scrutiny, for it testifies both to his innate sense of color-quality and color-power and to the tremendous obstacles which he encountered in converting paint into color. At this period he borrowed extensively from his predecessors in the matter of color-schemes, often following his sources very closely.[19] While it is usually possible to detect evidence of experimentation, of efforts to achieve individuality both in the actual colors and in the manner of their use, the outstanding fact about the experimentation is that Cézanne's failures were far more numerous than his successes. The intrinsically satisfying color-units are few in number and are usually surrounded by color which is unilluminated, muted, leaden, dull, dead; the color then fails in its plastic relationships, in the part it is designed to play in drawing, modeling and composition, and in its decorative and expressive functions.

[14] E.g., "Six Bathers" (100); "Compotier, Pitcher and Fruit" (128).
[15] E.g., "Herrings" (13); "Railroad Cut" (22); "Idyl" (26).
[16] E.g., "Red Roofs" (35) of the early 1870's; "Bibemus Quarry" (155) of 1898.
[17] E.g., "Venus and Cupids" (209).
[18] Cf., e.g., the contour of the clouds in Rubens' "Annunciation" (247).
[19] E.g., Daumier's in "Donkey Thieves" (18), Courbet's in "Two Strollers" (37).

Cézanne's inability to achieve a consistently high quality of color is usually compensated for by an array of other factors— the pattern of technique, the quality of surface, the thickness of impasto, the naïveté of drawing, the gross distortions, the sweeps and swirls of the composition—all of them so interrelated that a forceful individuality triumphs over the all-too-obvious defects and crudities.[20] The defects are perhaps most readily recognized in the light of a comparison with Daumier's form, to which many early Cézannes bear close resemblance in color-scheme, drawing, modeling, depiction of active movement, dramatic light-and-dark contrasts, silhouetted masses, and in essentially illustrative interest with a tendency to distortions productive of grotesqueness.[21] In Cézanne, the drawing and modeling by which a certain naïve expression is rendered are crude and heavy, with mechanically repeated distortions, radically different from those resulting from Daumier's highly skilled and subtle execution. Daumier's grotesque drawing, in other words, renders many and varied degrees of caricature, qualifies and defines the character of his figures as actors in a story; Cézanne's springs from an attempt to render the abstract basic essentials of things by a painter who reveals the fact that he has not yet at hand the necessary technical instruments.

Convincing evidence of Cézanne's innate artistry and of his assimilation of the spirit of the old masters whose work engrossed him at this early period, is provided by his "Artist's Father" (7), painted about 1866-1868.[22] The impasto is thick, the light-and-dark contrasts are much in evidence, a black contour-line outside the volume is relied upon to locate it in space, and faulty color-relations cause the shadow cast by the foot to sink beneath the level of the floor. Yet despite these crudities, the picture bears comparison with the best of the old masters in its grasp of the character of the sitter, its solidity of color, and the simplicity and fine integration of its component parts. A pervasive mosaic texture gives an individual charm to the entire composition. In power, dignity and majesty, the picture suggests Rembrandt, brought down to modern times by the color, drawing, pattern, technique, and vigorous painting which Cézanne had absorbed

[20] E.g., "Head of Man" (6); "Antony Valabrègue" (10); "Donkey Thieves" (18).
[21] Compare, e.g., Cézanne's "Donkey Thieves" (18) or "Two Men and Two Women" (25) with Daumier's "Thieves and Donkey" (267).
[22] Illustration, p. 151.

from Daumier, Courbet and Manet. In short, the influences of other painters, assimilated in essence and saturated with Cézanne's own individuality, have been fused into a new form, and though the painting is still in the tradition of the old masters, its content of values, its force and strength, are essentially the same as those which Cézanne realized when he was at the height of his powers.

A change from the general style described above makes its appearance between 1868 and 1872,[23] with the development of a transitional stage between Cézanne's earliest work, in which the influences of the old masters held sway, and his later paintings in which some of the radical innovations brought into being by his contemporaries began to show their effect, and the abandon of his early work is gradually replaced by the restraint, reflection and calculation which persist in all his subsequent painting. A mark of this transition is the predominance of the influence of Courbet and Manet over that of the older painters. Cézanne's pictures now contain few unaltered traits of Tintoretto, Ribera, the Dutch, or Delacroix. In "Railroad Cut" (22), a landscape of the late 1860's,[24] brighter colors enter into or replace the browns, blacks and grays of his earlier palette, giving a more colorful tonality to the ensemble. His former sharp contrasts of light and dark acquire, here, another character because both the light and the dark elements are rendered in positive colors, while the advent of this richer color-content is accompanied by a more legitimate plastic rendering of drama.

Akin to Courbet's at this time are Cézanne's hard, firm drawing, the matter-of-fact kind of everyday subject-matter, the emphasis upon the local color of objects, generally within a gray tonality, the grayish-tan flesh, and the tendency to a waxy surface-quality.[25] At times he utilizes also Courbet's familiar color-relationships between greens, blues, grays, and a particular shade of red.[26] These derivations from Courbet acquire a new cast from their union

[23] E.g., "Alexis and Zola" (12); "Black Clock" (14); "Boy Leaning on Elbow" (17); "Girl at Piano" (19); "Picnic" (21); "Railroad Cut" (22); "Green Jar and Pewter Pitcher" (27); "Boyer" (30); "Presumed Portrait of Valabrègue" (42).

[24] Illustration, p. 172.

[25] Compare, e.g., for general form, Cézanne's "Boy Leaning on Elbow" (17) or "Boyer" (30) with Courbet's "Head of Baby" (270) or "Wounded Man" (272).

[26] It is noteworthy that when Cézanne's borrowings from Courbet are predominant, the result, even in his mature years, is usually a picture of inferior quality, e.g., "Madame Cézanne with Striped Blouse" (98).

with traits characteristic of Manet: broad brushwork, generalization of detail, flattening of masses, internal illumination of color, lustrous blacks and whites, and the use of black accents for the purpose of increasing luminosity in surrounding colors.

In this blending of traits from Manet and Courbet, Cézanne's individuality is manifested in the greater power of the drawing and color. His color is more interesting and meaningful simply as color, and its greater solidity adds strength and vigor to the form as a whole. Perhaps the most striking departure from these predecessors appears in the distortion of shape, proportion, space, color, detail, and texture of objects, which does so much to establish the individuality of Cézanne's form and to bring out its distinctive conviction and power. The angular, rigid drawing, different from anything in Courbet or Manet, but henceforth a permanent feature of Cézanne's work, gives to the general expression a decidedly primitive feeling. Cézanne's plastic superiority to Courbet and Manet is best illustrated by his "Girl at Piano" (19) and "Picnic" (21), both of the late sixties.[27] In each of these the compositional organization is plastically dynamic, the color-ensemble is rich, powerful, solid, and deeply glowing, and the total form is dramatic and bizarre. Here, at an early date, he achieves the apparent paradox of making an intensely dynamic interrelationship of plastic units express a sense of dignified tranquillity—a characteristic of his best work at the height of his career.

At this period of experimentation with the Courbet-Manet form, Cézanne made a radical change in his use of light, obviously as a result of his contact with the impressionists.[28] Before this time he had resorted to the old masters' method of using local and focal points of illumination which, as already noted, emphasized light-and-dark contrasts, often with specious dramatic effects. The change consisted in an increase of general illumination throughout the canvas, by which the entire color-organization was raised to a higher pitch of color-and-light intensity. This departure was prior to his adoption of impressionism as a whole, the full-fledged technique of which had not yet been developed. Although Cézanne had begun his association with the pure impressionists, Pissarro and Guillaumin, in the year 1862, it was only about seven years later that the fruits of the association

[27] Illustrations, p. 157 and p. 160.
[28] E.g., "Railroad Cut" (22).

began to appear in his work.[29] This fact is significant as an indication of one of his fundamental psychological characteristics: the long period of gestation required for his assimilation of new ideas. This slow process enabled him to select and extract the features most relevant to his own purposes, and to forge them into an instrument for his characteristic personal expression. Indeed, a survey of the work of his entire career shows that his artistic coming-of-age dates from his assimilation and reorganization of what he learned from the impressionists. The years 1872-1874 are significant in this respect, for it was then that he actually copied Pissarro's paintings [30] and worked under his guidance at Auvers-sur-Oise. The influences did not exercise their full force all at once or in their entirety, for after he had painted landscapes in the impressionists' manner, he reverted to his earlier romantic type of subject-matter in such pictures as "Temptation of St. Anthony" (60) and "New Olympia" (34),[31] in both of which the composition, active movement and general feeling are very Delacroix-esque. The first of these pictures recalls the impressionists only in the perceptible brushwork, while in the second the drawing is like Manet's, the brushstrokes are like Monet's, and the generally light and delicate color-scheme and fluid rhythms are strongly reminiscent of Fragonard.[32] Another deviation from Cézanne's general direction at this period is represented by a number of landscapes which follow the styles of Courbet and of the Barbizon painters, notably Corot, Diaz and Dupré, sometimes very closely, and especially closely in color-scheme, and sometimes in a manner modified by the influence of Manet and Pissarro; but in every instance the original form is changed materially by Cézanne's bolder, terser drawing, by his color applied in broader areas, and by an organization more strikingly patterned than that in the Barbizon pictures.[33]

The grip of the impressionists upon Cézanne's vision in the early seventies was not loosened by his excursions into the more or less alien Barbizon field. The result of the specific influence of the impressionists' technique in Cézanne's work constitutes such an important factor that its full consideration must be reserved for

[29] E.g., "Railroad Cut" (22).
[30] E.g., Cézanne's "Louveciennes" (43).
[31] Illustrations, p. 181 and p. 179.
[32] See also Analysis, p. 314.
[33] E.g., Cézanne's "Autumn" (16); "Valley of Jas de Bouffan" (38); "Avenue of Jas de Bouffan" (41).

the detailed discussion of Cézanne's technique. He owed also to the impressionists the re-direction of his interest away from romantic fantasies to the realities of the objective world. This naturalistic strain had already been present in so far as he was influenced by Daumier, Courbet and Manet, but it became dominant as his own specific means were developed under the impressionistic influence. Cézanne's accentuation of the framework pattern is somewhat reminiscent of Guillaumin,[34] and the tendency toward an architectonic form in Bazille's "Family Party" (289) may have had its influence upon Cézanne's mature work. But among the pure impressionists he owed most to Pissarro, whose form is more forceful, positive and colorful than that of any other member of the school, and represents a more comprehensive and thoroughgoing integration of the plastic means.

Cézanne took over Pissarro's color-scheme with its interplay of many shades of green and orange, his pronounced pattern of color used in broad areas, the unctuous quality of his pigment, his vigorous painting, and his general type of subject-matter, drawing, brushwork, and composition.[35] Under Pissarro's tutelage he produced many pictures which depart little from the models except in their usually firmer drawing and more solid color.[36] As Cézanne gradually assimilated the essentials of Pissarro's work and of the impressionists' form in general, the changes he wrought in the borrowed features above noted are truly fundamental: they contribute vitally to the construction of a form plastically expressive of his characteristic power and they remain part of his equipment ever after.[37]

Notwithstanding his great indebtedness, Cézanne is not in any of his mature work an impressionist; in fact, he condemned the lack of solidity in the impressionists' modeling, and their neglect or abolition of the local color of objects. His volumes are vastly more solid than theirs, the color-areas are more positive and more definitely shaped by contour-lines, his space is deeper and its units or intervals are more sharply defined; fusion of light with color increases the activity of each of these elements, but rarely takes the form of a positive atmospheric haze or glow; there is seldom

[34] E.g., Cézanne's "Water Mill" (39).
[35] Compare, e.g., Cézanne's "River and Hills" (48) with Pissarro's "Garden" (273).
[36] E.g., "House of Père Lacroix" (44); "Suicide's House" (45).
[37] E.g., "Auvers-sur-Oise: Village Panorama" (47); "Val Harmé at Auvers" (70).

a shimmer of light to blur the outlines of his masses, to give the naturalistic effect of direct sunlight, or, as often in Monet, actually almost to efface the intrinsic quality of the color. Cézanne's work shares also the sense of the actual pigment, the "paintiness," which appears in all the impressionists, especially in Monet; but this defect was reduced as Cézanne's craftsmanship improved, although he seldom entirely eliminated it.

After assimilating what impressionism had to offer him, Cézanne never made any such extensive drafts upon other traditions as Renoir did upon the Venetians or upon the French painters of the eighteenth century.[38] By the end of the 1870's, in other words, he had in essentials attained to the distinctive artistic vision, beyond which he never went, though he did sharpen and improve it as time progressed. Simultaneously, he made specific adaptations from a considerable number of traditions which were in the natural line of his development, but his own form was so personal, both in conception and in technique, that everything he borrowed was completely transformed in his hands. The hatched brushstrokes, the solidity, the weight, the firm ceramiclike surfaces of his masses, all suggest Chardin.[39] The influence of Daumier, perceptible in his early work, became less evident as active represented movement gave place to poised and plastic movement; however, the forceful simplified drawing and the use of accentuated lines of contour, reminiscent of Daumier, remain.[40] The subject-matter of his still-lifes has an obvious affinity with that of the Dutch genre tradition, but of course without any of its elaborate literalness, and his technique shows the influence of Hals, though this doubtless reached him chiefly through Manet.[41]

Cézanne's many and important resemblances to El Greco would indicate a significant source of inspiration, but no evidence has yet been found that he had ever seen El Greco's paintings. Neverthe-

[38] The influence of the eighteenth century French painters appears in the delicacy of color and general fluidity of composition in a few of Cézanne's paintings of the early and middle seventies, e.g., in "New Olympia" (34), "Banquet Table" (50) and "Cupid's Arrow" (53). This French influence, which seems incongruous with the usual heaviness of his painting in oil, is an outstanding characteristic of most of his water colors of all periods.

[39] Cf., e.g., Cézanne's "Jug, Wineglass and Fruit" (46) and Chardin's "Various Utensils" (259).

[40] Cf., e.g., Cézanne's "Group of Bathers" (182) and Daumier's "Water Carrier" (268).

[41] Cf., e.g., Cézanne's "Provence Peasant" (151), Hals's "Dutch Burgher" (249) and Manet's "Soldier Examining his Rifle" (281).

less, there are a number of Cézanne's pictures, both of his early [42] and of his mature period,[43] which strikingly recall El Greco's distortions in drawing and modeling, his use of muscular accentuations, dramatic contrasts of light and dark colors, angular swirls and compositional planes, his activity of patterns, his exotic effect of color-relations, and the texture of his surfaces. If, as seems doubtful from these correspondences, Cézanne never saw El Greco's work in the original, the very close resemblance of the two men in plastic essentials can be classified only as a strange coincidence.

With all the similarities, however, the forms of the two men differ materially in their expression and in the use of the individual plastic means. The general expression of El Greco's form is that of an intricate and very active movement, often of excitement and turmoil, occasioned by the plethora of sinuous, writhing, serpentine effects of line, light and color. The associations it recalls are those of supernatural religious mysticism. Cézanne's mature form is tied to the everyday world with the bigness, broadness, majesty, simplicity, monumental character of a well-ordered and firmly constructed building that symbolizes composure and tranquillity. Color in El Greco functions most actively as a participant in the pervasive movement, not, as in Cézanne, primarily in building up the solidity and massiveness of volumes. The light in El Greco does not illuminate color to the depth it does in Cézanne, and its surface-pattern usually resembles the streaks of forked-lightning; in Cézanne the pattern of light is in broad patches and areas; it is organically bound up with the color, and therefore less isolated than in El Greco. As a result of the lesser degree of fusion of light with color in El Greco, his volumes lack the weight, the blocklike quality, the full internal solidity, the all-thereness of Cézanne's. El Greco's objects, for example, are more like painted surfaces than like actual things with all the qualities which a sensitive observer can discover in them in nature. No less different is their manner of using compositional planes in space. The space-composition in El Greco is usually constructed by an ascending

[42] E.g., "Picnic" (21); "Reading at Zola's" (23). Compare the latter with El Greco's "Nativity" (245); or Cézanne's "Don Quijote" (54) with El Greco's "Mocked Christ" (244).

[43] Compare, e.g., Cézanne's "Men Bathing" (164) with El Greco's "Laocoön" (243); or the girl's face in Cézanne's "Card Players and Girl" (141) with the Infant in El Greco's "Vision of St. Hyacinth" (246). See also the flesh-modeling by light and dark planes of color in El Greco's "Annunciation" (242).

succession of planes interrupted at various levels, which give the effect of an intricate, varied upward movement within comparatively shallow space. In Cézanne, the succession of planes extends from the very foreground into the deep distance, thus setting the composition in directly receding, fully three-dimensional space.

Broadly considered, Cézanne's fundamental design, based as it is upon the ordering of solid color-masses in deep space, is profoundly Venetian, and his use of color is an evolution, however indirect, of the structural, internally illuminated color of the school, especially of Tintoretto; but there is nothing in his paintings to correspond to the Venetian atmospheric glow, nor is there any pronounced effect of interflow of color or tone between masses and spatial intervals. Cézanne engrafts upon the Venetian space-composition a characteristic of sculpture; that is, a clear detachment of masses from each other and from their setting, as in a group of statues;[44] or an only partial detachment of sculpturesque volumes from their setting, as in high-reliefs.[45] Carpaccio's architectural designs are possibly a source of Cézanne's architectonic form, but the resemblance is in general effect, rather than in the means of compositional organization. The in-and-out compositional rhythms of Cézanne resemble those of the Venetians, but the volumes and spatial intervals which constitute the rhythms differ in that Cézanne's tend to be placed in receding parallel horizontal planes, somewhat in the manner of Poussin, but more emphatic.

In his clear-cut spatial intervals, Cézanne shows his debt to the Florentine school in general and, in his extensive use of line and distortion in the rendering of perspective, to Uccello in particular. With Michelangelo he shares the quality of weight and power, and his distortions play a part roughly analogous to Signorelli's and Michelangelo's muscular accentuations in modeling.[46] All three men derive much of their power from a generally sculpturesque character; but Cézanne's, in its fully-realized form, is sculpturesque only in broad essentials, and is rendered in terms more truly pictorial, while the power in Signorelli and Michelangelo is often actually sculptural in an imitative sense. Furthermore, Michelangelo's figures, like Signorelli's, depart only slightly from the

---

[44] E.g., "Bathers at Rest" (63).

[45] E.g., "Leda and the Swan" (68); "Five Nudes" (74); "Nudes in Landscape" (191).

[46] Compare, e.g., Cézanne's "Bathers at Rest" (63) or "Men Bathing" (164) with Signorelli's "Hell" (221) and Michelangelo's "Last Judgment" (227).

form of Greek statues; Cézanne's hark back to the more solid, massive, stable, and rugged early Egyptian sculpture.[47] In some pictures, most notably in his "Nudes in Landscape" (191), Cézanne, in a form which embodies the values of both ancient sculpture and monumental classic architecture, recaptures the effect of the metopes (211) and frieze of the Parthenon (210): the resemblance is not to the flowing graceful line but to the quality of massiveness and cumulative compositional power.[48] Cézanne's sculptural values, in a word, like his architectural values, are wholly re-created in the medium of painting, and involve no intrusion of alien elements.

[47] E.g., Cézanne's "Woman with Green Hat" (103); "Nudes in Landscape" (191).

[48] When Renoir uses qualities derived from classic sculpture, what is brought in from sculpture is saturated by the familiar characteristics of persons and objects in the world. In Renoir the reality of the figures is retained in terms of the comprehensive reality they have in life; in Cézanne the figures acquire a plastic life primarily by the part they play in terms of the values—weight, mass—more directly associated with architecture and sculpture. Compare, e.g., Cézanne's "Nudes in Landscape" (191) with Renoir's "Bathing Group" (292).

CHAPTER III

CEZANNE'S FORM AND TECHNIQUE

I. INTRODUCTION

THE reason why Cézanne's pictures seem to the novice strange, bizarre, exotic, and different from those of his predecessors is to be found in the prominence of both technique and distortion. In a Leonardo or Raphael, for example, the continuously rounded surfaces, the sharp contours, the rendering of space by linear perspective, invite no attention to the means of their execution. The means are there to be discovered by analysis, but they do not force themselves upon the attention of the ordinary spectator; and the same is true of most of the painters of the past, however varied in other respects their work may be. David and Courbet, great as is the difference between stiff formal neo-classicism and vigorous naturalism, have in common the fact that they never leave the observer in doubt about what is represented, or, like Cézanne, do such violence to the laws of nature as to show a volume—a piece of fruit, for example—poised without natural means of support. Even Rembrandt, probably the least literal of the classic painters, gives an impression of selection and emphasis rather than of distortion; and in his portrayal of human personality and character he is, in the broadest sense of the word, intensely realistic. All these painters seem to be speaking a recognized language, with a common grammar; Cézanne, however, appears to be inventing a language of his own, almost like James Joyce in literature. The nearest approach to him in this sense is to be found in El Greco; and El Greco himself, after centuries of neglect, regained recognition and influence only after Cézanne had reopened the critics' eyes. Cézanne, in other words, is in a superlative degree a painter whom it is necessary to *learn* to see; both his means and the ends for which they are used are highly individual; and at the same time they are so organically interrelated that failure to grasp either makes the other unintelligible.

Cézanne is in this respect akin to the impressionists, from whom,

22

as we have seen, he derived much of the raw material of his form. The technique of his work of the early seventies was extremely impressionistic in character, and he never discarded, though he adapted to different ends, the visible brushwork by which Manet, Monet and Pissarro built up their pictures. This technique had its origin partly in the color-division of Delacroix, which goes back to Constable and ultimately, in germ, to the broken color of Rubens and the Venetians; partly in the brushwork of the Spaniards and Hals, who were the chief sources of Manet. By the impressionists, this technique, however far from literal in details, was used for purposes much more closely akin to familiar appearances of things than in Cézanne, and hence they have often been classified as "realists" or "naturalists," whether the subject-matter depicted be the effects of direct sunlight, as largely with Monet, or the essential everyday quality of particular persons and things, as with Manet. What distinguishes Cézanne is that he used a technique developed from theirs for a much more profound reorganization of natural appearances, and one much more individual to himself, so that while the strangeness of impressionistic pictures was quickly dissipated, and they soon began to appear extremely "lifelike," Cézanne's work seems an authentic revelation of nature only to one who has learned to look away from the superficial qualities of the world, and to discover the way in which objects are interrelated and fused in a more definitely plastic organization.

Cézanne's paintings, in other words, are preëminently *composed,* and the analysis of his form is primarily an account of his composition. In many painters, especially those of the second or third rank, particular objects are obviously first conceived as individual things, and subsequently disposed about the canvas like articles of furniture in a room. Such arrangement or disposition is indeed, by many critics, considered to be the whole of composition, just as in literature the plot of a novel or play is often regarded as the series of incidents which befall the characters, instead of the way in which the characters display their inherent nature. Both books and pictures may be so loosely knit that such a definition does justice to their "plot" or "composition"; but it does no justice to Cézanne's work. Cézanne's form is, in conception at least, completely organic; the technique is used to build up units of color, light, shadow, line, and space; and the part which each of these plays in composition is so intimate that the brushstrokes which build up pattern also create volumes and set them in space; and the line that contributes solidity to objects and places them in perspective is itself usually color applied by an actual brushstroke or series of brushstrokes. In Matisse, in contrast, areas of color, brushstrokes, linear patterns, often diversify and ornament the surface of the canvas without playing any very essential part in expressive structure; in Degas—to take another example—line may convey a vivid sense of movement or gesture, and yet not be an indispensable part of the plastic architecture of the form as a whole. This is not true of Cézanne: all the threads in his composition are interwoven into a single fabric, the subdivisions of which—particular figures, natural objects, areas of pattern, segments of line, or intervals of space—have relatively little independent esthetic importance. Detail is not itemized, and often, as in landscapes, the important compositional divisions cut across individual objects. Through the technique, the color is integrated in the composition as a whole, and the separate units are chiefly stages in the organization. Particular colors, lines, areas of light and shadow, and intervals of space, in other words, acquire their esthetic importance primarily from the entire process of compositional integration.

Our analysis of Cézanne's form will consequently begin with an account of his technique, and indicate the way in which it is used to create an architectonic structure, the component parts of which are solid volumes in deep space. Color and light, as Cézanne uses them, are so intimately bound up with the technique and composition that they can be best treated as parts of these two general topics. Line and space, while also not strictly separable from the organic form, lend themselves better to separate study and they are discussed under their respective headings, although here also color and light must be dealt with as they affect and are affected by line and space.

II. TECHNIQUE AND PATTERN

The fundamental characteristic of Cézanne's technique is the application of color in perceptible brushstrokes, which he derived, as we have already noted, from the impressionists, and particularly from Pissarro and Manet. Another feature, scarcely less important, is his extremely frequent resort to spots, strips or areas of bare canvas, which play as essential a part in the drawing, modeling and compositional organization as do the brushstrokes of color. This use of bare canvas is, of course, also derived from the impressionists, but with the latter it is either an incidental or an accidental feature, while in Cézanne's fully-developed form it is an instrument deliberately and consistently employed for various specific purposes inherent in the nature of his design.

Cézanne's pattern of brushstrokes is much more constant and systematic than Pissarro's, the strokes themselves are more perceptible and more uniform, and they are organized in more definitely shaped areas. For Pissarro, as for the other impressionists, brushstrokes individually and in relation to one another are indispensable components of the design as a whole, and in Manet especially they are perhaps the chief instrument in drawing out whatever is characteristic and essential in the object depicted. Cézanne's brushstrokes are most active not in their particularity but as constituents of patches or areas, and in this respect are more akin to the units in a mosaic. In their individual shape, they most resemble Manet's, since they are usually flat and square or oblong instead of thin, elongated, curved, and produced by the tip of the brush, as in Pissarro or Monet. Their application on the canvas is more positive and deliberate in Cézanne than in any of the other painters in question; they are also more colorful, they impart a more intense structural conviction to the objects which they draw, and they are much more active compositionally, partly because of their specificity, partly because any illustrative or decorative part they may play is entirely subsidiary to their plastic function.

However, before Cézanne succeeded in making brushstrokes serve as an effective instrument for his individual purposes, he passed through a long, tedious, difficult stage of experimentation. In some of his pictures, painted several years after he had attained the basic essentials of his mature form, the unsuccessful adaptation of technique to expressive form is still clearly evident. In "Hill of Le Galet at Pontoise" (76), for instance, the parallel, mostly oblique brushstrokes, which were a rather constant feature in his work of the late seventies, appear throughout large areas, but accomplish little more than the formation of a lively surface-pattern. They fail to function as planes in the drawing and modeling or in the definition of space, with the result that practically all the trees, for example, are mere conglomerations of strokes of paint. Similar technique of slanting parallel strokes appears in

other landscapes [1] and in still-lifes [2] and figure-paintings [3] in the
late seventies and early eighties, either throughout entire pictures
or in large areas of them, and it recurs intermittently throughout
his career. If not sufficiently varied by other types of brushstrokes
or if inadequately adjusted to color, it is responsible for the
monotonous, mechanical surface-pattern in some otherwise good
pictures.[4] A number of pictures of the middle seventies and of
about 1877 exhibit an all-over pattern of broad, short, square,
individual touches of thick paint which produce a characteristic
mosaiclike surface.[5] Later in Cézanne's technical development, a
similarly decorative pattern of square units is produced by a great
variety of brushstrokes; it is infinitely richer in color content, and
its decorative aspect is secondary to its expressive contribution;
in other words, pattern of brushwork and color are organically
integrated in the plastic form.[6]

The most obvious and direct effect of Cézanne's brushstrokes
is their pattern: they are *grouped,* and the constituents or units of
each group are usually alike in a number of respects. They have
a common color, or tone, or direction, or degree of perceptibility,
and are generally distinguished in one or more of these aspects
from the patches or areas with which they come in contact. Frequently the brushstrokes making up a single patch are further set
off from the adjacent areas by a line of demarcation, sometimes
a linear band of color, sometimes a sharp circumscribing edge;
and it is the patch or area as a whole which constitutes the fundamental unit of composition. Such areas may be made up of hatchings, which serve to model volumes; or they may be stripes, which
function as lines; but they are usually definite planes, which are
so grouped as to build up the solidity of masses in a manner distinctive of Cézanne. This method of modeling represents his most
individual creative use of the impressionistic technique. When the
execution is successful, these planes are varied and distinguished
by changes in color, tone and linear direction; they are ordered in

[1] E.g., "Estaque" (66); "Val Harmé at Auvers" (70); "Bay of Marseilles
Seen from Estaque" (90).
[2] E.g., "Compotier, Glass, Apples and Knife" (64).
[3] E.g., "Leda and the Swan" (68) and "Five Nudes" (74), in each of
which, however, Cézanne realizes monumental solidity of volume and a dynamic space-volume composition, in spite of the mechanical technique.
[4] E.g., "Five Nudes" (74).
[5] E.g., "Choquet in Armchair" (52).
[6] E.g., "Bibemus Quarry" (155).

deep space, and by their intersection or, more correctly speaking, their collision, at various angles, they convey the effect of dynamic movement. This effect is heightened by the dramatic contrast consequent upon the manifold differences between the various areas, and the two factors, interpenetration and contrast, combine with the structural color to produce much of Cézanne's characteristic impression of power.

Cézanne's patterns are in the main angular: the lines do not flow like Botticelli's, for example, or Renoir's. When curvilinear elements occur, they are usually employed for purposes of contrast and not to set the general character of the design, while even in themselves they are rigid rather than fluid. The general quality of rigidity, even of severity, arises also from the sharp impact of one area or object upon another, an effect which persists even when there is interpenetration of brushstrokes across lines of division. Such lines are often broad and ragged, but these qualities do not in the least blur the difference between one object and another, or cushion the collision of the two. Within single areas, there is often a considerable degree of interpenetration and overlapping of brushstrokes, but even when a particular area is drawn and modeled with relatively less perceptible technique and has a one-piece effect (which, with Cézanne, seldom reaches complete homogeneity), the uniformity is usually itself a note of contrast with adjacent areas. The prevailing effect of contrast, together with the general ruggedness of surface, contributes powerfully to the drama of the design as a whole.

To enumerate all the varieties of Cézanne's pattern would be to anticipate our discussion of line, space and composition, but some of the effects directly connected with technique may be mentioned here. The grouping of brushstrokes into patches is constantly repeated on a larger scale, with single patches making up the units of more extensive areas, and often imparting to the ensemble the patterned character of a patchwork quilt,[7] or the varied effects of mosaics and tapestry.[8] The more extensive areas, like their constituents, are usually definitely shaped, angular and rigid even when curvilinear. All of these areas, in turn, are diversified in various ways. An area running in one direction may be executed in brushstrokes running at an angle to it as, for example, a horizontal area patterned by brushstrokes predominantly verti-

[7] E.g., "Mountains in Provence" (85).
[8] E.g., "Five Nudes" (74); "Bibemus Quarry" (155); "Well" (174).

cal;[9] similarly the brushstrokes that make up a strip functioning
as a line may be placed, not in the direction of the line, but at right
angles to it;[10] a generally circular area may be built up and patterned chiefly by square or oblong brushstrokes.[11] Innumerable
other variations of technique and pattern are adapted to draw out
the specific qualities of particular objects and situations, to accentuate, for example, either the continuity of space[12] or the beat of
volumes;[13] but whatever their individual function they are alike
in emphasizing the qualities of contrast, drama, power, and plastic
movement, and in establishing compositional order. Occasionally,
however, poor adjustment of color-relationships dissociates the
pattern from the form as a whole, with the result that the organization collapses into a series of isolated color-patches, which seem
to jump out of the canvas.[14]

The improvement of technique in Cézanne's later work consists
chiefly in the fact that the actual brushwork becomes more and
more organically combined with the effects of color and color-
relations, and that the pigment itself is less often heaped up into
functionless layers of paint. Indeed, in some of his mature pictures, the pigment is so thin that the individual brushstrokes, even
when they are superposed, have the transparency and delicacy of
water-color glazes.[15] In other paintings equally good, done after
1900,[16] the brushstrokes are still loaded with pigment, but the
touches have become more sure, and the impasto functions as
positive color in drawing, modeling and composition, whereas in
the early work it represents the accumulation of the repeated
touches of pigment which he was compelled to pile up in attempt-
ing to coördinate the technique with the color-requirements of his
design. Another common occurrence in his mature work is the
striation of volumes and contours by a parallel alignment of ribbonlike brushstrokes or long dashes, which establish a rhythmic continuity of the drawing and modeling of the volumes with the broad

[9] E.g., "Leda and the Swan" (68), see detail illustrated, p. 294; "Red
Earth" (111), see detail illustrated, p. 299.
[10] E.g., "River and Hills" (48), see detail illustrated, p. 294.
[11] E.g., "Ginger Jar and Fruit" (181), see detail illustrated, p. 300.
[12] E.g., "Well" (174).
[13] E.g., "Compotier, Pitcher and Fruit" (128) or "Oranges and Bottle"
(148).
[14] E.g., "Mount Ste. Victoire Seen from the Chemin des Lauves" (189).
[15] E.g., "Interior with Nude" (83); "Mount Ste. Victoire" (154); "Rocks
and Trees" (179), see detail illustrated, p. 295.
[16] E.g., "Skull and Fruit" (187); "Nudes in Landscape" (191).

contour-lines and the pattern of adjacent areas or masses.[17] This continuity of pattern frequently involves a subdivision of the broad contour-line into a set of multiple individual outlines which help carry the activity of one unit over into another.[18]

Cézanne's command of his medium was seldom uniformly perfect even at the end of his life, but as his technical proficiency improved, and his vision broadened, he was often able to subordinate obvious technique to the purposes of design by making the individual components of the technique less perceptible, without loss in decorative effect and with an enormous increase in expressive power. He learned to rely less on the pattern of individual brushstrokes, to avoid the necessity of applying repeated coats of pigment, to use thin glazes successfully, and to relate more skilfully his individual color-planes in a general space-composition.[19] Technique gradually becomes less and less monotonous: it is still perceptible, but individual areas are more precisely adjusted to the expression of the form as a whole, and there is greater feeling of continuity between them; the effect of solidity is obtained less by blocklike shapes and thick pigment than by incorporation of structural color in the substance of the object itself. These changes, of course, represent a refinement, not an abandonment, of Cézanne's earlier methods: his technique, organized in a very definite and positive pattern, remains the keystone of his form throughout his entire career.

III. LINE

The highly patterned character of Cézanne's paintings, the very distinct shape of their constituent areas, necessarily involves a constant emphasis upon line and linear effects. Line is indeed so vitally essential to the fabric of the picture that sometimes it is introduced without any warrant in representative necessity;[20] but at its best it is never merely a detail in a superposed pattern, but an inherent part of the substance of the plastic form. Cézanne's awareness that such linear effects were essential to his design showed itself in his unceasing efforts to make technique and color

[17] E.g., "Nudes in Landscape" (191), see details illustrated, p. 296 and p. 304.
[18] E.g., "Girl with Doll" (146); "Ambroise Vollard" (158); "Drinker" (177); "Nudes in Landscape" (191), see detail illustrated, p. 296.
[19] Compare, e.g., "Woman with Green Hat" (103) with "Head of Victor Choquet" (61).
[20] E.g., across the handle of the jug in "Jug and Fruit" (123), or across the leg of the figure seated by the tree in "Nudes in Landscape" (191).

his instruments in forging a kind of line that should distinguish each area definitely from adjacent areas, and should at the same time be an adjunct in the drawing, modeling and spatial localization of volumes.

The simplest form of line, in painting as in nature, is that produced by the contact of two areas or by their intersection, and is exemplified in the outline of a building or a mountain against the sky. This type of line occurs frequently in the painting of the Florentines, and the interplay of line, relatively independent of color, planes, or perceptible brushwork, is usually the groundwork of both the expressive and the decorative phases of their form. In Cézanne's best work no such isolation of line from form is possible, nor does his line function independently of the activities of color and technique: it is a by-product of the meeting of planes of color, and the interaction of the linear effects so produced constitutes the groundwork of his architectonic design. He does habitually make use of the clean-cut division of objects present in the Florentines which he sometimes accentuates by contrasts of light and dark adjacent areas.[21] Often, however, he lends additional emphasis and weight to his line by making it a narrow strip of color, which he adapted from the Venetians. Such actual, as distinguished from mathematical, lines are frequently ragged in Cézanne, much as were Daumier's, and are usually built up by perceptible brushwork. A series of brushstrokes running roughly parallel to one another may be aligned along the border of an object; the brushstrokes may be overlapping [22] or placed in a series of dashes.[23] This makes the actual line in one of its types, but a similar effect may be produced by a narrow band or succession of spots of bare canvas.[24] In none of these types does line ever extend very far without breaks, and occasionally, as when brushstrokes or alternate areas of light and dark overlap, it is serrated like the edge of a saw.[25] Sometimes the line consists primarily of a zone of deepened color extending into the object defined;[26] at

[21] E.g., "Valley of the Arc" (109).
[22] E.g., "Five Nudes" (74), see detail illustrated, p. 302; "Group of Bathers" (182), see detail illustrated, p. 302.
[23] E.g., "Nudes in Landscape" (191), see detail illustrated, p. 304.
[24] E.g., "Poplar Trees" (73); "Table, Napkin and Fruit" (172), see detail illustrated, p. 297; "Well" (174), see detail illustrated, p. 299.
[25] E.g., "Mount Ste. Victoire and Valley" (57), see detail illustrated, p. 296; "Five Nudes" (74), see detail illustrated, p. 302.
[26] E.g., "Valley of the Arc" (109), see detail illustrated, p. 293.

other times it seems to occupy the space between two neighboring objects; [27] and sometimes it lies outside the object altogether, as a narrow band of color or "area-line" [28] paralleling the actual boundary and forming an independent plane.[29] The area-lines frequently convey so emphatic an intimation of solid mass that they suggest an additional view of the object from an angle other than the one from which the main aspects are given; and it is possible that this device of Cézanne's suggested to Picasso the idea of combining, in a single view, aspects of things as they appear both from the front and from the side.[30]

When Cézanne's line extends into the object of which it is the contour, it is often an important adjunct to modeling; [31] when the line lies outside of the object defined, it affects more directly the location of the object in space; [32] but in each instance, it contributes to both modeling and spacing; and in all the cases mentioned, it participates in the compositional ordering of the canvas. Whatever the particular manner employed to emphasize contour and shape, brushwork is always a reënforcing agent. As already noted in a previous section of this chapter, linear contour is accentuated sometimes by multiple, more or less parallel, striations or streaks,[33] and sometimes by a further duplication of the contour in some part of the pattern of brushstrokes and color-areas which makes up the body of the object itself and the units surrounding it.[34]

What is chiefly significant in all these uses of line is the multiplicity of plastic functions involved. The line is never merely a means of indicating shape, but rather an essential means of drawing, modeling and composition. Its positiveness as well as its close relationship to light and shadow enables it to make an important contribution to the solidity of the objects which it outlines. It is

[27] E.g., "Plate with Grapes and Peach" (58), see detail illustrated, p. 292.

[28] An "area-line," as the term implies, is an element which fulfills the dual function of both a line and an area.

[29] E.g., "Oranges and Bottle" (148), see detail illustrated, p. 293; "Ginger Jar and Fruit" (181), see detail illustrated, p. 301; "Group of Bathers" (182), see detail illustrated, p. 302.

[30] Compare, e.g., Picasso's "Violin and Bottle" (353) with Cézanne's "Ginger Jar and Fruit" (181), see detail illustrated, p. 301.

[31] E.g., "Valley of the Arc" (109), see detail illustrated, p. 293.

[32] E.g., "Oranges and Bottle" (148), see detail illustrated, p. 293.

[33] E.g., "Nine Bathers" (107); "Girl with Doll" (146); "Peasant in Blue Blouse" (149); "Ambroise Vollard" (158); "Nudes in Landscape" (191).

[34] E.g., "Five Nudes" (74), see detail illustrated, p. 302; "Nudes in Landscape" (191), see detail illustrated, p. 296.

often in itself a plane in relation to other planes, and thus becomes an essential part in the spatial organization of the picture. Furthermore, as a color-area in relation to other color-areas, it enters into the color-composition of the form as a whole. Unfortunately these general formal relationships of line, especially as mediated by color, are not always successful in execution: Cézanne's imperfect control of his medium, most obvious in his use of line, frequently results in a tendency to an overaccentuated contour, often in the form of a lumpy or grainy ridge of paint, which fails to perform its function of spatial localization, remains an isolated element, and thus impairs the unity of the composition as a whole.[35] This break in unity is often aggravated by reliance upon very thick pigment to secure either spacing or the weight and plastic power which should have their source in the color itself and its relationships. Another peculiarity of Cézanne's use of line as an adjunct to the drawing and modeling of volumes and their location in space, is that the pigment of his broad dark outline sometimes sinks below the surface of the adjacent color-areas, thus creating a recession and projection of planes. This specious device appears intermittently throughout his entire work.[36]

Linear effects in Cézanne, in addition to defining the boundaries of individual objects, occur within the objects or areas and also extend over a number of them. Those within the objects are of particular importance in modeling; those embracing a number of areas function in placing objects in perspective and in general compositional organization. Both types alike, as well as the lines lying along boundaries, are usually constructed by perceptible technique. A succession of short parallel brushstrokes, as we have already noted, may constitute a general linear effect or strip, in which the individual brushstrokes are placed at an angle to the line as a whole.[37] To bind the entire strip more firmly together, Cézanne often makes one of the edges sharply continuous, leaving the other comparatively ill-defined and allowing it to taper off

[35] E.g., "Bathers at Rest" (63); "Mardi-Gras" (106); "Old Woman with Rosary" (178); "Three Skulls" (184); "Château Noir" (186); "Vallier" (188).

[36] E.g., the reclining figure in "Bathers at Rest" (63) of 1877, see detail illustrated, p. 292; several instances in "Jug and Fruit" (123) of c. 1890; "Skull and Fruit" (187) of c. 1904.

[37] E.g., "River and Hills" (48), see detail illustrated, p. 294; "Gardener" (130), see detail (a) illustrated, p. 298; "Eight Women Bathing" (161).

gradually into the adjacent area.[38] Sometimes, to emphasize still further both the sharpness of the one edge and the general linear continuity of the strip or patch, he intensifies the light or color along that edge,[39] or defines it by an actual brushstroke from which the other strokes then take their start.[40] When the strip is broad, the effect of the patch is that of a rigid fringe, a comb, or of one side of a quill, to the rib or backbone of which the brushstrokes, like the barbs or tufts of a feather, are attached. This combined effect of line, patch and brushstrokes, which we shall designate as the "quill-motif," is, of course, one variety of Cézanne's general organization of brushstrokes in patches forming planes : the sharp edge accentuates the space between the quill-like planes as well as the continuity of direction in the segments which make up the patch. Cézanne constantly uses this quill-motif in drawing, modeling,[41] and space-organization,[42] for which it is one of his most effective instruments.

In another organization of brushstrokes which emphasizes linear direction and spatial relationships, groups of parallel strokes are arranged with overlapping edges, so that the effect as a whole is that of a crenelated strip of color. The interpenetration is at times made more emphatic by areas of bare canvas between the strokes.[43] The general tendency of the crenelated edge, as of the quill-motif, is often to carry back into deep space the perspective of horizontal planes. Each of these motifs may be used also either to draw a particular object or to pattern a more vaguely defined area in the background, but the definiteness of shape and the continuity of direction are sufficient to maintain linear character in general, while the contribution to perspective exemplifies the basic compositional activity of Cézanne's line in all its forms.

Cézanne frequently employs, to discharge functions essentially linear, devices in which there is no actual line at all, but only a succession of spots or areas or accents of color or tone which define a direction and carry the eye along a single path up or down, to the right or left, or forward or backward in space. These spots

[38] E.g., "Gardener" (130), see detail (a) illustrated, p. 298; "Rocks and Trees" (179), see detail illustrated, p. 295.
[39] E.g., "Gardener" (130); "Bibemus Quarry" (155); "Well" (174); "Rocks and Trees" (179).
[40] E.g., "Gardener" (130), see detail (b) illustrated, p. 298; "Well" (174).
[41] E.g., "Woman with Green Hat" (103).
[42] E.g., "Gardener" (130) ; "Well" (174).
[43] E.g., "Mount Ste. Victoire and Valley" (57), see detail illustrated, p. 296.

or areas need not be precisely shaped or in immediate contact with each other, so long as their sequence is clearly marked and the observer's imagination fills in the gaps. Such broken or interrupted linear sequences may of course also include segments of actual line or continuous mass, as when the boundary of a clump of foliage continues the direction of a man's arm;[44] and from the compositional point of view line exercises in these sequences an important function. This is a traditional device used frequently by old and modern masters, but in Cézanne's hands it operates more obviously and more directly in establishing compositional integration.[45] In principle these linear sequences are identical with the sequences of brushstrokes and fragments of contour which make up his line on a smaller scale.

In the anatomy of Cézanne's form, in brief, it is the linear aspects of things, whether bounding contours, actual lines, strips of color, area-lines, or sequences of direction, that make up the bones and sinews. Inseparably merged with color, they emphasize the structure of his form as a whole, its basic architecture; and it is the systematic use of them, in subordination to the architectonic design, which occasions the omnipresence of distortion in his work. Objects as we ordinarily see them, the haphazard forms and arrangements of ordinary life, are neither shaped nor placed to build up formally organized and balanced designs. This is true, of course, of the raw material of any artist, but the transformation required by Cézanne's form is much more thoroughgoing and also more specific than that in any other painter of equal rank. In comparison with Renoir's, for example, it affects a different aspect of things, and one more immediately apparent to the ordinary eye. Renoir's interests were more universal and also more human: he could exhibit a vastly greater range of values in the world, but without altering so deeply the familiar shape of things to which our human emotions are primarily attached. It is the shape of things which ordinarily enables us to recognize them; and it is the violence which Cézanne does to familiar shapes that gives to his paintings their appearance of extreme and wilful distortion. His wilfulness, however, is in reality a manifestation of single-mindedness, a per-

[44] E.g., "Man Putting on Coat" (56).
[45] Compare, e.g., Cézanne's "Card Players and Girl" (141) or "Men Bathing" (164) with Tintoretto's "Two Prophets" (238), El Greco's "Mocked Christ" (244) and Renoir's "Bathing Group" (292) or "Two Women in Park" (313).

ception of what is needed if the raw material of perception is to be re-formed into the substance of his design. That design requires definitely shaped plastic units with the precise and emphatic contours and planes which will enable them to fuse in a firmly-knit architectural structure. Such a structure can no more be constructed out of the objects of nature, molded by forces that have no relation to art, than a suspension bridge or a skyscraper can be built out of iron ore.

IV. Space

Spatial organization includes both the shaping of individual objects into volumes which have depth and solidity, and the placing of such objects at various intervals and positions in two- and three-dimensional space. The first is what is usually termed "modeling," the second is the achievement of perspective; for Cézanne, however, not only are the means of both to a large extent the same, but the construction of a single object and its integration in the form of the picture as a whole are so much phases or stages of a single process that they cannot be adequately discussed in isolation from one another.

Cézanne's technique is directed from the start to the emphasis of spatial character. As we have already indicated, his brushstrokes, both singly and as organized in patches or areas, take the form of planes set in definite space. The accentuation of planes follows the French tradition, from the primitives to Manet;[46] but though the use of planes gives a flattened appearance to the rounded surfaces of Cézanne's masses, the masses as entities are not flat but three-dimensional. In other painters, when the continuous rounded swell of actual physical things, as represented in the modeling of the Renaissance painters, is discarded, there is usually also a reduction in the depth of the picture, as for instance in Manet; but Cézanne's space is as notable for its depth as his volumes are for their weight and massiveness. The massiveness does not arise, however, from the continuous change of illumination to be seen in Leonardo or Rembrandt or any of their modern followers, and though the ordinary devices of linear perspective are employed to some extent, they do not by themselves render the spatial effects characteristic of Cézanne's individual form. Pattern of line and of color, arising out of technique and conjoined with

[46] See Barnes and de Mazia, "The French Primitives and Their Forms," p. 34, Barnes Foundation Press, 1931.

the structural activity of the color-relationships, is the prime factor in creating and organizing massiveness.

The place of the traditional literal chiaroscuro is taken in Cézanne by the union of color and light in the hatchings or groups of brush-strokes out of which the surfaces of volumes are made up. Cézanne's typical use of these hatchings, in modeling and drawing, constitutes one of the distinctive contributions of his mature work. In these grouped hatchings, instead of successive tones of the same color with continuous and gradual increase or decrease in light-content, there is usually a modulated pattern of patches achieved by application of brushstrokes of different hue or tint, one color serving as light or as highlight, another as middle tone or as shadow. Of these varied effects of illumination, it is generally the middle tone and the shadow that are accentuated in terms of color, and the tonal transition from one area to the other is relatively abrupt rather than gradual.[47] Thus the indispensable contrast of illumination is secured in essentials without literal imitation, and when Cézanne is successful the result is an integral union of light and color which conveys with intense conviction the sense of sub-stantial reality. At the same time a decorative quality arises directly, without any superposed ornamental motifs, out of the structural color-pattern. It is seldom, however, that Cézanne realizes the degree of color-subtlety of the greatest masters of light, such as Renoir. Often, indeed, Cézanne fails almost entirely to integrate the light and the color, and as a result the color is dull, drab, muted, opaque, or totally lacking in luster or internal glow. The fault may appear in the picture as a whole,[48] or in parts of it;[49] sometimes it is found in only certain areas of a picture which elsewhere has deep, rich and glowing color.[50] Occasionally Cézanne's inability to control his medium leads him to pile up pigment where the highlight falls, so that the represented solidity

[47] In Renoir's modeling, by contrast, the tonal modulations are more subtly graduated from the darkest to the lightest color, and the highlights are more vividly accentuated both as light and as color. Compare, e.g., the trees in Cézanne's "Valley of the Arc" (109) with those in Renoir's "Bathing Group" (292).

[48] E.g., "Idyl" (26); "House at Auvers" (32); "Red Roofs" (35); "Louveciennes" (43); "Temptation of St. Anthony" (60); "Compotier, Glass, Apples and Knife" (64); "Bay of Marseilles Seen from Estaque" (90); "Girl with Doll" (146); "Ambroise Vollard" (158); "Millstone in Woods" (165); "Woods" (175); "Old Woman with Rosary" (178).

[49] E.g., "Hill of Le Galet at Pontoise" (76).

[50] E.g., "Woman with Shawl" (118).

depends upon actual physical bulk and projection of the paint.[51] Very often, also, in modeling, the color-relations make the spot on which the light falls appear to recede instead of to stand out. This "sunken light," it should be added, is not always a drawback: it often provides a note of unexpectedness or picturesqueness without detracting from the conviction of the modeling, as when the constituent planes of a solid object recall the values of landscape.[52]

The overlapping color-planes of which Cézanne's objects are composed sometimes produce a comparatively one-piece effect;[53] at other times, in contrast, they are sharply distinguished from one another and give the effect of depth not only by their light-shadow relations and the intrinsic weight of their color, but also by their intersection at various angles in space. The planes then appear as facets, like those of a roughly hewn block of wood, and the lines of their intersection often give the effect of hinges on which the planes may be conceived as turning.[54] The pattern then seems to reveal the internal structure of the object, and at the same time it heightens the three-dimensional character typical of Cézanne. This effect is produced not only by the actual formation of the brushstrokes and the planes which they make up, but by perspective established by the direction in which they are placed, and by contrasts of color, light and shadow. As such, the construction of the individual mass is the beginning, on a small scale, of the general compositional arrangement of volumes and whole areas of the picture which is fundamental to Cézanne's balanced, dynamic form.

Modeling as dependent upon pattern and intersection of planes necessarily involves line, but Cézanne's line also contributes to modeling in other ways, as when hatchings and patches of color within the area of an object are supplemented by a definite linear contour around the object.[55] Sometimes contour is sharp and clean-cut,[56] but more often it is achieved by heavy actual broad lines of

[51] E.g., "Cakes and Fruit" (51); "Bathers at Rest" (63); "Bay of Marseilles Seen from Estaque" (90).
[52] E.g., the piece of fruit in the foreground of "Fruit and Tapestry" (55); the door panel over the coffee pot in "Woman and Coffee Pot" (140); the table drawer in "Card Players and Girl" (141). Cf. a similar effect in the well in Tintoretto's "Woman of Samaria" (240).
[53] E.g., the face in "Girl with Bird-Cage" (97); some of the fruit in "Oranges and Bottle" (148).
[54] E.g., "Provence Peasant" (151), see detail illustrated, p. 300.
[55] E.g., "Five Nudes" (74); "Nudes in Landscape" (191).
[56] E.g., the left contour of the apple in the left foreground of "Ginger Jar and Fruit" (181), see illustration, p. 268.

color,[57] by area-lines,[58] or by outlines of shadow which appear sunken between, and below the level of, color-areas that come in contact along the line.[59] All these methods of using line add to the weight of the volume, emphasize its individuality, and establish its spatial relationships both internally and externally. The broad lines of contour and area-lines often themselves function as space and define the position of objects with reference to adjacent objects. In this again, pattern shows its tendency to extend beyond the flat surface of the canvas and to assume a character inherently compositional and expressive as well as decorative.

Another important function of linear pattern in relation to modeling sometimes appears, especially in spherical objects of still-lifes, in a particular use of intersecting straight and curved linear sequences of color-units within the area of the object modeled.[60] Around a nodal point, perceived as nearest the eye, a series of concentric bands of color are disposed at varying distances, like the parallels of latitude as they would appear to an observer looking down on a globe of the earth from a position above the North Pole. Because of the color-relationships established, each circular band, as the series extends, represents a greater depth of space; at the same time another series of comparatively straight lines, radiating like the spokes of a wheel from the same nodal point, correspond to the meridians of longitude. The "lines," in both cases, are rarely actual lines: they are rather the result of sequences of brushstrokes or of areas of light or color which, in spite of interruptions, maintain essential continuity in a particular direction. They are, in effect, lines of perspective used to organize the space in which a particular mass is set and at the same time to indicate the curvature of its surface, and in them modeling and space-composition coalesce.[61]

As we pass from Cézanne's construction of individual volumes to that of spatial order on a larger scale, we find the use of brushstrokes, planes, linear contour, and indications of direction no less ubiquitous or significant. Fragments of line or local linear pattern

[57] E.g., "Nudes in Landscape" (191), see details illustrated, p. 296 and p. 304.
[58] E.g., the upper right contour of the apple in the left foreground in "Ginger Jar and Fruit" (181), see detail illustrated, p. 301.
[59] E.g., the reclining figure in "Bathers at Rest" (63), see detail illustrated, p. 292.
[60] E.g., "Fruit and Tapestry" (55), see detail illustrated, p. 297.
[61] For further details see analytical notes on "Fruit and Tapestry" (55), p. 318.

contribute to the rendering of deep space by virtue of their organic connection with a network of lines and areas which extends ultimately to every element in the picture. The principle involved, here again, is that of linear perspective, and its consistent application by Cézanne, with its purposive distortions, results in a multiplicity of rhythmic space-relationships, not unlike those of Uccello, but far more bizarre and picturesque, and at the same time intensely positive, convincing and powerful.

Cézanne's spatial intervals, like those of the Florentines, are clear-cut and precise, with none of the pervasive atmospheric color-overtones found in the Venetians, Claude le Lorrain or the impressionists. In general, he disregards not only their methods, but aërial perspective itself : the outlines of far-away objects in his painting are practically as sharp as those in the foreground. In this respect, Cézanne's drawing of space differs from that of the Venetians and Renoir, and is primarily a by-product of the placing of volumes ; however, it is akin to that of the Venetians in the emphasis given to space by sharp contrast in the directions of volumes tending away from each other. In Cézanne, the resulting dynamic movement is of objects—fruit, houses, trees—in themselves inert, while in the Venetians it is usually of the represented movements of arms, legs and figures as a whole.[62]

The rhythmic movement of volumes and planes in space is so basic in Cézanne's design that it usually extends to the treatment of the background—whether that be sky, wall or drapery—and makes it serve the dual purpose of a screenlike area or space-boundary and of a rhythmic sequence of semivoluminous planes which continue the movement of the units in the middleground and foreground ; this sequential ordering thus contributes to compositional unity in the widest sense as well as to the expressive movement of the total form. Contrast between the three sections of the picture is established by a concentrated activity of distinct units in the middleground, and a relative coalescence of the voluminous planes of the background into a one-piece unit of sky, wall or drapery.[63] Both within particular masses and in the sequence of masses and large planes, the patches, strips and the quill-motif described in the preceding section are among the most

[62] Compare, e.g., Paolo Veronese's "Baptism of Christ" (241) with Cézanne's "Ginger Jar and Fruit" (181).
[63] E.g., "Red Earth" (111) ; "Compotier, Pitcher and Fruit" (128) ; "Card Players and Girl" (141).

effective means of establishing the general rhythmic continuity.

While the main compositional motif in Cézanne is that of the movement of volume-space units, it is the relationship of the planes in which the volumes are set which contributes most to the individuality of the bizarre, dynamic effect of the ensemble. Cézanne frequently accentuates receding space by an emphasis upon the definite location of an upright plane in the immediate foreground.[64] The plane may be a single object—a table cloth, a wall—or it may be composed of several objects, as, for example, a row of tree trunks. This vertical foreground-plane is often one of the features of his familiar plan of organization, in which upright volumes or wedgelike masses are set upon a roughly horizontal solid plane as on a table top, whether this plane be actually the top of a table in a still-life or the main oblique-horizontal plane of the ground or floor in a landscape or interior scene.

The problem of localizing the individual masses in deep space is fundamentally that of making the plane on which they are placed go backward. This problem is solved chiefly by the treatment of the color-pattern which makes up the fundamental plane as a whole. The smaller planes into which it is subdivided frequently intersect, much as do those within the individual objects, the faceted character of which thus recurs on a larger scale. The entire "table-top" plane, which occurs either in the foreground or in the middleground of the painting, is made to recede mainly by lines of direction extending across it, which may be the indications of linear perspective within an actual object—as when a road extends backward through a large area of a landscape [65]—or a series of areas so united to one another by similarity of technique, color, light, or shadow, that they establish the perspective of the entire section.[66] Sometimes a linear area, composed of parallel brushstrokes set at right angles to its general direction, may give the effect of perspective by tapering off gradually as it moves away into space; [67] or the sense of distance may be conveyed by a sequence of reced-

[64] E.g., "Six Bathers" (100); "Nine Bathers" (107); "Valley of the Arc" (109); "Mount Ste. Victoire with Pine Tree" (124); "House and Wall" (147); "Viaduct" (152); "Well" (174); "Ginger Jar and Fruit" (181). The plane is vaguely suggested in some of his earlier work, e.g., "Reading at Zola's" (23) of the late sixties.
[65] E.g., "Mount Ste. Victoire and Valley" (57).
[66] E.g., "River and Hills" (48); "Red Earth" (111).
[67] E.g., "Red Earth" (111), see detail illustrated, p. 299.

ing objects, with their different shapes and relative sizes specifically adapted to the attainment of this end.[68] Perspective in the
main horizontal plane of Cézanne's composition is often effectively
rendered by a pattern of parallel, relatively horizontal bands or
stripes which contrast with one another in color or tone, and are
usually made up of brushstrokes, also horizontal, which thus reenforce the composite rhythm of the color-bands. Varying degrees
of emphasis upon the perceptibility of the bands or the pattern of
brushstrokes result in a great variety of effects.[69]

General lines of perspective of any of the sorts above noted
may admit of many interruptions, provided there is essential continuity of direction, and their effect is as a rule conjoined with a
tilting of the entire planes on which they occur. Such general
planes, in addition, are usually bound together by some form of
homogeneous technique: their constituent brushstrokes may be of
approximately uniform size and shape,[70] or be placed in the same
direction,[71] or have a common degree of accentuation,[72] or be
dominated by the same general color or tone.[73] Sometimes, especially in landscapes, a whole set of particular objects, a group
of trees with their leaves and branches, for instance, may be regarded plastically as one plane with angular protuberances and
recessions; in this case the constituent brushstrokes interpenetrate
extensively and enforce the effect of continuity.[74] At other times,
as in some of his landscapes [75] and in most of his still-lifes,[76] the
beat rather than the continuity of volumes is emphasized, and then
the individuality of particular objects is made more obvious by
variations between their technique and that of adjacent areas, and
often also by positive contour-lines, either heavy or clean-cut.
Whatever the particular means, Cézanne inevitably makes use of
the general principle by which the illusion of depth may be produced: the principle involved is the fact that any object, placed
between the spectator and a more remote object, obscures the

[68] E.g., "Gray Jug and Fruit" (122); "Ginger Jar and Fruit" (181).
[69] Cf., e.g., "Near Gardanne" (93); "Normandy Farm" (114); "Plain,
Trees and Hills" (150); "Road at Marines" (153); "Big Trees" (160).
For comparative analytical notes see Appendix, p. 387.
[70] E.g., "Leda and the Swan" (68).
[71] E.g., "River and Hills" (48); "Five Nudes" (74).
[72] E.g., "Gardanne" (92).
[73] E.g., "Red Earth" (111).
[74] E.g., "Well" (174).
[75] E.g., "Valley of the Arc" (109).
[76] E.g., "Ginger Jar and Fruit" (181).

view of the latter. It is not, however, upon this principle, which of course is scientific rather than esthetic, that he relies for his own distinctive effects of three-dimensional space. His characteristic means, in this respect as in others, are continuity and contrast of pattern, lines of perspective created by specific uses of technique and color, emphasis upon planes and their intersection at various angles, contrast of light and shadow, and the intrinsic quality and relationships of color.

V. Composition

We have already noted the extreme selectiveness of Cézanne's form: the fact that from any object or situation he chooses only the traits or aspects adapted to a definite, extremely individual effect, reducing the associated values of subject-matter or of general human interest, distorting natural appearances often to the point at which only their broad general character is identifiable, and executing his designs by a technique equally selective and purposive in all its phases. The fact that this design or form is architectonic implies in addition that for Cézanne the supreme plastic function is composition, always basically space-composition of a monumental order, whether the actual scale be large or small. His use of the means already discussed—pattern of brushwork, line, space, color, and light—can be understood only if we grasp the relation of each of these means to the compositional unification of the form as a whole.

Cézanne's pattern of color and technique is, even apart from its other plastic functions, his most obvious and fundamental means of establishing compositional order. The surface of his canvas, as we have already seen, is divided into definite areas, almost always precisely shaped, usually bounded by strongly marked linear contours, and further distinguished by contrasts in color, in kind and degree of illumination, and in manner of execution. Homogeneity of technique in conjunction with line serves to unify particular areas, which are bound together sequentially by continuity of line, mutual adaptation of shape, and relations of color, of light and of shadow. The quality of his color, more often subdued rather than sparkling or glittering, never strident or flamboyant, is itself a means of direct sensuous unification. In spite of his abundant palette of seventeen pigments, Cézanne's color-schemes are generally restricted in range, with hues of blue, green, ivory, tan, and orange predominating. A variety of blues, usually deep in tone, sometimes grayish and often leaden, prevail in perhaps the majority of his pictures. These tones usually strike the keynote of the color-scheme, and by their pervasiveness assist in harmonizing the pattern of color-contrasts.[77]

Varying degrees of perceptibility of technique, and variations in the shape and placing of the brushstrokes, establish marked differences in the appearance of the patterned areas; but the patterned effect itself extends to every part of the canvas and, reenforced by color-relationships, establishes a basic unity apart from the use of any specific compositional device. This is akin to the unity of the mosaics, and occasionally it even suggests the effect of a continuous fabric—a textile with a basket-weave,[78] for example, or with herringbone stripes,[79] or a patchwork quilt,[80] or a piece of tapestry.[81]

The significant characteristics of Cézanne's composition are not grasped, however, until the ubiquitous pattern is considered as something much more than surface-decoration. The pattern is ingrained in the form, and only by an effort of abstraction which does violence to its intrinsic nature can it be isolated as an entity of two dimensions: the areas or patches of which it is made up are so definitely planes set at angles to one another that their spatial character appears even in extremely small areas. The problem of composition, for Cézanne, is one of organizing the spatial relationships between all the component areas: between the planes or facets of each object, between the larger planes occupied by objects or groups of objects as a whole, and finally between the main sections of the canvas, and thus bringing the pervasive plastic movement of every unit into an all-inclusive stable equilibrium. The nature of this equilibrium is prescribed by the architectonic character to which allusion has already been made, and is what distinguishes Cézanne's compositions from those, for example, of Renoir. There is no lack of equilibrium in Renoir, but it is balance of moving forces, a harmony of motion rather than

[77] In a few of the landscapes of his mature period—e.g., "Rocks at Bibemus" (170); "Rocks—Forest of Fontainebleau" (171); "Woods" (175)—a deep lavender tone dominates the color-scheme and gives it a distinctive character, totally different from his usual blue-green-orange-tan combination.
[78] E.g., "Well" (174).
[79] E.g., "Leda and the Swan" (68).
[80] E.g., "Corner of Quarry" (176).
[81] E.g., "Five Nudes" (74).

of rest. In the same way, a streamlined automobile, an aeroplane, a racing yacht, have a poise of their own; but it is not the poise of a suspension bridge. Even in architecture, a cathedral with its spires seems to soar, while a fortress or a pyramid stands four-square and conveys the impression not of movement but of power to resist movement. The power of active movement, as it appears in Michelangelo's "Last Judgment" (227) or, more plastically rendered, in Tintoretto or El Greco, is almost completely absent from Cézanne's work: his compositions suggest not hurricanes but mountains.

It is natural, therefore, that Cézanne's most characteristic compositional arrangement should be that of the stablest of all natural objects or architectural structures—the pyramid. The principle of the pyramid remains, even when Cézanne resorts to the use of an enclosure by a sequence of masses, of an area or volume of space, forming a sort of tent, and accentuating the enclosed space itself.[82] In either case, whether space or mass is emphasized, the individual wedgelike volumes that make up Cézanne's pyramid frequently seem to jut out of a solid setting like figures in relief.[83] The spatial and dynamic effects arise partly from the massiveness of the objects themselves, and partly from the varying intervals and angles at which they are set in relation to each other and to the planes below, above, in front of them and in back of them; and it is in the conjoined effect of these two factors—masses and interrelation of their planes—that the sense of thrust and counterthrust of forces, and of ultimate equilibrium, resides.

The general types of Cézanne's compositional order, however varied, represent no radical innovation. The pyramidal organization is in itself one of the oldest of traditional devices, and in its simplest form is represented by the Gothic ogives and the familiar Crucifixions and Madonnas of the old masters. It has been employed by painters of every school, and it may, in the hands of an academic painter, sink to the lowest depths of banality. In Cézanne's hands it is seldom banal, partly because it is so obviously the form which his design must inevitably take, partly because the details are treated with such originality, force and imagination that picturesqueness of the whole is developed. The general

[82] E.g., "Five Nudes" (74); "Three Bathers" (82); "Large Bathers" (190).
[83] E.g., "Five Nudes" (74); "Four Bathers" (75).

form is modified according to the relative emphasis put upon the beat of the volumes or upon their continuity.

Sometimes, especially in his decentered compositions, there is no actual object to serve as the apex of the pyramid, and the masses on the two sides are directly united by plastic links of various sorts, so that they become bilaterally balanced units enframing an area of central space. In "Man and Skull" (142),[84] for example, the balance is effected by successive rhythmic thrusts and counterthrusts connecting the figure on the right with the series of objects on the left that function plastically as another figure. The same general type of composition is employed, with wide variations in detail, in a number of Cézanne's other pictures, notably still-lifes, but in none of them do the variations affect the essentially architectural character of the composition, its balance, or the complete subordination of all elements and aspects to the form as a whole. In "Gray Jug and Fruit" (122),[85] for instance, the two groups of masses which enframe the central space to right and left are supplemented below by a third group, consisting of the drapery, table and a few pieces of fruit; the general effect is that of a beat of volumes proceeding downward and upward across the picture, and counterbalanced in the upper part of the canvas by a pyramidal arrangement of planes patterning the background. In "Ginger Jar and Fruit" (181),[86] the principal masses right and left—the fruit on one side and the fruit and jar on the other—are connected by the overhanging table cloth below and by the volumes of its folds within the central space, so that the beat of volumes follows a lateral as well as a receding sequence. Here too, further compositional balance is achieved by a pyramidal arrangement which includes the jar and the shovel-like unit in the background. In "Table, Napkin and Fruit" (172),[87] the composition is doubly divided into foreground and background and into right and left sides. The foreground presents a continuous throb of masses, placed in directions at various angles to one another, which move in and out and across the canvas from the circular group at the right—the plate and fruit—to the other circular group on the left—the platelike table cloth and fruit. The background is sharply divided by a series of vertical broad bands, which function as hinges, and the receding and advancing planes, meeting at an apex on these bands, form a sub-composition not unlike a partly folded

[84] Illustration, p. 259.
[85] Illustration, p. 274.
[86] Illustration, p. 268.
[87] Illustration, p. 227.

screen, or a series of accordion pleats. The pattern of color-areas in this background is rhythmically related to that in the foreground and more or less duplicates it, so that continuity is established throughout the varied areas of the entire canvas.

Cézanne's compositions always bear the marks of reflection, of calculation in the disposition of particular components,[88] and their general form does not vary greatly in his different paintings. In his still-lifes, for example, there is usually a vertical plane, the foreground of the picture; then a roughly horizontal plane, on which the details of subject-matter—plates, fruit and the like— are placed; then a vertical background-plane which brings the recession of deep space to an end and thus shuts in the composition as a whole.[89] Both in a literal and in a figurative sense this may be termed a "table-top" composition; and the same general arrangement, in which a central plane containing most of the detail of the picture is sandwiched between upper distance and lower foreground-planes, is also extensively used in his landscapes. Often an accentuated effect of spatial depth is produced by direct recession, from the immediate foreground, of the horizontal tabletoplike plane.[90] This vertical-horizontal-vertical sequence of the main compositional planes (referred to throughout this book as the "table-top" type of arrangement), which produces the general effect of rising and receding space, is obviously a repetition, on a much larger scale, of the intersection of planes at definite angles which occurs in the modeling of single objects and also in particular groupings of objects. Conversely, the upward and backward rhythm of the main planes may recur again and again on a smaller scale, giving to the whole of the landscape the effect, for example, of a flight of steps.[91] Such planes, whether vertical or horizontal, extend laterally across the part of the canvas on which they occur; in other instances, planes formed by figures, trees or other upright objects, extend up and down, and are frequently set at such an angle to each other, and at such rhythmic intervals both in deep and in lateral space that their compositional relation-

[88] In this respect, Cézanne is the antithesis of Renoir, whose compositions are not only more varied but more spontaneous, often to the extent that they seem casual.
[89] E.g., "Ginger Jar and Fruit" (181).
[90] E.g., "Mount Ste. Victoire and Valley" (57); "Gardanne" (92); "Red Earth" (111).
[91] E.g., "Gardanne" (92).

ships follow what may be termed an accordion-pleat or folded-screen type of design or motif.[92]

The base of Cézanne's pyramid of masses is usually set upon the intermediate or horizontal plane, and the pyramid itself is often elaborated and counterbalanced by another extending downward from the first, so that the two together form what is approximately a diamond.[93] This diamond-shaped organization, like the pyramidal, has analogues in the traditions from the early Italians to the moderns; it occurs, for example, in Renoir;[94] but in Renoir its corners are linked together by a continuous flow of color-and-light units even when space separates them, whereas in Cézanne the course of the pattern is usually more definitely indicated and more forcefully punctuated with distinct volumes and space intervals.[95] Cézanne's diamond-pattern, in other words, is characteristically rigid and angular, Renoir's, curvilinear and fluid. In Renoir also, as for example in "Woman at Rest in Landscape" (314), in which the main figure is actually set within the diamond shape, the diamond-motif is felt as a very subsidiary and unobtrusive agent of composition, mainly because it is less obviously defined along its outlines than Cézanne's. Moreover, its use conveys no sense of premeditation, but rather of something casual, and this increases the naturalness and spontaneity of the expression. In Cézanne, by contrast, the compositional diamond gets its character from the definiteness and positiveness of the units, and its activity as a compositional agent is clearly the result of calculation logically determined by the geometric nature of the pattern and design.[96] When, as sometimes happens, Cézanne departs from his usual practice and makes the boundaries of his compositional pattern curvilinear, the diamond-motif is transformed into a laterally extending oval,[97] and the pyramid or tent sometimes becomes an overarching sequence of masses which, like an umbrella,

[92] E.g., "Five Nudes" (74); "Men Bathing" (164). See analyses, pp. 334-335.
[93] E.g., "Modern Olympia" (33); "Mount Ste. Victoire with Pine Tree" (124); "Card Players and Girl" (141); "Man and Skull" (142); "Men Bathing" (164); "Ginger Jar and Fruit" (181).
[94] E.g., "Mother and Child" (305); "Seated Nude" (309); "Woman at Rest in Landscape" (314).
[95] Compare, e.g., Cézanne's "Man and Skull" (142) with Renoir's "Seated Nude" (309).
[96] Compare, e.g., Cézanne's "Man and Skull" (142) with Renoir's "Woman at Rest in Landscape" (314).
[97] E.g., "Oranges and Bottle" (148); "Men Bathing" (164).

covers or encloses the main compositional organization.[98] Even under these circumstances, however, it retains a pervasive feeling of angularity in the pattern and a staccato quality in the rhythm.

The same principle applies also to the triangular motif that appears as a factor in another traditional type of order characteristically used by Cézanne. This is the hub-and-spokes pattern, which, as the name indicates, consists of units that tend to radiate in all directions from a focal point, and which, as an aggregation of triangular areas, is obviously a variant of the pyramid-theme.[99] Both the pyramid-theme itself and all the variations of it which have been noted are as a rule rhythmically repeated throughout the picture in which they are used, and are so related to other units, similar and contrasting, as to establish a symphonic organization of pattern and compositional form.

Because of the essential self-enclosure of Cézanne's compositions, there is little attempt to convey, even in landscape, the sense of infinite space, as it appears in the Renaissance artists or in such a modern painter as Renoir. Even when the horizon is visible the rearward plane has more the effect of a screen than of illimitable distance, so that the space of the composition in its entirety is relatively limited. The shut-in feeling of the composition, however, is modified by a rendering of the background-plane as a series of subsidiary receding planes, which, paradoxical though it may seem, do not interfere with the continuity of the entire background as one of the basic compositional planes.[100] This is really an application of the same principle as the modeling of solid volumes by sunken light: the constituent planes, at one and the same time, build up the forward projecting object or the solid mass, and create within the mass an internal composition of receding planes.

Particularly striking in Cézanne is the absence of features or aspects in individual units of the picture which would divert the observer's attention from the formal effect as a whole. From many paintings, even great paintings, a particular episode, a figure or group of figures, can be cut out and still constitute a picture in itself; in Cézanne such an area, detached from all the rest,

---

[98] E.g., "House on Hillside" (131); "Men Bathing" (164).
[99] E.g., the patterning areas in the foreground-plane in "Red Earth" (111); the spatial relations of the heads in "Card Players and Girl" (141); the space-pattern of the arms and hands at the center in "Nudes in Landscape" (191).
[100] E.g., "Red Earth" (111).

has no such esthetic fulness as it has as a unit in the total composition. There are, of course, sub-compositions, subsidiary groups of objects, pieces of fruit on a plate, the features of a human face, or even areas of brushstrokes, that have a distinct formal organization of their own; but their independence is never more than relative, and their full significance in the picture depends upon their connections with the design in its entirety.

Composition in Cézanne, we thus see, is not a separate plastic function, but the sum and substance of his use of all the plastic means. His types of order are extremely limited in number: his importance does not lie in the range of his invention, but in the completeness with which his forms, creative and individual, dominate every part and phase of the matter organized. The magnitude of his achievement will appear as we observe his progress toward the full expression of his powers in the treatment of landscape, still-life and figure-painting.

CHAPTER IV

THE EVOLUTION OF CEZANNE'S FORM

I. Introduction

THE evolution of Cézanne's form is far from a continuous process. After making an advance in control of technique or synthesis of the plastic means, he was extremely prone to revert to an earlier, less adequate form of organization and execution, and this tendency, which we have already noted in the work of his apprenticeship, persisted all through his life. At no time was his command of his medium sufficiently sure to guard him against descents into mediocrity. Gradually, however, his distinctive form emerged and perfected itself, and its character and significance can be adequately grasped only if it is seen as the outcome of a long and painful struggle. The history of this struggle, as it is revealed in Cézanne's works of every type, is the subject of the present chapter.

Landscape, still-life and figure-painting have their own individual problems, which require solution by a distinctive use of the plastic means in each field, and accordingly it will be convenient to discuss the evolution of each in a separate section. Basically, however, there is no fundamental difference in plastic form between the three as Cézanne treated them: his interest in subject-matter *per se* was so slight that he made little effort to draw out the qualities in objects which lend them interest as particular things in the real world. The fruit in his still-lifes is not designed to appeal to the appetite; the esthetic content of his landscapes is not due to the charm of actual scenery, the warmth of sunlight or the specific attraction of a spring or autumn day; and the persons in his pictures do not suggest an invitation to human companionship. Natural landscapes, objects on a table, persons, are all treated as the elements in a plastic architecture which retain their natural character primarily in broad universals, with emphasis chiefly upon their voluminousness as color-masses, their position in deep space, and their union in a structure preëminent for its formal balance and compositional integration. The inevitable loss of a certain kind of spontaneity, and the quality of deliberation which often seems to rob intime subject-matter of its natural charm, are essential to the majestic power of Cézanne's mature organizations of volumes in deep space.

II. Landscape

The salient characteristics of Cézanne's earliest painting are, as we have observed, a feeling of intense activity, largely representative and often exaggerated into violent turmoil, and a ubiquitous use of light-and-dark contrasts which frequently degenerate into plastic melodrama. There is a general obviousness, both of effects and of means, and often an extremely incompetent handling of paint. His development consisted partly in an improvement in execution, partly in a more adequate integration of the plastic means. This integration eventually reached a superlative degree of unity, one which indifferent execution was almost powerless to affect in its intrinsic force and conviction. The beginning of it took place when Cézanne discovered in impressionism the raw materials for a technique which became the appropriate instrument for his own distinctively personal vision.

Prior to his adoption of impressionistic technique, Cézanne's interest in landscape painting *per se* scarcely existed. His work in the 1860's shows a preoccupation with narratives in which figures were the chief actors, and the landscape, when present, either is a neutral setting or is so treated that its components participate with the figures in an illustrative rendering of drama. It was in 1870, at the time of the Franco-Prussian war, that Cézanne began his systematic efforts to grasp and interpret the essentials of natural landscape. He escaped military service, lived at Estaque, on the Mediterranean coast near Marseilles, and devoted the years 1870-1872 to an assiduous study and painting of the sea and shore of that region from various viewpoints. His "Red Roofs" (35) of this period [1] still shows the influences which dominated his earlier pictures; it repeats the accentuated light-and-dark contrasts of the seventeenth century Dutchmen, but the fougue and romanticism of his earlier work is tempered by the Courbetesque matter-of-fact kind of painting. The color is dead and unillumi-

[1] Illustration, p. 159.

nated and the drama rendered speciously by large sweeps and violent contrasts of light and dark areas.[2]

Cézanne's attempts prior to 1870 to depart from this early form toward the painting of pure landscape and to utilize part of the early impressionists' technique are well represented in "Railroad Cut" (22), of the late 1860's.[3] In this picture the tumultuousness of the earlier work has been toned down, and though there is a greater amount of obvious drama than in his mature painting, the drama is more akin to Manet's than to that of the late Venetians, the Spaniards or the Dutch. The violent contrasts of light and shadow are likewise softened and enriched by a much more extensive intermixture of color, and the orange-tan which is so important a feature in his later characteristic works dominates a large part of the picture. Already in evidence, though in an embryonic stage, is the patterned compositional framework of color-bands and color-patches so typical of his mature form. The technique resembles that of Manet in that it is individual brushstrokes, rather than groups or areas of strokes, that function principally in drawing and modeling, although here and there definite hatchings of color establish planes and build up volumes in Cézanne's characteristic later manner of projecting and receding facets. Color is sufficiently permeated with light to make the entire picture luminous, but there is still reliance upon Manet's use of pure black, which here, as a set of contrasting accents, emphasizes the luminosity of the other colors. Broadly considered, this landscape represents a creative transformation of Cézanne's earlier old-master form effected by the use of part of the impressionists' technique, especially Manet's. The color is brighter and more solid than at the earlier stage, and the spirit of landscape is rendered in an individual and forceful manner.

"Autumn" (16), of the late 1860's, a nondescript assemblage of features taken from Courbet, Monticelli, Diaz, and other Barbizon painters, exemplifies Cézanne's failure to maintain the general high quality of "Railroad Cut" (22), and to progress consistently toward an individual expression. In "Road" (36), of about the same period, Cézanne resorts to his earlier use of Dutch traits and of the Delacroixesque swirl, but an anticipation of the future appears in the grouping of parallel hatched brushstrokes into areas, which function as planes. Another landscape, "Avenue

[2] See analysis, p. 312.
[3] Illustration, p. 172.

of Jas de Bouffan" (41),[4] painted about three years later than "Railroad Cut" (22), represents the general Barbizon form greatly strengthened by features which remained part of Cézanne's working capital throughout the rest of his career. These are the parallel slanting brushstrokes, grouped into strips and patches, and functioning as planes distinctly set in space; a sharp edge on one side of the patch forecasting the quill-motif; silhouetted shadows on the ground constituting definite units in the total pattern of areas; and a directly receding ground-plane which anticipates his familiar table-top type of space-composition. The picture is basically a Courbet form, as interpreted by Pissarro in his pre-impressionist period, and it is stamped with Cézanne's individuality chiefly by the character and function of the brushwork.

The majority of Cézanne's landscapes of the early seventies bear witness to the fact that his main concern was with the form of the impressionists, especially of Pissarro. He rebelled, however, against the impressionists' reduction of the natural solidity of volumes, and their suppression of the local color of objects in favor of emphasis upon the effect of the varied colors of adjacent areas upon one another. The changes he sought to achieve in the impressionists' form was to restore local color to objects, to build up volumes with structural color, and to establish dynamic relations between the volumes and their spatial intervals. He was, in other words, interested not in the surface appearances of nature, but in the profundities; not, for example, in the fugitive effects of sunlight on objects, but in the permanent and essential qualities of their basic structure, imaginatively recast in an ordered, dynamic relationship in space. His constant effort was to make color the primary instrument in a compositional organization monumental in character. When he did succeed in attaining to a personal expression, he accomplished it by the substitution of brighter colors—notably red, green and orange-yellow—for his earlier somber tones, and by reduction in the size and sweep of his strokes of brush or palette knife.[5]

Cézanne actually worked with Pissarro at Auvers-sur-Oise in 1872 and made copies of his preceptor's pictures which depart from the models only in minor details.[6] When he follows Pissarro

---

[4] Illustration, p. 174.

[5] E.g., "Railroad Cut" (22).

[6] Compare, e.g., Cézanne's "Louveciennes" (43) with Pissarro's "Louveciennes" (274).

closely, and has good control of his medium, his color is richer, deeper, more solid, and the picture in its entirety is stronger than the prototype.[7] When he interprets Pissarro's form, the results vary greatly in degree of originality, technical skill and general strength of plastic expression. His variations from the model are usually effected by the use of devices reminiscent of Corot and Courbet;[8] sometimes these pictures are dominated by Pissarro's characteristic green and orange-tan color-scheme, but they are usually more strikingly patterned and their color-contrasts are more pronounced.[9] His expansion of Pissarro's form is well illustrated in "River and Hills" (48), painted about 1875,[10] in which the impressionistic technique is drawn upon more freely than hitherto, and is also more specifically adapted to Cézanne's own purposes. In the color-scheme of green and orange-coral, as in the uniformly rich and glowing color, and in the positive and forceful pattern, the influence of Pissarro takes precedence over that of the other impressionists. The strokes are more like Manet's than Sisley's or Monet's, and the "paintiness" (the actual feeling of the pigment), always characteristic of the impressionists in general and of Monet in particular, is strongly in evidence. Cézanne's brushstrokes have become both more perceptible and more regular in shape than those of the impressionists, so that the surface is patterned by more definitely shaped and clearly outlined areas of contrasting color. The emphatic patterning in Cézanne, together with the greater solidity and weight of his color, reënforces his use of hatchings or overlapping brushstrokes in his modeling.

Compared with Cézanne's earlier paintings also highly patterned,[11] "River and Hills" reveals a much richer infusion of positive color, with reduction in the vividness of the light-dark contrasts, and absence of heavy dark contour-lines. The movement and drama, no longer specious and turbulent, are balanced and convincing; and the brighter, clearer, more vibrating, and better coördinated colors add a decorative reënforcement to the expression of the form as a whole. Technically also the picture

[7] E.g., "Suicide's House" (45); "Ile-de-France" (77). A characteristic Cézanne feature appears in "Suicide's House" in the drawing and modeling of the tree trunks by long, roughly parallel streaks and bands of color.
[8] E.g., "House at Auvers" (32); the landscape in "Bathers at Rest" (63).
[9] E.g., "House at Auvers" (32).
[10] Illustration, p. 176.
[11] Cf., e.g., "Railroad Cut" (22).

represents an advance in that the brushstrokes are more sure, more meditated, so that while the impasto is thick, it is relatively free from the piled-up layers of pigment to which he had earlier been obliged to resort in order to make pigment or color discharge the plastic functions required of it. Cézanne's control of the medium has in this picture reached the stage at which harmonious relationships of color become the fundamental instrument in his drawing, modeling and compositional organization.

"River and Hills," compared with a representative impressionistic painting such as Monet's "House Boat" (288), shows, in the painting of the water, for example, a more complete union of light and color, a greater amount and effectiveness of color-contrast, and a sharper distinction between the patterned area of the water as a whole and the rest of the picture, as these are related in the architectonic design. Compared with a typical Pissarro, such as "Garden" (273), this Cézanne is less literal in its rendering of detail, although it is not yet so broadly generalized as his later work. Most of the brushstrokes are grouped into areas within which, and partly overlapping, they lie parallel to one another; thus aligned, they form stripes which, as planes, build up the structure of the masses. In addition, the distribution of light and shadow, added to the continuity of the stripes themselves, forms diagonal lines extending into three-dimensional space and introducing spatial order into the composition. Corresponding parallel brushstrokes in typical Sisley units, as for example in the trees in "River Scene with Ducks" (287), are so shaped, placed and related to each other as to give the effect of a continuously rounded surface rather than of an organization in accentuated planes. In Degas, van Gogh, and occasionally in Manet, the perceptible technique of parallel strokes of pastel or brush shows a decidedly greater decorative than expressive emphasis.[12] Cézanne's use of the parallel brushstrokes, in brief, is more fully expressive and more specifically an instrument of drawing, modeling and composition; and his more systematic organization of these strokes in "River and Hills" constitutes an important plastic advance over both the impressionists' form and his own previous work. A significant fact is that even at the early stage represented by this picture, there is no imitation of the impressionistic effects of direct illumination and glowing haze: both

[12] E.g., Degas's "Dancers with Hair in Braids" (285); van Gogh's "Factories" (317) or "Houses and Figure" (319); Manet's "In a Boat" (279).

light and atmosphere are part and parcel of the total color-form, not, as in Monet and Sisley, separate entities.

The compositional function of the technique in "River and Hills" is especially manifested in the division of the entire canvas into three patterned areas—the water, the landscape proper, and the sky—dominated, respectively, by brushstrokes predominantly horizontal, vertical and oblique. The continuity within each area, and the contrast between the areas as a whole, extending to their color, shape and size, and the direction of their constituent plastic units, establish the general compositional scheme; to this the brushwork, varied in each area, contributes an additional motif of dynamically related rhythms and contrasts. Furthermore, the disposition of the rocks to right and left in the area of the land, supplemented by the activity of planes produced by the pattern of brushstrokes, forms a bilaterally balanced sub-composition which brings into compositional focus and equilibrium the sand-wichlike and table-top arrangement of the three main areas extending laterally across the picture. "River and Hills" thus achieves a systematic integration of technique and formal organization, and illustrates the emergence of one of Cézanne's typical forms of composition. In short, Cézanne's transformation of the impressionists' technique results here in expression of a higher order than theirs, while a finer decorative quality is attained by more varied color and a more orderly, purposive and meaningful arrangement of brushstrokes. Nevertheless, the form is still immature: the color, the organization of masses and space, and the definiteness of units are much less powerful and convincing than they ultimately become.

A more organic assimilation of the impressionistic technique is shown in "Mount Ste. Victoire and Valley" (57), painted probably in the middle seventies.[18] The free intermingling of positive and glowing colors creates a rich series of color-modulations, which build up volumes by changes of color as well as of tone, and by patterns of mosaiclike chords, which are more solidly structural than the more uniform, less glowing tones in "River and Hills" (48). These color-chords are derived basically from impressionism, but their structural quality and the increased emphasis on planes replace the superficial impressionistic color-effects by a convincing realization of massiveness and monumental character. The technique itself is more varied, vigorous, resourceful, and

[18] Illustration, p. 177.

purposive than in "River and Hills"; the rhythm of the brush-strokes is more complex, the interaction of planes more pronounced, the location of volumes in space more precise, and the movement of the whole composition is more forceful and dynamic. Moreover, the gain in definiteness of spatial relations makes the recession of planes and volumes decidedly more emphatic: the road, for example, a long tapering strip of color extending very definitely backward, accentuates the direct recession of the foreground-plane as well as the depth of the total landscape, and makes the sandwichlike and table-top character of the composition much more emphatic and effective than that in "River and Hills."

Compositionally, "Mount Ste. Victoire and Valley" is a much more elaborate arrangement of triangular and pyramidal motifs than "River and Hills." These motifs vary widely in size, color, definiteness of shape and degree of voluminousness, and embrace an intricate network of relationships in both two and three dimensions. The two main pyramids—the mountains—are comprised in an all-inclusive compositional diamond-pattern by linear directions which extend, through space, from the sides of the middleground to the area of light in the central upper part of the sky, and to the starting of the road in the foreground. The skeleton or framework of linear directions is also far more comprehensive than in "River and Hills," and is accentuated throughout the pattern by the brushstrokes, singly and in alignment, as well as by modulations and focal accents of color and light. The lines and continuities of direction vary from the severely straight to the serpentine, and are present in all degrees of perceptibility and accentuation, giving to the design a bizarreness and an elaborate compositional diversification unapproached in the simpler and more conventional "River and Hills." The linear effects are executed in many different ways, sometimes by a deepening of color on the edge of an area or mass which contrasts sharply with the lighted area of the adjacent unit; sometimes by the sharp collision of differently colored areas, often with jagged or crenelated contours; sometimes by alignment of brushstrokes in adjacent strips of different color. In "River and Hills" the plastic problems are much simpler, and their solution involves no comparable versatility in the use of means, nor does it yield any such variety of effects; linear effects, for example, result much more frequently from the unaided and unvaried contact of areas and brushstrokes, or simply from the alignment of the strokes. Occasionally, in both pictures, line is detached from the object to which it belongs, and occasionally also a narrow strip of bare canvas plays the part of color, light and actual line. Nevertheless, at the stage reached in "Mount Ste. Victoire and Valley," linear effects have a richer color-content than in Cézanne's earlier work, and are capable of discharging the complex plastic functions characteristic of his mature form. They not only delimit areas, enter into patterns, and themselves form planes, but they create planes that serve as adjuncts to modeling and space-composition; they are further from their sources in the traditions, from Daumier's, for example, and they are a more integral part of a genuinely Cézannesque design.

In this "Mount Ste. Victoire and Valley," Cézanne's typical architectonic form is realized to a marked degree, and he has achieved a systematic integration of forceful technique, striking pattern, structural color, accentuated lines and planes by which solid objects are ordered in space, and modeling by color-modulations. Henceforth, his general landscape-form remains fundamentally the same, though its scope is extended, details are varied and refined, and technique is less an independent factor, more an aspect or phase of the total effect. Without ever attaining the perfect unobtrusiveness, the supreme transparency, of Renoir's technique, Cézanne's becomes, to the trained eye, so organically fused with the plastic beat or throb of solid volumes in deep space that in his best work its existence as a separate entity becomes negligible.[14]

The outstanding fundamental principles of Cézanne's painting of landscape may be illustrated by a chronological study of a number of his pictures in which the most important variations of his characteristic form, outlined in a previous chapter, are to be observed.

Cézanne generally, in his landscapes as in his still-lifes and figure-paintings, placed the focal point of composition near the front of the picture rather than in the distance, in this respect apparently following Courbet, who, like Dutch painters of the seventeenth century, laid emphasis upon near-by objects. This effect is apparent also in Renoir, but with him there is a compositional focus also in the deep distance, as in Claude le Lorrain and Poussin, so that the foreground scene is not only realized in its own relatively episodic character, but is felt to be an integral part of nature

[14] Compare, e.g., "Valley of the Arc" (109) with "Mount Ste. Victoire and Valley" (57).

as a whole, in all its wide expanse.[15] In Cézanne the plastic activity is more accentuated in the foreground and middleground, so that the effect is largely that of a fragment of nature placed against a setting, and the plastic terms are much more nearly those of still-life. The difference is not absolute, but it is sufficient to give to the work of the two men contrasting sets of plastic values. In Cézanne, also, there is no such fluid intermingling of landscape proper and infinity of distance as there is in Renoir: in spite of connecting links, there is a decidedly more definite distinction between the two parts of the picture. The general difference in feeling, in the work of the two painters, is that between a continuous flow and a staccato throb.

The organization of Cézanne's compositions in three distinct general areas, a central area sandwiched between background and foreground, has already been noted in "River and Hills" (48) and reappears constantly in his landscapes. At times the area of sky is reduced in expanse or altogether omitted and a part of the landscape proper functions then as setting to the rest of the picture.[16] In "Plaza, Auvers-sur-Oise" (87) of the early eighties,[17] the general type of organization is diversified by a duplication of the receding foreground-plane in a second receding plane higher up in the picture. This is formed by a mass of foliage extending so continuously across the middleground that it appears as a canopy, which heightens the effects of pattern and contrast by its relation to the vertical rhythm of the tree trunks below, and the houses, steeple and other trees above. The contrast-theme is further carried out by the technical execution, which varies, in different areas of the canvas, in the specific character and placing of the brushstrokes and in the degree of their accentuation.

"Gardanne" (92), of about 1885,[18] follows the same general design of accentuated contrast between successive areas or planes which alternately rise sharply and recede; indeed, in this picture, the entire composition may be regarded as a series of steps, the spatial order of which is accentuated by the general emphasis on planes and lines of perspective, and specifically by the pattern of the brushstrokes themselves, which reënforce the general direction

---

[15] Compare, e.g., Renoir's "Bathers in Forest" (291), "Peninsula of St. Jean" (308) or "Two Figures in Landscape" (312) with Cézanne's "Bathers at Rest" (63) or "Bibemus Quarry" (155).

[16] E.g., "House of Père Lacroix" (44); "Well" (174).

[17] Illustration, p. 210.

[18] Illustration, p. 221.

of the areas in which they occur. Diversity in detail is secured by differences in technique from one area to another, and by the introduction of oblique or slanting areas which relieve the succession of vertical and horizontal units.[19]

"Red Earth" (111), of 1889-1890,[20] exemplifies clearly Cézanne's growth since his earlier use of essentially the same compositional plan in "River and Hills" (48). The foreground, middleground and background are arranged in the familiar sandwich fashion, with most of the subject-matter and the most active pattern of technique on the central plane, which rises and recedes by a series of subsidiary, subtly marked, steplike planes. The disposition of masses and areas follows both the pyramidal and the hub-and-spokes organization, and as in "River and Hills," and indeed in most of Cézanne's compositions, sequences of light, shadow and color in the pattern of the brushstrokes form lines of direction which give the effect of perspective. A marked advance over earlier landscapes appears in the much greater control of the medium, the subtlety of effects, and the extent to which the impressionistic technique has been assimilated and individualized. The impasto is thinner and more even in texture; color and light are better integrated, so that their combination produces a deep rich glow, even a translucency; the modulations of color are subtler and more numerous, and the color itself is more fluid, of richer sensuous quality, and more firmly integrated in the structure of planes and masses. There is even some degree of color-suffusion, and this, though on the whole alien to Cézanne's form, plays an important part in the total effect. In general conception, there is no point of outstanding originality, but the picture shows both Cézanne's usual ability to lend distinction to a familiar general design by picturesque treatment of detail, and a very appreciable advance over his early work in command of medium and in finesse of execution.[21]

In "Red Earth" Cézanne's landscape-painting has reached its mature and fully realized form. From this period on, his landscapes fall more clearly into two types of composition, distinguished by broad general characteristics which, however, may and often do overlap, so that traits belonging to each type sometimes occur in the same picture. In one type, the beat of separate volumes is emphasized; in the other, objects are used primarily as parts of

[19] For further analytical data see Appendix, p. 343.
[20] Illustration, p. 229.
[21] See also analysis, p. 357.

still larger aggregates, in which they tend to interpenetrate and lose their individuality. The difference corresponds roughly to that between a series of columns and a wall. When separate masses are made the compositional units, they are usually set off by heavier or sharper contour-line, which makes a relatively clear-cut division between one area of brushstrokes and another; within the areas the perceptibility of the brushstrokes is usually diminished, so that the modeling approaches a homogeneous or one-piece effect. The latter type of landscape-painting is best exemplified in "Valley of the Arc" (109); the former in "Red Earth" (111), "Bibemus Quarry" (155) and "Well" (174), in which more perceptible technique accompanies greater emphasis upon division within the volumes themselves, as well as a higher degree of continuity in a general all-over pattern of small units.

"Valley of the Arc" (109), painted about 1888-1892,[22] is also highly patterned, but the pattern is less one of brushstrokes than of geometrical areas. In fact, the brushstrokes are so unobtrusive as to escape notice except upon close inspection; in the quill-motif, for example, emphasis is upon the rib and not upon the barbs, so that the effect of the motif is primarily linear and accentuates the hinges upon which the planes appear to move. The technique as a whole is more completely fused with the total form than in "Red Earth" (111), for example, or "Bibemus Quarry" (155) : it is toned down to meet the requirements of a design different in character from that in either of the other landscapes. This picture represents the distinctive features of Cézanne's landscape-painting, and his architectonic form in general, at an extremely high level of power and conviction.[23]

"Well" (174), painted in the late nineties,[24] represents still another variation of Cézanne's usual compositional arrangement in three large, distinct, contrasting planes. The novelty consists in the placing of most of the masses in the foreground and background, with a large area of free space about the focal point—the well—in the middleground. The general foreground-plane rises rather abruptly, shutting off, like a fenestrated curtain or screen, the recession of space not far from the front of the picture; but on close examination the foreground appears as a series of upright planes set behind one another by the pattern of light and shadow,

[22] Illustration, p. 228.   [24] Illustration, p. 241.
[23] For analytical data see Appendix, p. 355.

so that they recede as they rise. The open space in the center is converted into the familiar effect of Cézanne's tentlike enclosure, largely by means of the twigs, leaves and branches which enfold it in a three-dimensional pattern, the outstanding characteristic of which is the perspective attained by lines crisscrossing as they go back, in a manner reminiscent of Uccello.[25]

The surface of the picture is highly animated by ubiquitous small interpenetrating patches, lines and brushstrokes. The technique, instead of being generally uniform in direction throughout large areas as in "Red Earth" (111), is extremely varied, and so also is the color: the result is a much more active movement throughout the composition. The quill-motif is especially prominent, with both color and technique varied in practically every area, and the geometrically shaped individual patches are frequently set apart by lines or areas of bare canvas. The unusual lightness and delicacy of the execution result in a general effect more reminiscent of water color than of painting in oil.

In "Bibemus Quarry" (155), painted in 1898,[26] the composition includes several of Cézanne's most frequently used devices: the majority of the active masses are concentrated in the middleground; the distant sky serves chiefly as a setting, a kind of backdrop marking the confines of the stage on which the action takes place; the foreground, by its position, formation in planes, and contrast of color and light, functions as a screen- or curtain-like space-boundary, a starting point which emphasizes the receding rhythms of space-volume units that constitute the basic motif of the composition. The relationship of the screen-effect of both the background-sky and the immediate foreground to the space-volume theme in the central unit of the organization, constitutes a variety of the familiar sandwich theme; the individuality of the composition arises from the fact that the volumes and the intervals of space are more definite and clean-cut in the foreground than in most of Cézanne's landscapes. The masses throughout are very angular and blocklike, contrasting sharply with one another in shape and in the way in which they are placed, but collectively they form a staccato, roughly circular sequence around the focal area in the middleground. This plan of circular organization—a variation upon the hub-and-spokes motif—is not new either in Cézanne

[25] Cf., e.g., Uccello's "Rout of San Romano" (215).
[26] Illustration, p. 255.

or in the traditions.[27] Compared with Cézanne's previous use of it, the device in "Bibemus Quarry" is more complex in pattern and in construction of the units than in his "Bathers at Rest" (63) or "Card Players and Girl" (141); it is less obvious, less mechanical than in "Five Nudes" (74); more powerful in color, more forcefully dynamic than in "Well" (174).

The general improvement noted in "Red Earth" (111) continues in "Bibemus Quarry," especially as regards the intensity, the luminosity and the structural quality of the color, all of which reach in this landscape their highest level of excellence and place Cézanne on a par with the greatest colorists of all time. Moreover, he displays a superlatively effective control of paint in rendering the voluminousness of masses and the strength and conviction of spatial ordering. As in "Well" (174), there is a pronounced and actively dynamic movement which results from the concerted interaction of the patterns of light, color and technique throughout the composition; but the pattern itself is secondary in importance to the effect produced by the numerous rhythms of color-planes and color-volumes sweeping in space through the picture as a whole. Particularly to be noted in "Bibemus Quarry" and in other landscapes of about the same period,[28] is the tendency of the brushstrokes to be grouped into patches preponderantly square in shape and lending a mosaic- or tapestry-like appearance to the ensemble, a richer form of the pattern of individual square strokes frequently used in Cézanne's work of the seventies.[29]

The four landscapes just discussed, "Red Earth" (111), "Valley of the Arc" (109), "Well" (174), and "Bibemus Quarry" (155), are instances of Cézanne's final triumph in the struggle, which endured through his entire career, to make paint function as color and serve the ends of expression. Each of these pictures is a symphony of clear color, each different from the others in key, in relation of color to technique, in thickness of impasto, in composition, and in expression and feeling of landscape; and each is free from that feeling of paint so often noticeable in his otherwise great pictures of all periods. This high level of technical proficiency, however, was not consistently attained by Cézanne even in the pe-

[27] Cf., e.g., the mechanical and conventional forms of it in the Flemish "Crucifixion" (216), in the South German "Last Supper" (217) and in Benozzo Gozzoli's "Madonna and Angels" (220).
[28] E.g., "Red Earth" (111); "Red Rock" (169); "Well" (174); "Corner of Quarry" (176); "Rocks and Trees" (179).
[29] See detail illustrated, p. 295, and cf., e.g., "Choquet in Armchair" (52), illustration, p. 193.

riod from 1888 to 1898, during which these pictures were painted. In much of his work of every type, painted up until the very end of his life, his control of the medium was so faulty that the pigment is piled up, the pattern isolated from the form, the space-composition "jumpy," the brushwork overaccentuated and unrelated to the compositional organization of color, and the color-relationships are inharmonious.[30] Cézanne himself was conscious of this lack of uniform quality of execution, complained bitterly about it to his friends, and boasted extravagantly when he succeeded in making his brush do on canvas what he saw and felt in nature and wanted to express. The advance in craftsmanship represented by the four landscapes discussed above, is unquestionably due largely to Cézanne's extensive and long-continued work in water color. He had painted in that medium in the early seventies, continued to experiment with it more or less regularly until the late eighties, and then concentrated his energies upon it and practiced it assiduously until the year of his death.

III. STILL-LIFE

Cézanne's still-lifes are in general distinguished from his landscapes by the much greater emphasis upon individual units of subject-matter. In his landscapes, as already noted, the compositional units often include a whole group of trees or bushes or other natural objects, merged to the point at which their individual boundaries are scarcely perceptible, and the particular identity of each is almost lost. Plastically, such units are patches of brushstrokes, planes, or color-areas, rather than separate objects; and it is the continuity or contrast of patterned areas rather than the individuality of the object depicted that is of importance. In still-lifes, on the contrary, the main pattern is of whole objects—plates, draperies, pieces of fruit—which are as a rule sharply marked off from one another. The distinction, however, is relative, for in those landscapes in which the beat of volumes is accentuated there is naturally more emphasis also upon the individuality of the separate objects. Furthermore, the general architectural quality of Cézanne's design introduces a common factor into the treatment of every type of subject-matter: landscape, still-life and figures, all have this architectural quality in common, but the individuality of par-

[30] E.g., "Mount Ste. Victoire Seen from the Chemin des Lauves" (189).

ticular objects, naturally more apparent in still-lifes and figures, is more emphasized in Cézanne's treatment of these than in his landscapes.

Because of the definite individuality of particular objects, Cézanne's still-lifes exemplify in a high degree the general principles of his use of space. As was pointed out in a previous chapter, his space-composition is Florentine in the sharpness and clearness of the spatial intervals, Venetian in the construction of volumes out of solid color, though it has none of the interflow of color between space and volumes which characterized the Venetians and was carried to its greatest heights by Renoir. The line, which plays so important a part in Cézanne's rendering of space, owes something to both the Florentines and the Venetians: it resembles that of the former in its clean-cut character, but is broader, like that of Titian and Tintoretto, and more broken into sections, like Daumier's. The light-dark contrasts, which are essential in his building-up of flattened masses in space, are derived from Manet, as are also the diminution of half-tones and the broadening of highlights into comparatively large areas. All these features, of course, appear also in Cézanne's painting of landscape, but the distinctness of the units in still-life makes the spatial intervals, the relations between them, and the method of modeling more definite and striking.

Composition in his still-lifes follows essentially the same principles as in the landscapes. It is preëminently stable and balanced, usually based upon the principle of bilateral symmetry, with striking and picturesque variations in detail lending distinction to the pyramidal disposition of units. The table-top type of compositional arrangement and the general intersection of planes in deep space, noted in his landscapes, reappear, with the difference that the focus of compositional activity is, in the main, placed nearer the front of the picture. In the treatment of both types of subject-matter, there is also the same accentuation of the first fundamental plane, to divide the extreme foreground from the space of the composition proper; but in the landscapes the background, whether of sky or natural setting, is usually rendered with greater contrast to the main compositional masses; the enclosing walls or draperies in still-lifes are more nearly equal in weight and voluminousness to the units in the foreground. The difference, however, is again one of degree; as we have seen, there is little or no essential variation in Cézanne's basic compositional form in his treatment of any type of subject-matter.

Cézanne's still-lifes of 1869-1870 are chiefly interesting as evidence of his innate sense of color-power; in other respects, they follow closely the models of antecedent paintings, and show little or no trace of individual creativeness. "Black Clock" (14) and "Green Jar and Pewter Pitcher" (27), for example, both of 1869-1870,[31] scarcely deviate from Manet's color-scheme of black-and-white effect, luminous quality of pigment, brushstrokes generalized in large areas, and type of drawing and compositional arrangement. Both of these pictures are superior in color-power to Manet's work, and their boldness and striking drama make up for what they lack of Manet's subtleness and finesse of execution.[32]

In the early and middle seventies Cézanne had come nearer to a personal expression in still-life painting. The sources in the old masters are still quite obvious, but they are more integral parts of the new form, and their modifications, however slight, forecast some of his later characteristics. A typical still-life of this period is "Plate with Grapes and Peach" (58).[33] Like many of Cézanne's other early paintings, this picture recalls Tintoretto and El Greco in dramatic light-effects, muted luminosity of color, and perceptibility of pattern formed by the shapes of areas of high and low illumination. Colors alternatingly very bright and very dark continue the light-shadow contrasts of Cézanne's earlier modeling, with the areas of light and shadow clearly distinguishable. The obviousness of the drama has been reduced, the general tendency is toward the continuous one-piece surface of Chardin and Courbet, and there is not yet any evidence of the interpenetrating contrasting colors, that is, color-chords, which are so characteristic of Cézanne's method of modeling after he had achieved the ability to infuse more positive color in both the light and the shadow. The grapes are flattened in the manner of Manet, with an exaggerated emphasis on both highlights and adjacent darker color, and a broad dark line around each grape heightens the effect of solidity and at the same time functions as intervening space. The device is specious here, but it is the germ of Cézanne's later important use of line in spatial organization. The shadow cast by the plate on the table has an independent dark line of contour, and that cast by the peach on the plate is outlined by a strip of light. By such use of light, shadow and line, an obvious pattern is secured, together with a sense of depth; but the facility of the means robs the effects of

[31] Illustrations, p. 162 and p. 163.   [33] Illustrations, p. 188 and p. 292.
[32] Cf., e.g., Manet's "White Peonies" (283).

any profound conviction. Though the tendency to a continuous surface predominates in all the particular objects depicted, the background is patterned with parallel streaks which form receding planes and thus anticipate a subsequent habitual practice.

The influence of impressionism appears later in Cézanne's still-lifes than in his landscapes. "Plate with Grapes and Peach" shows none of the influence of Monet or Pissarro, but its conglomerate space-composition, especially in the area of the grapes, is close to that in Cézanne's definitely Pissarroesque "River and Hills" (48) of about the same period. Manet's influence, as noted above, is still very much in evidence, but its adaptation, in spite of deficiencies in color, results in an individual form, stronger in all plastic essentials than Manet's.[34] Deliberate distortions are already introduced when necessitated by design: among them is the break in continuity in the upper edge of the table which makes the section at the right counterbalance an opposing slant in the mass and shadows of the still-life objects; it also brings the more horizontal direction of the upper part of the table at the left into rhythmic relationship with the pattern formed by the stem of the bunch of grapes and the shadow on the plate. The defects of this picture are typical also of other still-lifes of the period: while color is completely integrated with light and shadow, the color-scheme is heavy, a leaden tone pervades the various colors, especially in the background, the compositional units are imperfectly individualized, and the result is an inadequate realization of three-dimensional spacing.

Compared with Cézanne's landscapes, this picture shows a heightened individualization of objects, achieved by reduction of internal pattern and greater emphasis upon bounding contours, so that its compositional pattern is one of relatively large, positively shaped color-areas, rather than of the constituents of objects. Within the areas, brushstrokes are less perceptible than in Cézanne's landscapes, and contrasts of color are not sufficiently striking to interfere with homogeneity of effect, while the individuality of each area is further heightened by contrast with adjacent areas both in color and in degree of illumination. These contrasts, together with the clean-cut or positive linear demarcations, result in the type of pattern of color-areas upon which the forms of Matisse, Picasso and the semi-abstract contemporary painters are largely based.

Several of Cézanne's distinctive ways of modeling masses and

[34] Cf., e.g., Manet's "White Peonies" (283).

locating them in space may be observed in some of his early still-lifes. In the picture just discussed the volumes and their spatial relationships follow, in the main, traditional forms: the masses are of the one-piece type, with weight given by the structural quality of the color, and the chief instrument of their construction and spatial organization consists of light-shadow contrasts. In "Plums and Pears" (79) of the late seventies,[35] a pattern of overlapping contours coöperates with the pattern of highlights to establish spatial order, but is effective chiefly from the standpoint of representation. Most of the highlights are flat patches, abruptly changing in tone with the transition to shadow, so that the modeling is really a matter of light-dark contrast. In some units, because of ineffective color-relations, the illuminated areas appear to recede into the body of the object rather than to rest upon it, thereby impairing the solidity. The heightened effect of pattern thus gained suggests that some of these areas of sunken light may be intentional distortions; this presumption gains plausibility from the fact that areas of sunken light function definitely as components of the design throughout Cézanne's career. In this picture, however, as in many others, most of the sunken lights bespeak technical incapacity, since when Cézanne uses this distortion effectively, he secures activity of pattern and contrast with no sacrifice of solidity.[36]

In "Fruit and Tapestry" (55), of the middle seventies,[37] as also in Cézanne's mature work generally, the highlighted area of an object is formed by a definitely shaped patch of positive color, which acts as one of the component planes. Thus not only do the volumes and the intervals between them become more clearly defined, but so also do the elements within them. The increasing activity of color and planes extends its influence to the enclosing space, and plays a proportionately more important part in the rendering of space than does the comparatively mechanical overlapping of contours noted in "Plums and Pears" (79). Moreover, the contribution made by cast shadows to the space-organization of masses becomes less obvious; the dark shadows play a part in the color-pattern, as do their determining contours in the pattern of line, while the shadows themselves are subdivided into minor planes. This more precise and integrated definition of spatial intervals is accompanied by a more positive recession in depth, achieved mainly by color-relations and deliberately distorted linear perspective.

[35] Illustration, p. 189.   [37] Illustrations, p. 190 and p. 297.
[36] Cf., e.g., "Woman and Coffee Pot" (140).

Additional anticipations of Cézanne's later work appear in "Fruit and Tapestry" in the use of contour-lines to individualize masses, but they are still overaccentuated: the less emphatically outlined volumes of his later painting at its best are more convincing and esthetically more effective.[38] The same picture also forecasts familiar later effects in its strongly marked interweaving of curvilinear and rectilinear patterns of line, and in the presence of the table-top motif as the characteristic basis of a pyramidal composition. The background is welded with the solid components of the foreground into a continuous structure by the pattern, which echoes in the background the shapes of the main masses, even suggesting some of their actual solidity. Although the execution is decidedly clumsy, the clumsiness is itself a part of Cézanne's distinctive form, and cannot be accounted an unqualified drawback.

In the stage of development represented by "Fruit and Tapestry," the general contrast between Cézanne's still-lifes and his landscapes has taken definite form. As already noted, the compositional units in the landscapes tend to include several items of subject-matter, while in the still-lifes the plastic units usually coincide with individual objects; and it is the interrelation of these objects, their shapes and their constituent color-areas and brushstrokes, that makes up the compositional pattern of the picture. The composition in "Plain, Trees and Hills" (150),[39] for example, is an organization of wedgelike volumes, a slanting pyramidal ensemble of trees and mountains, the perspective of which converges toward an apex high up and far back in the picture. In conformity with this design, the central tree is executed as a pair of juxtaposed upright bands, one functioning as light and the other as shadow; and both of them, by their upright position and bandlike character, emphasize the wedgelike characteristics in the tree. The internal organization of brushstrokes, many of them quill-like, which radiate from a central rib running the whole length of the tree, make up a herring-bone pattern and further emphasize the wedgelike character of the tree itself. All the aspects of the tree, in other words, color, line, light, shadow, and pattern of brushstrokes, are conceived in accordance with the part played by the tree in the composition as a whole, and it is only in a limited and qualified sense that the tree can be regarded as an independent entity.

[38] Cf., e.g., "Oranges and Bottle" (148) or "Ginger Jar and Fruit" (181).
[39] Illustration, p. 244.

In "Fruit and Tapestry," in contrast, the units, though organically interrelated, maintain their separate individuality to a much greater extent. The green fruit on the right, for example, is built up of concentric circular stripes, the smallest of which is nearest the eye, and the largest, the heavily accentuated contour, is in deepest space. In spite of brief interruptions and minor irregularities in tone and color, each stripe forms a plane, and the whole series of stripes, closely packed together, both model the volume and give its surface a continuity much more compact and solid than that of the tree described above. The variations within the stripes form a second pattern in the modeling of the same piece of fruit, and its components radiate from the center of the mass like the spokes of a wheel or the ribs of an open umbrella. These two series of patterning elements set all the parts of the volume in perspective, by the latitude-longitude device described in the chapter on space.[40] Each spot or patch plays its part in both patterns, and also enters into the scheme of light-dark contrasts and color-relations which forms the more general means of modeling. Very ingenious variations of the same principles of modeling appear in each of the other pieces of fruit, and the particular adaptation of the method coöperates with the quality of the color and the adjustment of light and dark to give to each volume its own solid, independent reality.[41]

Notwithstanding all the above-noted devices, three-dimensional solidity in the majority of Cézanne's still-lifes painted during the seventies is derived to a great extent from the thick impasto rather than from that finer adjustment of color, line, light, and space, characteristic of his successful late work. Other marks of his immaturity appear in overdependence upon light-and-dark contrasts and upon heavy contour-line; and the sum of these shortcomings results in ill-organized composition and imperfect integration of expressive and decorative features.[42]

"Compotier, Glass, Apples and Knife" (64), of about 1877,[43] is a typical example of the plastic inadequacies mentioned. The color is dull and leaden, the impasto is very heavy, color and light fail to reënforce each other, solidity is obtained largely by thick, heavily striated pigment, space is jumbled, and the surface and texture of

[40] See p. 38.
[41] For further analytical details see Appendix, p. 318.
[42] For an exception to this general character of the still-lifes of this period, see analysis of "Jug, Wineglass and Fruit" (46), Appendix, p. 315.
[43] Illustration, p. 191.

the whole canvas are "painty." This picture illustrates also a characteristic stage in the evolution of Cézanne's brushwork: the accentuated individual strokes are parallel to each other, and practically all of them slant in the same direction. Technique of this sort naturally produces a uniform pattern throughout the canvas, but while it serves to tie the units together compositionally, its effect is one of facility and speciousness. When, in contrast, in "Red Apples" (84) and "Four Peaches" (129), for instance, the uniform brushwork takes its proper place in relation to color and spatial organization, it supplies a positive contribution to individual and highly expressive forms.

When the basic plastic essentials of Cézanne's still-lifes of the late seventies and early eighties are considered apart from the unsuccessful or indifferent efforts of execution, the fact emerges that at this stage he had attained to a characteristic and individual form of expression. This form is further modified and developed in the still-lifes of his later periods, in which a number of outstanding features may be distinguished.

The character of Cézanne's still-life painting makes it inevitable that line should serve, perhaps even more than in his other work, to model, to set in space, to bind together compositionally, as well as to fix the boundaries of objects and areas. Used to give the effect of perspective, line extends all over the canvas and produces innumerable geometric shapes, set at angles to one another, which form an organic part of the rhythmic compositional pattern of the picture. This pattern of angular shapes helps to establish continuity between foreground and background in Cézanne's still-lifes; and this continuity, as already noted, is more thoroughgoing than that in his landscapes. The succession of volumes and intervals appears as if uninterrupted through walls and draperies, with only enough diminution in solidity and voluminousness to secure the effect of contrast; in landscape the transition from solid objects on the ground to the distant sky is much more marked; and though continuity is not lost it is the contrast and not the continuity which is primarily apparent.

The complete integration of foreground and background, which is a characteristic of the best of Cézanne's mature still-lifes, seems to have been his main difficulty from the period when he had arrived at his characteristic expression until the end of his life. And the occasions on which he failed to obtain the sought-for perfect coördination are far more numerous than those on which he succeeded. Indeed, it seems to be the rule in Cézanne that the plastic problems which he often solved superlatively are also those in which he frequently failed lamentably, a condition which prevails in his late no less commonly than in his early work. The failures are due usually to bad relationships between color and light which make areas appear as mere masses of pigment, not as color functioning adequately in drawing, modeling and compositional organization. In "Geranium and Apples" (121) and in "Onions and Bottle" (167), for example, the waxy paint in the background acts as a sort of screen which interferes with the color and pattern in the rendering of receding space. At whatever period of his career, this defect, like most of Cézanne's other shortcomings, is due to his uneven control of the medium of paint. It is only when he is skilful in this respect that the background is felt to be a cognate unit with the main part of the composition, contributing its share to a rhythmic continuity of color-units which then embraces the entire organization.

Interaction between foreground and background reaches a high degree of effectiveness in "Ginger Jar and Fruit" (181), of the early 1900's.[44] This composition is organized about a shaft of space receding from the center of the table in the foreground to a focal point—the green lemon—in the distance; and the rhythm of color-masses which punctuates the foreground-space is carried back into the setting chiefly through the intermediation of plastic relationships established between the constituent planes of the still-life objects, the large jar in the middle distance, and the pattern of lines and planes in the background. Another form of plastic linkage between foreground and background appears in "Oranges and Bottle" (148), painted, probably, in the middle nineties.[45] In this, the organization is closely akin to that of the familiar decentered portrait.[46] There is a continuous diminution in solidity of volume and in positiveness of color as the eye passes from the oranges, table cloth and bottle, to the detached motifs on the wall paper and the patches of bare canvas functioning as solid units of light on the wall; but the rhythmic interaction between the volumes in the main part of the composition and the pattern of shapes in the setting is so thoroughgoing as to make the setting seem like a cloudy or otherwise imperfect mirror, which repeats, not the literal detail

[44] Illustrations, p. 268, p. 300 and p. 301.
[45] Illustrations, p. 226 and p. 293.
[46] E.g., Tintoretto's "Venetian Senator" (239).

of particular objects, but their generalized shapes, a sense of their massiveness, and a rough reproduction of the intervals between them. The composition thus resolves itself into an uninterrupted succession of volumes, moving from the lower left to the upper right and from the lower right to the upper left, within a roughly diamond-shaped or angular-oval compositional framework that includes both foreground and background.

We may sum up the subject of Cézanne's still-life painting by saying that the best of it is built upon an architectonic conception of volume-and-space units which is made particularly dynamic by the interaction of pattern, picturesquely distributed objects, and color of appealing sensuous quality, structural solidity and multifarious compositional activities. Each of these is organically adapted to the main purpose of the design: a space-and-volume composition in which all the units are constructed and distributed to bring about Cézanne's characteristic effect of power and force. In his most successful work, the pattern in the modeling, or rather the composition, of the units, is adapted to the composition of the whole picture: the pattern in the different areas or masses, similar as far as shapes are concerned but different in quality of color, yields a varied series of cognate forms that reënforce one another and constitute a rich unified totality. The still-life "Compotier, Pitcher and Fruit" (128) illustrates, perhaps better than any other of Cézanne's still-lifes, the fertility of his imagination in making these highly patterned and picturesque elements coöperate in innumerable ways to further the main purpose of the design.[47]

IV. FIGURE-PAINTING

With few exceptions, Cézanne's landscapes and still-lifes were painted after his contact with the impressionists; in contrast, his earliest figure-paintings fall in the period when the old masters' influence upon him was at its height. This, as already noted, is the period of his overt romanticism, of exaggerated drama, both literary and plastic. Not only do the pictures, unlike those of his mature years, tell an obvious story, but they do so by means which are overemphatic, crude, often specious and flamboyant.[48] Contrasts of light and dark are violent to the point of stridency, broad rhythms

[47] For details see analysis of "Compotier, Pitcher and Fruit" (128), p. 374.
[48] E.g., "Donkey Thieves" (18); "Murder" (20); "Idyl" (26).

sweep across the canvas in sharply opposed directions, and the same sweep and extensity appear in the strokes of brush and palette knife. Drama and vigorous movement are portrayed by representative factors, not by coördination of plastic means: line, piled-up pigment, and alternating light and dark are relied upon almost entirely, and color-relations play a secondary rôle. In spite of the crudity in both conception and execution, these early figure-compositions already show the power inherent in everything Cézanne ever did; the overaccentuated technique is itself in harmony with the vehement drama; and the compositional distribution of masses, while bizarre, already has the picturesqueness which springs from unexpected departure from comparatively conventional general forms.

The development of Cézanne's figure-painting appears chiefly in the transformation of represented drama into plastic drama, in the replacement of turmoil by composure, with power not lost but heightened, and with an immense gain in depth of expression. The early pictures are primarily illustrations which represent a specific episode or situation; those of his mature years are plastic organizations in which the particular action or scene represented is irrelevant esthetically. Even in those late pictures in which figures are shown as actually doing something, the essential activity resides in the interaction of color-masses in space, not in the represented narrative.[49]

Cézanne's early portraits are definite delineations of particular individuals, with emphasis upon the peculiarities of the sitter, his cast of countenance, posture, or psychological disposition.[50] The means have the speciousness of those employed in his figure-compositions painted at the same period; and these portraits also have Cézanne's characteristic force, and show in germ the qualities that distinguish the work of his prime. Even when most literal, they are not photographic. In the early portrait, "Head of Man" (6), for example, painted about 1865-1867,[51] the head is brought into vivid relief by an intense, Rembrandtesque illumination which makes it stand out as dramatically as does the head of the kneeling figure in Masaccio's "Saint Peter Healing the Sick" (219), or that

[49] E.g., "Five Nudes" (74); "Group of Bathers" (182); "Nudes in Landscape" (191).
[50] E.g., "Uncle Dominique" (5); "Head of Man" (6); "Artist's Father" (7); "Achille Emperaire" (9).
[51] Illustration, p. 149.

of Saint Paul in Dürer's "Four Saints" (226).[52] The drama, in other words, is not merely an emphasis upon one of the details of subject-matter, but serves to focus and organize the composition, and shows Cézanne's ability, even during his apprenticeship, to provide a plastic foundation for his literary effects.

These early portraits are executed mainly by broad strokes or dabs of the palette knife which give a decided mosaic effect to the whole surface. The form is, in general, close to that of Courbet, or of Manet, or to a form combining effects from both these men; but despite the crudity of execution, it is expressive of more power than are its prototypes. The expressive force and the defective craftsmanship in these early portraits are alike illustrated in "Antony Valabrègue" (10), painted about 1868.[53] The contours of the strokes are raised edges of paint which make the surface indented; and while in the flesh the strokes form a striking pattern they fail to bind the texture of the flesh into a single volume with the head. The disproportionate pigment, very thick in the lighted areas and very thin in the shadows, contributes to defects in drawing and modeling which make the head appear to project forward without a corresponding indication of the three-dimensionality of the back of the head: the forehead seems to be a volume separate from the hair, and the latter appears as a depressed surface; hence the face is like a mask placed in front of an area of dark color. In other words, a break in the proper relationships between color, light, line, space, and technique, interrupts the continuity of the total volume of the head as well as the color-composition of the picture. The blacks sink in and the highlights project inordinately because no middle tones establish a bridge between the two. Cézanne's late portraits, in contrast, reverse the method of modeling: pigment is piled up in the shadows, and the lights and highlights are either thinly painted or taken care of by spots of bare canvas, while numerous modulations in color establish connecting links, intermediary tonal relationships, which enliven and enrich as well as make more convincing the elements of drama retained by the light-and-dark contrast. In spite of the change of method and better control of pigment, he often failed to set volumes in space through the medium of color-relationships, and resorted instead to such

[52] Rembrandt's "Head of St. Matthew" (257), painted in broad brush-strokes which function as planes, may indicate that Rembrandt, through Daumier, exerted an early influence upon Cézanne.
[53] Illustration, p. 152.

specious means as accentuated areas of light [54] or exaggerated contour-lines.[55]

An intermediate stage in the transition to Cézanne's distinctive form in figure-painting may be illustrated by "Man Putting on Coat" (56), painted probably in the middle seventies.[56] In this picture the change from represented to plastic activity is well under way but not yet complete. The action—putting on a coat—is depicted with considerable verisimilitude, but it is quieter, more poised than in the very early pictures, it is free from flamboyance or grandiosity, and is no longer confined to the acting figure itself; that is, the figure is an organic part of the composition as a whole, to all of which the action is plastically communicated, so that in a very real sense it is the whole picture that may be said to put on the man's coat. Movement, in other words, is extended to the conception and execution of the entire picture; and it is this quasi-metaphorical extension that constitutes the plastic as distinguished from the illustrative character of the expression. Such plastic expression, unmistakably present in "Man Putting on Coat," reveals Cézanne's distinctive way of seeing, which eventually enabled him to lend an intense pictorial drama to things and episodes in themselves often inert, commonplace, or trivial. As yet, however, the plastic expressiveness is far removed from the completeness and conviction achieved in the work of his prime.

The traditional influences in this picture which have intervened and curbed the turbulence that Cézanne took over from Caravaggio, the late Italians, and, possibly, El Greco, as well as from Delacroix, are clearly Daumier's and Manet's. Daumier's influence is apparent in the choice of a comparatively trivial episode for subject-matter, in the poise of the movement itself, and in the integration of figure and setting in a comprehensive design, in which the movement is extended to all parts of the ensemble.[57] Technically, it appears also in the simplified drawing of the figure, the tendency of dark areas to be silhouetted against lighted color, the accentuated and sometimes broken line of contour, and the black-ivory-brown effect of the color-scheme especially in the figure. Chiefly because neither the structural quality of color nor the dynamic interrelation of volumes is as yet adequately achieved,

[54] E.g., "Woman with Shawl" (118).
[55] E.g., "Man and Skull" (142).
[56] Illustration, p. 171.
[57] Cf., e.g., Daumier's "Don Quijote in the Mountain" (264) or "Water Carrier" (268).

the picture is inferior in sense of power, plastic strength and fulness of expression to Daumier's or to Cézanne's own mature
work: pattern remains comparatively superficial, as does integration of detail in the whole.

In technique, the painting has affinities with both the work that
precedes and that which follows it. To a considerable extent, especially in the figure, brushstrokes exercise their function individually rather than as elements in areas, so that their contribution to
illustration and decoration takes precedence over their specifically
plastic activity. This testifies to the influence still exerted over
Cézanne by Manet, which, however, is already tempered by Cézanne's greater natural feeling for structural color.[58] Like Manet's,
Cézanne's brushstrokes here show clearly the tendency to flatness
and a square or oblong shape, attributes which qualify them to
assume the function of planes. In some parts of the landscape-
setting, the organization of the brushstrokes into larger areas or
patches has already appeared and made considerable advance; in
these areas Cézanne's personal adaptation of the impressionists'
technique in a form more fully expressive, more structurally convincing than theirs, is clearly in evidence; but the organization of
the brushstrokes is as yet only partial, and the command of color
and color-relations is still insufficient to achieve adequate solidity
of mass or definiteness of spatial position. The color-scheme is
at a transitional stage in that it combines features taken from
Daumier, as in the figure, with the color of the setting which is
dominated by the blue so characteristic of Cézanne's mature work.
Space is rendered by conventional symbols and technical devices—
as, for example, by cast shadows, sharply silhouetted color-areas
and alternation of strongly contrasting light and dark—rather than
realized plastically, that is, by organic relationships of line, light,
color, and pattern.

In spite of this imperfect realization of space, many aspects of
the technique, such as the definition of the figure and its parts by
clean-cut contour and the rendering of depth by lines of perspective, anticipate in essentials some of the distinctive means of
Cézanne's ultimate form of plastic organization. Compositional
unity, likewise as in later pictures, is achieved largely by the pattern
of brushstrokes and the shapes of particular objects, though eventually, of course, these factors play their part as elements in a

[58] Compare, e.g., with the figures in Manet's "Tarring the Boat" (282).

much more solid and closely-knit ensemble. The same is true of the
compositional effect of linear directions, sequences of line in which
interruptions occur but which nevertheless maintain an essential
continuity. That is, here as later, they are an important means of
indicating spatial depth and of interweaving separate areas into a
unified whole, but their relative isolation leaves the composition in
this picture comparatively loosely knit. Well-integrated areas alternate with others in which both conception and execution fail to
carry conviction, so that Cézanne's own distinctive form appears
sporadically and rather as a promise or anticipation than as an
accomplished reality.[59]

How the promise was fulfilled may be seen in "Gardener"
(130),[60] a much later picture but one presenting the same plastic
problems as "Man Putting on Coat" (56), and containing similarities in the drawing of the figure. "Gardener" shows a still
further reduction of emphasis upon representation, and a much
more thoroughgoing organization of solid volumes in deep space.
The plastic rather than illustrative character of the movement appears in the later painting, in that the figure, while not itself engaged in active movement, sets the total organization into an all-
embracing rhythmic movement of plastic units. The figure is the
most voluminous and most clearly defined of all the units; both the
voluminousness and the clarity of definition diminish continuously
as the eye passes outward through the setting to the boundaries of
the picture. This is plastic movement; in "Man Putting on Coat"
there is no comparable contrast in solidity, and the activity is
largely the representative movement of actual events in the subject-
matter. In "Gardener," with the clear definition of the figure and
its parts, the emphasis on individuality of units is carried further
than in "Man Putting on Coat," so that compositionally and technically these units are more like those in Cézanne's still-lifes, and
tend to form definite color-areas. This tendency is characteristic
of Cézanne's figure-paintings as it is of his still-lifes; and as his
command of color increased, the lines enclosing the figures became
more definitely color-areas in themselves, more positive adjuncts
in the modeling and drawing of masses and space, and more important agents of compositional unification.

The actual technique shows a corresponding advance. In "Man
Putting on Coat," as in the work of Hals and Manet, individual

[59] See also analysis, p. 317.
[60] Illustrations, p. 233 and p. 298.

brushstrokes have a high degree of plastic activity, though they are here more rigid and naturally less illustrative in function. In "Gardener," not only is the activity of the individual brushstroke determined by that of the group of strokes to which it belongs and with which it functions, but the rigidity is decidedly greater, in accordance with the more static, more Cézannesque design. Moreover, variation in the perceptibility of technique to emphasize the relationship of figure and setting appears to a greater extent: in "Man Putting on Coat" the perceptibility is approximately the same everywhere in the canvas, but in "Gardener" it is decidedly more pronounced in the setting. At the same time, as in Cézanne's still-lifes, echoes of the more obvious parts of the pattern, reappearing in the more smoothly painted areas, help maintain compositional unity. This heightened contrast between figure and setting becomes increasingly prominent in Cézanne's mature form, and correspondingly the pattern that links together the contrasting areas grows more and more organic, so that, in a constantly higher degree, it is made one of the fundamental means of drawing, modeling and compositional integration in all its phases. The relative haphazardness of technique in the earliest stage, which though diminished is still evident in "Man Putting on Coat," is reduced in "Gardener" by a precise adjustment of means to ends, a design evolving from mature reflection; and this is preëminently distinctive of Cézanne in his most characteristic work.[61]

In Cézanne's portraits or paintings with a single figure, the problem of composition centers about the relation of figure to setting; the figure is of course always a subsidiary composition in itself, and in a completely characteristic Cézanne the unification of the parts of the figure, and of the figure as a whole in the entire composition, are phases of a single continuous process. In compositional themes of single figure and setting, Cézanne's means of unification, together with different degrees of success in its achievement, are well illustrated by four pictures, "Madame Cézanne with Drapery Background" (113) and "Woman with Shawl" (118) both of the late 1880's, "Provence Peasant" (151) of the middle 1890's, and "Woman with Green Hat" (103) of 1888—all examples of his mature form.

"Madame Cézanne with Drapery Background" (113) is in design a typical Cézanne composition, but in execution it is appre-

61 See also analysis of "Gardener" (130), p. 380.

ciably below the level of his best work. Its surface consists of the familiar pattern of color-areas, with contours of objects markedly accentuated, and linear sequences and rhythms playing their usual part in binding the compositional elements together—one part of the figure with another, and the figure as a whole with the background. The linear framework and the adjustment of volumes to one another in deep space are forceful and picturesque, with a bizarre effect arising from the contrast between the stably drawn and placed figure itself and the pattern of slanting units in the background. Technique is strongly accentuated and its compositional function is very important: its patterning motifs are repeated over and over in both the figure and the setting. The shape of the head, likewise, recurs rhythmically in subsidiary parts of the figure, in the shape of the body as a whole, and in the setting. These unifying effects of technique and pattern, however, remain superficial, chiefly because of the comparatively inadequate color. In its intrinsic quality the color suffers from an excess of heavy leaden tone, which makes it, for Cézanne, dull and lifeless. Not only is color-power lacking, but also harmonious interrelation of colors with one another and with the other plastic means. The pattern of technique, because of both its own accentuation and the lack of support by color, stands out in isolation, and the rhythmically repeated elements in various parts of the picture tend to be mere shapes, with little individual force or distinction of expression. This lack of vitality in the parts of the form, together with the ineffective total color-organization, makes unity superficial and the whole picture comparatively diffuse and lifeless. Cézanne's characteristic static quality reaches here the point at which the figure has the rigidity of a wooden image.

In "Woman with Shawl" (118) [62] the figure itself has none of the halting and disjointed character of the portrait just discussed, but the excellence of the picture as a whole is impaired by lack of color-quality in part of the setting. The figure is clean-cut and convincing and all the elements are rich and solid in texture, chiefly because color is fine in quality and is so well related to light, line, mass, space, technique, and pattern that every part of the figure harmonizes with and reënforces every other part. There is much less rigidity than in "Madame Cézanne with Drapery Background" (113), and the characteristic power is tempered with a fluid grace rare in Cézanne. Indeed the poise, grace and general expressive-

[62] Illustration, p. 231.

ness of the hands, as well as their delicacy and skilful technical execution, have rarely been excelled by any painter. The main mass in the composition is roughly pyramidal in shape and is unified partly by the pattern of technique with which it is drawn, and partly by the color, which lends to it as a whole and to every part of it a high degree of life and reality. Through the planes, which delimit the surface of the figure and build up its constituent volumes, extends a sequence of gently contrasting rhythms in subtle space, and from a point about the center of the woman's waist a general hub-and-spokes pattern radiates in all three dimensions, adding a further linkage between the compositional elements.

The background is much less well organized. In the lower third of it an attempt is made to achieve compositional unification by extension and repetition of the color-pattern of the figure, but, while the color itself is appealing and of unusual tones, the plastic units lack distinctness. Above, the background suffers from disorganization because of ineffectual use of light. The accentuated area of light back and to the left of the figure's head designed to convey the effect of space—one of Cézanne's frequently used devices—is here esthetically unsatisfactory because of the sharp drop in color-quality between the lighted area on the left and the inadequately illuminated color on the right; the relationship between the right and left portions of this part of the background thus goes beyond contrast and becomes discrepancy, and the sense of depth is gained at the expense of compositional continuity. The linear sequences and rhythms between the upper part of the setting and the figure are likewise effective only in part, and no organic union is established between the convincing figure itself and the unsuccessfully realized background.

"Woman with Shawl" is thus a notable advance upon "Madame Cézanne with Drapery Background" (113), but the improvement is for the most part confined to the treatment of the figure. Pattern, color and light join in creating a high degree of plastic reality and compositional unity there, and the technique is used in due subordination to these ends Although the defects of the setting impair total compositional unity, the high level of quality in the figure proper imparts to the picture a delicate fluid grace unusual in Cézanne, combined with the dignity and stateliness like that in good Renaissance portraiture.[63]

[63] See also analysis, p. 361.

"Provence Peasant" (151)[64] has a decidedly more sculptural quality than either of the pictures just discussed, and the in-and-out movement of its planes is much more active. The head, especially, is like a carved block extending forward into space, as are also the arms, body, and objects in the background; and all of these, modeled with many facets, jut forward at angles contrasting with one another. Both planes and volumes participate in this in-and-out movement, which extends in varying degree to all parts of the canvas, and its unifying effect is further heightened by the equally pervasive contrast-motif. An unusual and striking color-scheme, with a much more extensive and assertive infusion of reds than is usual in Cézanne, adds to the bizarreness arising from the distribution of lines, planes and masses. The degree of compositional unification attained by all these means is very high, though it is somewhat adversely affected by defective relationship of the bright red stripes of the dress to other colors and to the texture of the volume in which the stripes occur.[65]

"Woman with Green Hat" (103),[66] with the same general scheme of compositional relations as the foregoing three portraits, marks a great improvement upon any of them in the level of its plastic quality. This is primarily due to the superb quality of its color, and especially to the harmonious compositional activity of color-relations. The actual color, the intermixture of light, and the use of the pigment itself, all combine to give to every color-area an extremely high intrinsic excellence. The correlation with light is such as to lend to the focal points of the composition a greater degree of glow and luminosity than to areas of secondary importance, which have proportionately less illumination; and this adjustment is so finely graduated that there is a continuous crescendo or decrescendo of light as the eye passes from any point on the canvas to any other. Even in the darkest areas there is no such descent of color-quality into mediocrity as that which appears in the background of "Woman with Shawl" (118). The dominating blue-gray tones of the color-ensemble pervade in varying degree and unify every part of the picture; the variations are sufficient to provide adequate drama without the obvious and often specious contrasts in "Provence Peasant" (151). The color, in short, though retaining its prevailing Cézannesque restraint, is, in its immediate

[64] Illustrations, p. 258 and p. 300.   [66] Illustration, p. 230.
[65] See also analysis, p. 383.

richness and glow, in its depth, and in its multiform plastic activity, of the very highest order.

Brushwork, individual to Cézanne, with scarcely a trace of its traditional origins, is used to unify the composition in a degree proportional to its general importance in the picture. Indeed, in perhaps no other picture by Cézanne is the technique so thoroughly integrated, so variedly and effectively instrumental, in the total form. The pattern of brushstrokes is not accentuated, and is so merged with the other aspects of the form that it is felt primarily as an organic element in the general harmony of effect, though it can be discerned as a separate factor if looked for. Practically all types of Cézanne's brushwork occur in it, such as broad short strokes, long ribbonlike strokes, straight or curved, and organized either in a curled-up spring-motif or in patches of hatchings and quills—all of them present in varying degree of emphasis, and making up a continuous texture with diversified surface extending over and binding together the entire canvas. Because of the perfect integration, the pattern so constituted is perceived as a reënforcement of the design of color and light, and it is only in the hands and part of the lap that the technique stands out prominently, not as an overaccentuation but as an element of contrast to the comparatively uniform adjacent areas. This submergence of obvious pattern of brushwork, together with the diminution of the emphasis upon definite planes of thick paint, is very possibly an effect of Cézanne's extensive work in water color.[67] The planes exist and function actively and organically, but the even thickness of the impasto and the lack of accentuation of their contour give in essence, though, of course, with added solidity of substance, the feeling of translucent water-color washes. This is characteristic of some of his best work of the late period.[68]

Throughout the entire painting of this canvas the structural quality of the color causes the technique to coalesce with the substance of the volumes themselves, so that the surface-pattern is no longer merely such, but an integral part of the objects depicted. This more organic integration of pattern and structural color makes the head more solidly voluminous than that in "Provence Peasant" (151), which in comparison seems, in spite of its accentuatedly

[67] See p. 94.
[68] E.g., "Red Earth" (111); "Well" (174); "Corner of Quarry" (176); "Rocks and Trees" (179).

jutting character, like a hollow box, in which attention is called to the ins and outs of the surface rather than to the solid underlying substance. The torso in "Woman with Green Hat" also presents a higher degree of plastic excellence than that in "Woman with Shawl" (118) : the effect is of a column of granite rising and projecting massively into space, while in "Woman with Shawl" voluminousness of substance is secondary to a rather realistic rendering of texture of fabric. A quivering character, arising partly from the spots and areas of sunken light, is present in both portraits, but in "Woman with Green Hat" the function of the pattern is to lay stress, not upon surface-texture, but on the planes which bound the solid mass and by their intersection determine its organization in deep space. The fundamental purpose of the pattern is thus to emphasize the architectonic character of the design, as well as the solidity of the masses, so that the form as a whole is more fully expressive, in a typically Cézannesque manner, than that of any of the other three portraits discussed above.

The movement of planes and semivolumes in the background of "Woman with Green Hat" repeats that in the figure, but in an appropriately lesser degree. Largely by means of the technique, the linear shapes, the protuberances and recessions of the figure are echoed in the background as rhythmic repetitions and variations. The background maintains its identity, with as much distinctness of parts and intrinsic conviction as the design requires, but it never competes with the figure for the observer's attention or dislocates the center of gravity of the picture.

The compositional use of lines and planes in "Woman with Green Hat" shows the same superiority over that in the other pictures of this group. The lines which specify direction and determine perspective, as well as the planes which fix the position of the body and of its various parts, and relate it dramatically to the background, are subtler, less accentuated as individual devices, more organically merged in the form as a whole; and they, too, gain from the more structural color a higher degree of plastic conviction. The use of all the plastic means, in brief, while essentially the same in kind as that in the other portraits, has reached a perfection of coördination that makes "Woman with Green Hat" supremely expressive and powerful. Cézanne's control of his medium and the quality of his color reach their greatest height in this picture, and so too does his unification of all the parts and areas in a single compositional whole.[69]

Before proceeding to a consideration of Cézanne's figure-groups, we shall consider in some detail his "Man and Skull" (142), of about 1892,[70] partly because it embodies so many of the characteristic compositional devices already discussed, and partly because it illustrates the fertility of his imagination in achieving a great variety of individual effects by a relatively limited number of means.

This painting contains actually only one figure, but the table, books, skull, and drapery are more than mere accessories: taken together, they are virtually the compositional equivalent of a second figure. As in Cézanne's other paintings, the figure of the man is a subsidiary composition in itself, as is also the unit of drapery, table and skull; and the composition as a whole gathers up and further organizes the relations that bind together each of these sub-designs. This duplication of figure-units greatly heightens the complexity of the space-composition. The man himself, by his being placed at a definite angle to the frontal plane of the picture, establishes an organization of masses not unlike that in "Provence Peasant" (151), while the other unit, with the table projecting at its own angle and having its movement continued and varied by that of the skull and drapery, establishes a second organization which both strikingly contrasts with and strongly reënforces the first. The succession of abrupt positive thrusts and counterthrusts throughout the composition interact with one another in an extremely dynamic design, with a total effect radically different from that in "Provence Peasant." This difference depends, as usual with Cézanne, not upon any basic divergences in the conception or execution of the component parts—in spite of minor individual differences the objective aspects selected for emphasis do not greatly vary in any of his pictures—but upon the way the parts are put together, and especially upon the mode of spatial synthesis. It is, in other words, the network of relations which an object acquires in each organization that determines its specific character, and therefore the character of the form as a whole. In "Man

[69] See also analysis, p. 348. The fact that "Provence Peasant" (151) was painted about six years later than "Woman with Green Hat" illustrates once more Cézanne's habitual failure to maintain a continuous improvement in either technical execution or expressive power.

[70] Illustration, p. 259.

and Skull" the plane of the table top corresponds to the plane of the book in "Provence Peasant"; each throws into relief the vertical position of the near-by figure, accentuates its recession in space, and combines with adjacent objects in a compositional series of units which are rhythmically echoed in other parts of the picture; but in spite of these resemblances the plastic part played by the plane in the total design is quite different in the two pictures. In "Man and Skull" its compositional function is much more basic and far-reaching: it orders and sets in equilibrium the other elements in the design to a far greater extent than does the relatively incidental plane in "Provence Peasant."

"Man and Skull" is a characteristic Cézanne form in its vigorously dramatic movement of sharply angular masses in deep space, and it also incorporates a type of compositional arrangement familiar in all the traditions of painting from the very earliest. The decentered figure, balanced either by another figure or by a vertical sequence of masses which function as a figure, appears in Giotto, van Eyck, the early Florentines, the Venetians, El Greco, and the work of numberless other painters.[71] It is really only a variation of the pyramidal or bilaterally balanced form, with the central mass replaced by a shaft or area of space. The enframing figures or other compositional units are related to each other by resemblances, contrasts, rhythms of various sorts in their constituent elements, or by direct links extending, in varying degree of continuity, across the intervening space.[72] In this picture, both the units participate in the movement of planes advancing, receding and intersecting at different angles, out of which arises the general effect of dynamism and drama. Not only does this movement embrace the relations of all parts of each unit to one another, but the figure as a whole forms one wall of the area of

[71] E.g., Giotto's "Saint Francis, Supporting the Lateran, Appears to Pope Innocent III" (213); van Eyck's "Jan Arnolfini and Jeanne de Chenany, his Wife" (214); Botticelli's "Saint Augustine in his Study" (223); Ghirlandaio's "Saint Jerome" (224); Giorgione's "Two Saints" (229); Tintoretto's "Susanna at the Bath" (237) or "Two Prophets" (238); El Greco's "Vision of St. Hyacinth" (246).

[72] An example is Tintoretto's "Two Prophets" (238) in which the figures form upright, roughly parallel masses, each dominating half of the canvas; at the same time the relations of color and linear pattern, and the placing of subsidiary masses such as forearm, loaf of bread, shoulders and heads, unite the two in a single revolving movement. From the continuous circular arrangement, the volumes project into space in all directions, yielding a definite and characteristic effect of dynamic power. In Giorgione's "Two Saints" (229), an analogous composition moves quietly and gracefully because of

enclosed space, the plane of the right side of the table a second, and the side of the table at the left a third, so that all three are held together by their relationship to this enclosed space. They thus constitute an instance of the accordion-pleat motif, illustrated also in a number of Cézanne's bathing groups.[73] In "Man and Skull" it is made more complex by a steplike arrangement of horizontal and vertical planes in many ways like that used in his still-lifes and landscapes; and within this general framework a number of other Cézanne types of compositional linkage occur. The familiar diamond-shaped pattern includes the skull, the man's head, the corner of the back of the chair, and the hand on the lap. Individual areas are joined by more or less continuous lines of direction, and the surface of the canvas is interspersed with patterns of roughly triangular or oblong areas alternately curvilinear and rectilinear, together with specific motifs, such as that of the accolade or cupid's bow, the decorative character of which is extended to include also a compositional function. The more comprehensive form of this picture is as perfectly unified, in conception at least, as are the simpler compositions containing only one figure; compared with "Woman with Green Hat" (103), however, it is less uniformly successful in execution, chiefly because of occasional lapses in color-relations. Around the head and shoulders of the figure, for example, such indifferent relationships, together with overaccentuated contour-lines of thick pigment, fail to establish adequate spatial order.[74]

Cézanne's mature, large-scale treatment of a group of figures in an interior, is best represented by his "Card Players and Girl" (141), of about 1892,[75] one of several versions of similar subject-matter.[76] The major theme here is the rhythmic beat of fully three-dimensional masses in clean-cut space which, reënforced by

a different type of interaction between the component parts: the headdress of the saint on the left is joined by a hyphenlike ribbon in the central space with the garment of the saint on the right. The gradual transition from the color of one figure to that of the other has the same gentle quality, as have also the pattern of light and the other means of unification. In the accentuated space-composition of van Eyck's "Jan Arnolfini and Jeanne de Chenany, his Wife" (214), the pattern of light, as the chief unifying instrument of the centrally divided organization, finds its most obvious exemplification in the bright illumination of the hyphenlike joined hands.

[73] E.g., "Five Nudes" (74); "Men Bathing" (164).
[74] See also analysis, p. 368.
[75] Illustration, p. 276.
[76] Some of the other versions are "Card Players" (125), "Two Card Players" (127) and "Two Men Playing Cards" (143).

dramatic contrasts, produces Cézanne's characteristic effect of power.[77] Contrast is ubiquitous: it extends to the color-scheme, in which tones of red, green and orange-yellow relieve and diversify the prevailing blue; to the kind of rhythms and the degree of their perceptibility; to the alternation of angular and oval motifs in the pattern of lines and planes; and to the degree in which volumes, planes and spatial depth are accentuated in the group of figures and in the setting, respectively.

The composition combines Cézanne's familiar pyramidal and enframing types of order. The pyramidal embraces the group as a whole and the individual figures; it is reversed in the V-shaped compositional motif, which has its apex at the center of the lower edge of the canvas and interlocks with the upright pyramid in a diamond-shaped pattern; it is repeated in the converging sequences of oblique lines, planes and areas of light and shadow which make a roughly triangular pattern in the background. Within the area at the center common to both the main and inverted pyramids, the details—objects on the table, hands and arms—combine in a hub-and-spokes pattern which radiates out through various continuations to all parts of the picture; and the treatment of these details, by emphasis on planes, solidity and perspective, extends the pattern into the third dimension and coöperates in giving to the whole composition its powerfully dynamic character.

The other compositional theme, that of the bilaterally enframing motif, is really, as we have seen in the discussion of "Man and Skull" (142), a modification of the pyramidal. It appears in the two-dimensional relation of the seated figures, at the right and left, to the central figure, and in the tri-dimensional relation of these three figures to the central space they enclose as within three solid walls; it is repeated in the tri-dimensional hub-and-spokes motif formed around the central figure by the other four. It occurs also in a number of subsidiary details of the canvas, for example, in the light and dark planes in the midst of which the head of the central figure is placed; and again in the compositional organization of the background by which the slant and pattern of the folds of drapery on the right balance the pattern and slant of the shad-

[77] This major theme of grouped forceful beats, deployed throughout the composition and used to effect dramatic contrasts, finds its counterpart in musical composition, in the ponderous rhythmic beats in the first movement of Beethoven's "Fifth Symphony."

ows on the left. The drapery and the shadows tend to converge on the upper center of the canvas, and thus function in both the enframing and the pyramidal compositional devices. In addition to these two general means of organization, the pyramidal and the enframing, many individual links are, as usual with Cézanne, introduced between particular objects or areas, such as lines of direction varying in degree of continuity, incidental patterns of light and shadow, and rhythmic reduplication of voluminous foreground-masses by semisolid planes in the background.

"Card Players and Girl" illustrates Cézanne's ability to introduce. coherence, order, power, and drama into a composition on a large scale; it suffers, however, like many of his otherwise successful pictures, from imperfect coördination of light with color, with the result that color lacks the effulgence, depth, solidity, and thoroughgoing organic activity found in his best work. The pattern of shapes and the perspective consequently carry more of the burden of lending solidity to masses, depth to space, and compositional order to the form as a whole, than they do when color and its relations to light play their full part.[78]

The essential features of Cézanne's form may, in conclusion, be brought out clearly by a comparison of two of his groups of bathers, "Bathers at Rest" (63) and "Nudes in Landscape" (191). The first was painted in 1877,[79] when his command of the medium was still very halting; the second was finished nearly at the end of his life, and more than any other picture it sums up and crowns his whole career. The later picture [80] is characterized by a mastery of composition, a complexity of organization, and a wealth of transferred sculptural and architectural values which go far beyond anything in the earlier painting. However, the fundamental Cézanne form, the convincing qualities of power and drama, were already achieved, despite the differences in technical skill, in the picture of 1877. The intervening development was in many ways of great importance, but the traits in which Cézanne's significance ultimately inheres, the force and coherence of his compositional design, are as unmistakably present in the early as in the late picture.

In both these paintings, a group of figures is placed in a natural setting, and the form as a whole is a fusion of figure-composition with landscape-painting. In both, also, the familiar sandwich-

[78] See also analysis, p. 365.   [80] Illustrations, frontispiece, p. 296 and p. 304.
[79] Illustration, p. 198.

arrangement of the main compositional planes of the landscape occurs; but the relations between the figures so definitely determine the design that the three planes combine in what is essentially a single compositional element, the function of which is to set off the principal masses, accentuate their position and dynamic movement, and at the same time bring them more completely into equilibrium. In both, the volumes, intensely weighty and massive, are placed in deep space, and the series of strains and tensions set up by their dynamic movement balance one another so perfectly that each composition has the stability of a fortress or pyramid, planned and executed on a monumental scale.

In the 1877 picture, Cézanne's own form may be seen taking shape out of the contributions of Courbet and Pissarro. The stark naturalism of Courbet is preserved, though Courbet's reproduction of representative detail is discarded in favor of an emphasis upon those traits of objects which give them solidity, weight and structural strength. Cézanne's objects are not reproduced from nature, they might more appropriately be said to be quarried from nature and then employed as building-stones for an edifice to which no structure actually existing in nature corresponds. Similarly, a color-scheme of blue, orange-yellow and green, largely taken over from Pissarro, is distributed through the picture with little regard for natural local color or for temporary accidents of illumination, in order to bind together various areas compositionally, and at the same time, by increasing contrast, to heighten drama and power. This compositional function of color is coordinated with distortions of line to emphasize contour, and of surface to emphasize planes; in consequence, a pattern of shapes is produced which is bizarre, picturesque, and a highly effective instrument of compositional unity; while the placing of planes at various angles to each other in all three dimensions makes the areas and masses thus delimited advance, recede, collide with, balance, and support one another.

An example of these varied interactions is offered by the main compositional plane of the foreground—a grass-covered area upon which the figures stand as upon a platform—which moves backward and upward in a continuous sweep to meet the plane of the sky; the joint movement of the two is continued right and left to embrace the other chief planes of the picture in an unbroken roughly circular motion which has the completeness, the finality, of the movements of the solar system. Within the area thus circumscribed, the masses—figures, trees, clouds—are set in relation to each other like the sun and the planets: a sort of centrifugal force seems to pull them outward at the same time as they are kept firmly in balance by the effect of a centripetal counter-force and by the massive weight of each unit. The counter-action of opposing forces thus establishes equilibrium, which is further maintained by counterbalancing tensions between groups of individual objects. The dynamic power of this composition is re-enforced by the ruggedness of the objects themselves; and the absence of fluid grace, of natural charm, far from detracting from the total esthetic effect, heightens Cézanne's distinctive forcefulness. So great is the power of the picture and so organically unified is its design that the fairly numerous faults in execution—notably the sculptural use of piled-up paint and the occasional failure to achieve successful spatial ordering of objects —are felt to be negligible, incapable of disturbing the profound sense of conviction conveyed by the organization in its entirety.[81]

The later picture, "Nudes in Landscape" (191), is the work of a more profound observer and an older, wiser and more experienced painter; it represents the complete flowering of Cézanne's genius. Cézanne's enduring concern with power achieved through dynamic space-composition finds in it expression on a larger plastic scale, in a more complex organization revealing richer plastic vision and a wider range of human values, than ever before. Indeed, many of Cézanne's other important paintings seem to be essentially studies for, or experiments looking toward, this final realization:[82] the particular plastic insights in them are here fused in a single all-embracing vision. In sustained perfection of execution, "Woman with Green Hat" (103) is a superior achievement, but its scope is so much smaller that the two paintings can hardly be weighed in the same scales.

Although this "Nudes in Landscape" is Cézanne's greatest imaginative triumph, both the materials involved and the principles of organization are essentially the same in kind as those in his other work. The dramatic contrast between dark-colored setting and light-colored figures goes back to his earliest period, though the color has become infinitely richer and more active plastically. The consistent encircling of areas by broad contour-lines,

[81] See also analysis, p. 324.
[82] E.g., "Study of Bathers" (156); "Eight Women Bathing" (161); "Bathers" (180).

together with the glowing color-quality of both the areas and the contours, imparts to the ensemble the rich, lustrous quality of stained glass. This emphasis upon contour, and the general contrast above noted, serve to give to the figures a more positive individuality and to set them off more distinctly in space; such distinctness, of course, was at all times an aspect of Cézanne's sculpturesque form, which varied from complete detachment to a degree of independence comparable to that of the volumes in a bas-relief. Here the closest resemblance is to the figures in a high-relief, more specifically, to those of the metopes (211) or the frieze of the Parthenon (210), in which, as in "Nudes in Landscape," solid masses both project from a background and move across it in a series of powerfully dynamic rhythms. In the painting, however, the composition of figures is repeated in a rhythmic in-and-out movement in the setting near by, and echoed a second time, with a lesser degree of emphasis, in the background proper.

The compositional scheme in general incorporates much of the framework of Cézanne's landscape-designs; in the placing of figures back of each other, it also resembles his still-lifes, but is incomparably more dynamic: the directions in which the figures are placed set up an interplay of forces which, apparently clashing, are harmonized in the compositional equilibrium of the total organization. The result is a staccato throbbing movement of rigid volumes which recall Egyptian sculpture, as well as the pyramids. The organization of the figures and other masses carries out both the frieze-motif and the pyramid-diamond motif; and it is the compositional interweaving of these themes in deep space, supported by deep, rich, solid color, effective color-relations and an unusually varied pattern of line and technique, which strikes the keynote of the architectonic form as a whole. Not only is the general compositional theme less stereotyped, freer, than in most of Cézanne's pictures, but all of the units show a corresponding enrichment of plastic content and flexibility of execution, so that the balancing of different aspects, the coördination of all the plastic means, is varied to give to each area its own appropriate kind and degree of solidity, movement, textural quality, and transferred values. To his supreme expression of power and epic quality Cézanne has thus added a decorative richness and a completeness of plastic realization that makes this "Nudes in Landscape" unique among all his pictures. However, even in this supreme triumph, the heavy pigment, the numerous crudities in drawing and modeling, bear witness to Cézanne's life-long struggle to master the medium of paint.[83]

V. Aquarelles

The physical properties of water-color washes on paper lent themselves admirably to Cézanne's efforts to fix by quick touches of color his immediate reactions to his subject-matter, and to add substance to forms previously indicated by contour-lines. The nature of the medium enabled him to apply several successive coats of color and make use of transparent glazes for plastic effects, with no such interference of the pigment as when he had to pile up his oil-paint in repeated attempts to obtain a particular quality. Constant experimentation and practice with water color not only developed his appreciation of the possibilities of color *per se* as an instrument of drawing, modeling and compositional organization, but it helped make his individual touches of color, in his work in oil, more definite, positive, purposive, and sure.

At times, his aquarelles consist of washes of color so thin and so sparingly used that the representative matter is extremely vague and sketchy; [84] but under close examination both the contour of objects and their substance appear with sufficient distinctness to become positive factors in an adequately expressive and uniquely personal form. It is in water colors of this type that Cézanne's form attains an extreme degree of abstract expression, often enhanced by clear, luminous, jewel-like colors, which are not only of a fine intrinsic sensuous quality but are organized in a color-form of high expressive and decorative value.[85] The best of these water colors reveal Cézanne's familiar planes so interrelated that they produce the same dynamic movement of volumes in space that is characteristic of his work in oil, but with a lightness and delicacy not exceeded by any other painter. In a great number of these aquarelles,[86] the distinctive dabs of color are more varied in shape and more individually active than are the brush-strokes in Cézanne's typical technique in oil; in others [87] they are organized in groups and function collectively as hatchings, strips,

[83] See also analysis, p. 393.
[84] E.g., "Mountain Range" (198) ; "Park of Château Noir" (201).
[85] E.g., "Park of Château Noir" (201).
[86] E.g., "General View of Aix from the Garden of Les Lauves" (193).
[87] E.g., "Trees" (204).

quills, bands, and compositional planes, just as they do in his oil
paintings.

The simplicity of the use of pigment makes these water colors
extremely enlightening as evidence of the essential nature of Cézanne's technique and drawing. The location of the washes of
color in relation to adjacent blank areas frequently indicates his
concentration on fundamental nodal units, the hinges which serve
to set his planes in motion; [88] the individual planes of color,
clearly perceptible and transparent, often overlap and thus create
additional plane-effects; [89] the linear framework characteristic of
his work in oil is also apparent with aspects of the line, in pencil
or in paint, which include the more or less continuous single linear boundary, [90] the broken outlining strips, [91] the alignment of
dashes, [92] the parallel multiple series of thin lines, [93] and the scalloping edges of foliage. [94]

The characteristics of Cézanne's aquarelles are recognizable in
a great number of his successful oil paintings executed after 1887,
including "Valley of the Arc" (109), "Red Earth" (111), "Pine
Tree at Montbriant" (115), "House at Bellevue" (126), "Provence Landscape" (138), "House and Wall" (147), "Bibemus
Quarry" (155), "Mount Ste. Victoire through Trees" (166),
"Well" (174), "Rocks and Trees" (179), "Ginger Jar and Fruit"
(181). In these pictures the technique is smooth and direct, the
pigment is relatively thin and at times transparent, and the color-
relations between contrasting patches in the pattern or in the
modeling of masses have an effect of fluidity, even though the
compartmental patchwork-pattern of the brushstrokes is still in
evidence. Earlier in his career, Cézanne had occasionally obtained
with oils the distinctive effects of water color as, for example, in
"Red Apples" (84). "Banquet Table" (50) and "Interior with
Nude" (83)—experiments obviously designed to achieve that specific purpose—stand apart from the general run of his work in oil
by their delicacy and freshness. In them, as in his work in water

[88] E.g., "Mountain Range" (198) ; "Mount Ste. Victoire with Tree" (199) ;
"Peak of Ste. Victoire" (202) ; "Smoker" (203) ; "Woodside" (205).
[89] E.g., "House Tops" (195) ; "Trees" (204).
[90] E.g., "Mountain Range" (198).
[91] E.g., "Trees" (204).
[92] E.g., "House Tops" (195) ; "Park of Château Noir" (201).
[93] E.g., "Garden at Les Lauves" (192) ; "House Tops" (195) ; "Nudes in
Woods" (200).
[94] E.g., "House Tops" (195) ; "Mountain Peak" (197).

color in general, there is a pervasive feeling of the French eighteenth century tradition, a feeling of grace and lightness which otherwise seems incompatible with the usual heaviness of his form.

VI. Conclusion

In this account of the types of Cézanne's painting we have laid primary stress upon composition. Composition, as we have seen in an earlier chapter, is for him the all-important plastic function: his pictures are conceived as plastic structures in which every part is designed with the utmost care to fit together with every other in building up an organic whole. This is the end which determines his selection of aspects from nature, his abstractions and his distortions. His pictures lack suavity or ingratiating charm, they make no attempt to convey the appeal of natural scenes or persons, and the transferred values which they recall from other realms of experience are primarily the abstract qualities of solid masses architecturally organized in deep space. At best, the richness and depth of his color add a powerful decorative force to his plastic organization, but the decorative interest is strictly secondary: nothing is put into his pictures that does not contribute directly to the essential expressiveness of their basic form.

While the foregoing chapters cover the general types of Cézanne's painting, they should be read, for particular variations within each type, in connection with the analyses of individual pictures in the Appendix. These will make apparent the wide variations in compositional unity, in expressive power and in technical rendering of the different plastic means. The analyses will reveal also the evidence of Cézanne's habitual reversion to early practices, both in the use of technique and in the interpretive use of traits from other painters' forms. This constant reversion, together with Cézanne's frequent failure to maintain levels of excellence previously achieved, makes it impossible to determine the date of many of his paintings more closely than within a period of several years.

CHAPTER V

CEZANNE'S LIFE AND PERSONALITY

PAUL CEZANNE was born in Aix-en-Provence on January 19, 1839. His father, though of humble origin, had made himself a prosperous banker, and Paul received, at the Collège Bourbon in Aix, the classical education customary for members of well-to-do families in his day. He showed an early fondness for poetry and literature, learned Latin so thoroughly that fifty years later he could repeat from memory whole pages of Virgil and Lucretius, and himself composed verses in Latin as well as French. While at school, he made the acquaintance of Emile Zola, with whom he quickly formed an intimacy that lasted many years, and profoundly influenced Zola as well as himself. With many common interests and ambitions, the two mapped out their future together, planned a joint career that should revolutionize both literature and painting, and probably did much to confirm one another's vocation. Cézanne's interest in art had declared itself when he was very young, and he had begun the study of drawing while still a schoolboy. He continued as a pupil in the Academy at Aix, where he succeeded in winning a prize; however, conformity to academic rules was distasteful to him even at that early age, and he never took this particular success seriously.

After his graduation from college, Cézanne wished to go to Paris, where Zola had preceded him, to fit himself for a career in art. His father, to whom such an ambition was unintelligible, wanted him either to enter the paternal bank or to undertake the profession of law. A compromise was reached: Cézanne agreed to attempt the study of law, while his father fitted up a studio for him at Aix and allowed him to paint in his leisure hours. The study of law progressed slowly and laboriously, though at the end of two years he passed his preliminary examinations. All his real interest was in painting, but the museum at Aix, and such guidance and companionship as he could find in a small provincial city, were totally inadequate to his needs. At the same time he

was constantly receiving letters from Zola, describing the oppor-
tunities that Paris offered and urging him to come there and begin
the career on which he had set his heart. Finally, in April, 1861,
his father relented, assured him of the necessary financial support, and Cézanne took up his residence in Paris.

Here disillusionment followed quickly. He entered the Atelier
Suisse, a free studio where models were provided, but neither
instruction nor criticism. This had the merit of leaving him to
paint as he wished, but offered nothing else of the slightest value.
Zola had his hands full to keep himself alive, and could be of little service to him. For the conventional *vie de Bohême* Cézanne
had as little taste as he had for any other form of conventional-
ity; his self-distrust made him morbidly fearful of any associations that might develop into entanglements; the confusion of
Paris so bewildered and distressed him that he became doubtful
of his vocation; and after four months, in spite of Zola's vehement protests, he confessed himself defeated and returned to
Aix. Convinced that he had no future as a lawyer, he entered his
father's bank; but a second revulsion of feeling took place almost
immediately. He found finance as repugnant to him as the law;
he could not put the memory of Paris out of his mind; and when
he attempted to paint in his own studio he became acutely conscious of his isolation from the masterpieces of the Louvre, in
which he had at hand the traditions of painting that he needed
for the nourishment of his growing mind. After a year in Aix,
he persuaded his father to allow him to abandon business as he
had already abandoned his legal career, and he made his second
venture in Paris.

This time there was no vacillation or thought of again retracing
his steps. A few months after his arrival the famous *Salon des
Refusés* was held, where he saw and immensely admired Manet's
"Luncheon on the Grass" (280) and other paintings belonging
to the new "realistic" movement. He saw, perhaps for the first
time, that he was not alone in rejecting and despising the mori-
bund tradition of David and Ingres, which still dominated official
art and the academies, and before long he made the acquaintance
of Pissarro, Guillaumin, and a number of the other young painters
who were later to become known as the impressionists. Later on
in the sixties, he met Manet, and also Monet, Sisley and Renoir;
he came to be on intimate terms with all of them except Manet,
who was an older man, fond of the sort of society in which

Cézanne was ill at ease and toward which he felt contemptuous. Cézanne, indeed, though his relations with the other painters as individuals were cordial, was never really a member of any group. He was always afraid that others would, as he expressed it, get their *"grappin"* (hooks) into him; furthermore, Manet, Monet and Pissarro were disposed to be revolutionaries in principle, and Cézanne, though he bitterly disliked the traditions of painting that happened to be in power at the moment, was far from objecting to authority as an idea or ideal. He had applied for admission to the Beaux-Arts and been rejected; later on, he sent his pictures to the annual Salon year after year, and year after year saw them refused; but he never questioned the propriety of an official school or salon as an institution. This was one of the contradictions of his nature, as were also his political conservatism and his Roman Catholicism. When it was a question of submitting his own perceptions and judgments, in a field in which he had first-hand experience, to the judgment of others, he rebelled at once; in most matters, however, feeling himself feeble, he craved something stronger than himself to lean upon, and for such support authority was indispensable.

In 1866 the jury of the official Salon rejected many, and in 1867 all but one, of the works of the younger painters with whom Cézanne was associated, and Zola came to their defense on each occasion with a series of articles in which the insurgents, especially Manet, were eulogized and the official tradition caustically attacked and ridiculed. These articles produced no change in official policy, but did much to rally enlightened opinion to the side of the new movement. Unfortunately, Cézanne individually profited little from the change. Zola, whose perceptions in the field of plastic art were at bottom conventional, did not really care for his work and scarcely alluded to it; furthermore, Cézanne himself was still far from having discovered his distinctive vein. He had not yet learned to abandon entirely the literary strain in his painting; the influence of Delacroix upon him was not altogether outgrown; he had still to catch up with his own contemporaries. This was the period of his melodramatic narrative pictures, some of them patterned very closely after Manet as well as Delacroix. His development was slow: he had not yet acquired even the limited mastery of paint to which he later attained, and the critics who charged him with crudity, however blind they may have been to the personal force and distinction always present in his work, were not wholly wrong. He himself was perfectly aware that he had not completed his apprenticeship, and though his steadfastness did not really falter he was the victim of constantly recurring fits of uncertainty and depression.

During the rest of the 1860's Cézanne continued to work steadily, producing pictures of the same general sort, spending part of his time in Paris, part in Provence. This alternation between the north and the south of France continued for nearly all the remainder of his life, or at least until failing health kept him permanently at Aix. He preferred nature as it was in the Midi, but his need for contact with the masterpieces of art in the museums attached him to Paris. He required long periods of retirement, but sometimes found the society of his family more oppressive than the crowds in the city. During the Franco-Prussian war he remained continuously in Aix and its vicinity, but afterward rejoined his friends and resumed his former way of life at Paris. At this period he formed an association with Hortense Fiquet, whom he eventually married. Their liaison had little or no direct effect upon his work, but indirectly it was the cause of an experience which was of great value to his development. Since he was still in complete financial dependence upon his father, who would have refused to sanction either an irregular union or a marriage with a dowerless girl, Cézanne could not visit Aix in the summer of 1872, especially as a son had been born to them the winter before. Accordingly he went to Auvers-sur-Oise, near Pontoise, where Pissarro lived. The two men began to work together constantly, and Cézanne doing for the first time most of his painting in the open air, really assimilated the impressionistic technique, or as much of it as he needed for his purposes. Pissarro was the strongest of the impressionists, and by far the most congenial to Cézanne in the particular bent of his mind; he was never so preoccupied with immediate light-effects as Monet; and in addition to what he actually communicated to Cézanne, he helped him form the habit of painting his landscapes directly from nature. The association continued until 1874, and in its course Cézanne became more and more conscious of "the magnificent colorfulness of nature," which was to set the standard for his painting in all his later years; he also began to modify the very heavy, lumpy impasto of his first period, and to apply pigment in the smaller regular brushstrokes which are characteristic of his mature work.

By this time, Cézanne was definitely on the way to his own

distinctive achievements. Popular recognition, however, was still a long way off. He had pictures in the impressionists' exhibitions of 1874 and 1877, but the official attitude toward the members of the group was unchanged, and it was especially hostile to him as an individual. He did not prevail over the indifference even of those whose attitude toward Manet, Monet, Pissarro, and Renoir had become genuinely appreciative. For years thereafter he exhibited nothing publicly and it was not until 1895 that the first extensive showing of his pictures was held in France. He continued to send regularly to the Salon paintings which were returned with equal regularity. During the next years he kept up his personal relations with Pissarro, Monet, Renoir, Zola, and a few other intimates, but ceased to be regarded by the public as one of them, and gradually sank into deeper and deeper isolation and obscurity. Those of his old friends who were painters never wavered in their admiration for him, regarding him as one of the outstanding figures of his age, an artist of the same order as the great painters of the past; but the academic critics reviled and ridiculed him when they mentioned him at all, and most people forgot his existence.

As the years went by, he saw even his old friends less and less frequently, though occasionally he visited Zola, and Monet and Renoir came to see him in the Midi. In 1886 he was finally married to Hortense Fiquet, and shortly thereafter his father died. This left him wealthy, but he was indifferent to money, except as it assured his independence, and he had had that for a long time. In the same year occurred his break with Zola. The immediate occasion of this was the publication of Zola's "L'Œuvre," the central figure of which, a painter whose career ended in failure, was generally regarded as modeled after Cézanne. Cézanne was wounded, but in fact the intimacy between the two men had been withering away for a long time, and not much was needed to bring it to an end. No actual quarrel took place, and there were no subsequent signs of animosity on either side, but their visits to each other and their correspondence came to an end.

In the late eighties and early nineties Cézanne became more and more isolated, and not long afterward the decline in his health began. He had always been a Catholic, but with the first intimation that his days were numbered his interest in religion became much more intense and he reverted to a closer communion with the Church. Badly as he needed its support, it was characteristic of him that he was extremely suspicious of the clergy and constantly on guard against what he imagined to be their intention to get their "hooks" into him. He had now achieved the full command of his powers, and much of his very best work was done during these years of loneliness. It brought him no tranquillity of spirit. He never outgrew his inability to work rapidly, and many of his paintings displeased him so much that he destroyed them before they were finished. At times he felt his isolation as exile: though he was incapable of sacrificing his integrity to secure recognition, the absence of the recognition was a source of pain and mortification. At other times, as on one visit to Paris during which he refused to speak to his oldest friends when he passed them on the street, the desire for solitude, for the opportunity to work without distraction from any quarter, made him almost completely a recluse.

However, the period of obscurity gradually came to an end. In 1894 the Caillebotte bequest of impressionist and post-impressionist pictures to the French Government drew some attention to him again, and in the same year Gustave Geffroy published an article on him full of enthusiastic appreciation. The next year marked the turning-point; Vollard arranged the first exhibition devoted wholly to his pictures. In the controversy which followed, his detractors were as much in evidence as usual, but an important body of public opinion made itself heard in his defense, and wealthy collectors, such as de Camondo and Pellerin, began to buy his pictures. At least a decade was still to pass before the immense vogue began which for a time made him the most discussed painter in the world, but a measure of recognition in many quarters came quickly. Other exhibitions in which his pictures appeared were held in 1899, 1900 and 1901, and in 1905 and 1906 the *Salon d'Automne* opened its doors to him. In 1907, after his death, the same salon had a retrospective exhibition in which appeared many examples of his work both in oil and water, covering all the periods and types of his painting. In 1936, the comprehensive exhibition of his work at *L'Orangerie* in Paris revealed to the public for the first time what a monumental figure Cézanne is in the history of painting.

After 1900, whether or not because of the increasing recognition accorded him, Cézanne became less a recluse, and began to establish cordial relationships with a number of his younger contemporaries. None of his characteristics—his aversion to associations which threatened to compromise his independence, his intolerance of opposition, his sense of "feebleness in life"—disappeared, but his suspicions were less easily called forth, his attacks of rage were less frequent, and he was more willing to believe in the good will and esteem of others for him. After his long years of loneliness, he enjoyed greatly the companionship of a number of younger writers and painters who admired his work and wished a better understanding of it. Though his mother, to whom he had always been deeply attached, died in 1897, his grief was alleviated by the fact that his son had already relieved him of the direction of his finances, his negotiations with picture-dealers, and the other practical affairs to which he felt himself unequal. On the whole, the last decade of his life was probably the most peaceful and cheerful that he ever had.

After 1904 Cézanne's diabetes, with which he had long been afflicted, grew rapidly worse and hastened the oncoming of the other infirmities of old age. It seemed to him that he was only then attaining the full maturity of his powers as a painter, but that his bodily weakness had reached a point at which he could no longer control his brush as he wished. In the summer of 1906 the approach of the end was unmistakable; he suffered constant discomfort and frequent attacks of severe pain; but the increasing exhaustion of his energies brought no enfeeblement of his will and he refused to sink into the passiveness of senility. In October, 1906, while painting in the open country, he was caught in a heavy storm, suffered a chill, and was brought home unconscious. The next day he rose early and attempted to go on with his work, but he collapsed almost at once, and died before his wife and son could reach him from Paris.

Although Cézanne's painting received a measure of recognition before his death, no observer who viewed his career wholly from the outside could have judged it to be, in the conventional sense of the word, a success. A few enlightened critics had in the end acclaimed him, but the public as a whole knew little of his work and cared nothing for it; his hoped-for conquest of the authorities had certainly never been made. Though he had repeatedly announced himself to be "the only painter," and no doubt on occasions felt the fullest assurance that this was the truth, his unceasing suspicion of others, his terror of the "hooks," would long since have been laid to rest if he had been able to feel certain about himself. The contrast with Renoir in this respect is illuminating. Renoir knew his own mind perfectly and could carry out his intentions with consummate mastery. His designs seem to have taken form in his mind with little or no inner conflict, and they were no sooner conceived than executed. Almost from the start he enjoyed a command of technique which Cézanne, after years of toil, never equaled or even really approached. Renoir was unperturbed by hostile criticism because no sense of failure, of inadequacy within himself, responded to it or corroborated it: the academicians were in his eyes too obviously unimportant to be given a second thought. Cézanne, on the contrary, wished to "make the officials blush with rage and despair," and in one of his late letters to his son he proclaimed that all his compatriots were dirt compared to him. These are the attitudes and expressions of a man whose conflicts were never solved, who never succeeded in being at peace with himself.

Nevertheless, Cézanne's claims on his own behalf cannot be dismissed as neurotic delusions of grandeur, and the measure of their validity must ultimately be judged by an analysis of his work itself. Their psychological grounds, however, lie within Cézanne's own experience, and these must be understood in the light of his personal history, the environment in which he grew up, the influences to which he was subjected, the goal which he set for himself, and the success of his efforts to reach it. In its broad general outlines, Cézanne's life was far from unique; it was a typical adventure in romanticism; and it can be made intelligible and judged only with the aid of a psychological account of romanticism in general.

The romanticist may be defined as one who lives only partly in the real world which we all share, the world of eating and sleeping, of making money, keeping engagements, and paying bills. Another part of his life, the part he is likely to regard as the more real and important, goes on in a world far more responsive to human wish and aspiration, a world from which boredom, defeat and disillusionment have been banished—in brief, a more glamorous world. Because he is more imaginative than the average man, the romanticist usually seems to the average man a visionary, and only too often it is his tragedy that the average man is right, that he *is* a visionary, that his ascent into his more glamorous world is a mere flight from reality. If the romanticist's intelligence is crippled, he becomes the dreamer too absorbed in his dreams to make them real; if it is entirely paralyzed, he becomes the lunatic for whom dreams are the only realities.

Romanticism and realism or naturalism are often regarded as opposites. The truth is that romanticism can only justify itself, can only prove itself valid, by having its nucleus in the realistic or naturalistic, a nucleus which is expanded by the imagination until it embraces the world of reality itself, and becomes a part of universally verifiable experience. This process constitutes the essence of artistic creation. What is fundamentally opposed to romanticism and realism alike is passive acceptance of convention. To conceive a world more rational than that habitually taken for granted, capable of arousing more vivid interests and yielding more profound satisfactions, is not an indulgence in illusion if the dream or vision is used as an instrument for the discovery of realities here and now. Subject to this control, the art of the romanticist becomes analogous to the art of the scientist, a process of exploring the environment and bringing to light in it things to which the conventionally minded are permanently blind. When the romanticist has proved his case, established the reality of his own conceptions, the stigma of illusion rests not upon him but on the follower of authority. Now that the insurgents of the 1860's and 1870's have made their ways of seeing things a matter of common perception, it is Cabanel, Meissonier and Bouguereau—the painters acclaimed in their day as "sane," "sensible," "normal"— who are felt to be unreal. The conceptions of the artist, in a word, are verified in the same manner as those of the scientist—by experiment, by the production of objective facts which vindicate their standing in the real world.

Cézanne's original romantic bent is incontestable. He grew up in a provincial Philistine environment, in a family in which the only comprehensible ambition was that for financial success and a substantial bourgeois position in society. Nothing which the natural course of events in that society offered him could conceivably have engaged his interests and energies. His mind fed naturally upon the images of art and literature, and at his most impressionable age he was brought into constant and intimate association with Zola, a youth of boundless ambition, immense energy, unbridled imagination, and an intelligence greatly superior to any other that Cézanne was likely to encounter at Aix. Many men in their youth, of course, have been dissatisfied with their surroundings, formed vague aspirations, and remained mediocrities all their lives. Cézanne, however, had not only extraordinary potentialities as an artist, but an equally extraordinary degree of integrity and force of character. He owed much to Zola for personal stimulus and encouragement, as also of course for assistance in practical affairs, but probably nothing in his actual career as a painter. Perhaps even less than nothing, for Zola may well have been largely responsible for the literary preoccupation which distracted Cézanne's properly plastic perceptions for years before he could entirely rid himself of it.

As we have seen again and again in the analysis of his painting, Cézanne was anything but precocious; he went through a long period of trial and error, studying the work of various painters and even copying from them for the purpose of trying out possible lines of advance, before he discovered the form in which he could embody what he himself and only he was able to perceive. Had he ever rested content with another painter's perceptions, he might justly be charged with a fixation, an arrest in development, but he was always aware that his ventures into imitation were temporary exercises, incidents in his own personal quest for reality.[1] He was perpetually in search of the objective facts from which alone his mind could draw its sustenance.

Thus Cézanne's romanticism, his fidelity to his own inner vision, if it was the cause of his tribulations, was also the sustaining force which drove him on to his ultimate victory. When at last he found the kind of objective fact that his individuality could make its own—the colorfulness of nature as a revelation of its form and architecture—his romanticism was fully transformed into a grasp of essential substance. The interaction between his mind and his environment became cumulative, and his growth, the enrichment of his background, was thereafter assured. The interpretation of objects in terms of color-planes, and of total situations in terms of dynamically interacting color-volumes, offered unlimited potentialities, to the exploration of which the rest of his life was devoted. In his letters and conversations he commented constantly on the varied aspects—he called them motifs—of nature at various times, as he observed them in the light of his varying interests and per-

[1] E.g., his free copies of Sebastiano del Piombo's "Christ in Limbo" (232), Rubens' "Disembarkation of Marie de Médicis at Marseilles" (248), Lancret's "Hide and Seek" (258), Delacroix's "Agar in the Desert" (260), "Dante's Boat" (261) and "Medea" (262), and Pissarro's "Louveciennes" (274). Compare these with Cézanne's "Hide and Seek" (1), "Christ in Limbo" (11), "Dante's Boat" (29), "Louveciennes" (43), "Agar in the Desert" (157), "Medea" (196), and "Three Nereids" (208).

petually expanding experience. It was the constancy and continuity of his own growth that enabled him to treat the same subject over and over without monotony, and notwithstanding his limited repertoire of plastic means, to create individualized forms of great variety.

To his romanticism, and the unremitting effort required to bring it to plastic fruition, Cézanne owed also the power which is the outstanding trait of all his characteristic painting. In order to pass from the superficial literary romanticism of his early period to the profound grasp of nature which he ultimately achieved, he was compelled to make a thoroughgoing reconstruction of his whole artistic personality. Not only were the paintings of his apprenticeship crudely executed, but their plastic structure was loose, and their force constantly degenerated into flamboyance and melodrama; and although, beneath all this crudity and literary romanticism, the feeling of power emerges, the perceptions, the forms of organization embodied in his mature work were present only in germ. Cézanne himself, recognizing as he did the unsatisfactory result of his efforts, was conscious only in part of his underlying purpose, and though he used his awareness for guidance as best he could, it was mainly the systematic *push* of his unconscious that furnished the drive toward his ultimate goal.

This unconscious, refusing to be deflected, overrode every obstacle that came in its way. It was manifested in his concentration of purpose, his capacity to undergo endless labor and hardship, his self-imposed isolation, his renunciation of every interest that could have detracted from his singleness of mind. These were the qualities involved in his ability to transform and give substance to his romanticism; they are also the qualities which, psychologically, constitute power; and ultimately, therefore, Cézanne's romanticism was the source of the power which makes his work unique in the whole history of art. Because of the power in himself, he had an incomparable eye for power in nature, for the qualities which can make the simplest material object seem massive, immovable and immutable. Because of it, he discarded in his work all the aspects of things which are accidental, superficial or fugitive—the play of light as it changes from hour to hour or from season to season, the expression of transient emotion on a human face, as well as all preoccupation with incident or narrative. Only what was permanent and essential, basic structure unaffected by momentary circumstances, finally found a place in his mind and work; the search for that generated his strength, and his strength in turn made the search successful. That Cézanne's strength was inherent in him, and likewise his responsiveness to the same quality in the world about him, is evidenced by the fact that in his early treatment of romantic subject-matter, inspired by the forms of Delacroix or Rubens, his paintings have a new and strange feeling of power, not even hinted at in the prototypes.

This power governed not only his choice of aspects for emphasis, but also the mode of organization in which they were arranged. The composition of all his characteristic paintings is, as we have seen, highly architectonic. They are intensely dynamic and full of drama, but in his successful work the operative forces are always brought into equilibrium, and the drama is that of thrust met and stabilized by counterthrust, not that of energy unleashed and set in motion. The deep space, the solid weighty masses, the strongly emphasized lines linking the masses together and lending them support and rigidity—all these are the characteristics of architecture conceived on an epic scale and executed with conviction and power. They appear not only in his large landscapes and figure-compositions, but in his small still-lifes, which, irrespective of their physical dimensions, have all of Cézanne's typical scope of conception and vigor of execution. The strangeness, the departure from conventions, the distortions in Cézanne's painting are, psychologically, akin to his behavior in social life; what his whole career, no less than his work, proclaimed to the world, might justly be given expression in these words: "I won't conform, I'll interpret imaginatively, my hand will put down what my eye, experience and feelings, all working together, say is real, sincere, myself." The point here is that the strangeness of his work is part and parcel of a self, an original self: his deformations of naturalistic appearances are akin to the brusque remarks made by Cézanne which, when sociability is the rule, project new interpretations upon conventionally accepted ideas, or redirect traditional feelings into new channels. The significant fact is that when he made these remarks, or dressed badly, or secluded himself, the members of the Batignolles group—Renoir or Monet, for example—thought Cézanne's conduct strange, yet did not utterly condemn it; but when he put into painting the psychological equivalent of this social strangeness, they admired it, saw in it a personality doing and revealing something new, individual, fundamentally significant, with the very subject-matter, technique, independent spirit, honesty, sincerity, which they looked upon as their very own. They prized it so much that persecution by either critics or public never swerved them.

Cézanne, like every other artist, had the defects of his qualities. The concentration of energies out of which his power arose entailed also many renunciations; indeed, a greater number of them than would have been necessary for a man less at war with his surroundings and hence less compelled to find self-possession by exclusion. Titian and Renoir, to take only two examples, show in their unlimited mastery of their medium, their capacity to realize an intended effect, a kind of power less accentuated, less intense, than Cézanne's, but in its own way not less real. At the same time, their more comprehensive interests enabled them to incorporate in their work a whole world of values, human and decorative as well as plastic, that are not even suggested in Cézanne's. The glow of diffused light bathing and transfiguring an entire landscape, the warmth of human flesh, the textural quality of silk or velvet, of flowers or jewels, have a reality of their own, a legitimate esthetic appeal that is not necessarily and under all circumstances inconsistent with the expression of power. Cézanne, however, because he felt himself "feeble in life," because he could not sufficiently control his human emotions to be indifferent to the "hooks," was obliged to shut out from his work innumerable qualities which more fortunate painters were able to admit without detriment to the balance of their feelings or the integrity of their minds.

Cézanne's vision, to sum up, because of the inherent character of his personality and the experiences involved in its successful growth, was extraordinarily penetrating. "The magnificent richness of color which animates nature," in so far as it can be used to build up solid masses and to organize them in space, was assimilated and made a part of his own mind with extraordinary completeness and with supreme power. In this sense his judgment upon himself— "I am the only painter"—is anything but an unqualified overcompensation, or a delusion of megalomania: it approaches closely to the literal truth. Little qualified as he was to do justice to painters who had other interests than his, he was not mistaken about himself. As regards sensitiveness to the specific form of reality in which Cézanne was interested above all others, and the ability to give it plastic realization, no other painter has ever equaled him. Whatever his difficulties, frustrations and doubts about himself, Cézanne did in essentials bring his romanticism to fruition, make his dreams a part of nature itself.

CHAPTER VI

CEZANNE AND RENOIR

THE characteristics on which Cézanne's real greatness depends, and those which limit his greatness and make him an easy prey for imitators, are thrown into clear relief by a comparison between him and Renoir. Both men were artists of the first rank, both had their essential origin in the Venetians, both took impressionism as their point of departure, both made color the fundamental means of all their plastic effects. These resemblances were accompanied by differences almost as basic. Renoir's natural endowment in the matter of craftsmanship was of the same magnitude as Rembrandt's or Velásquez': by the early 1870's he was able to paint whatever he wished without any visible sign of effort. His ability to take for granted the means of execution left his energies free thereafter for the work of broadening and deepening his perceptions themselves, and this growth in artistic stature proceeded uninterruptedly his whole life long. What he had once mastered became his permanent possession; Cézanne, in contrast, was perpetually confronted with the necessity of solving the same problems over again. This struggle seems to have left him with little opportunity for more fundamental development. He did outgrow the literary preoccupations of his earliest period—Renoir's sense for the authentically plastic seems to have been innate, for he had no corresponding literary period to outgrow—but once Cézanne had found the form natural to him he never made any further advance in essentials. As we have already seen, his "Bathers at Rest" (63) of 1877 is as original and powerful as his "Nudes in Landscape" (191) of 1890-1906. The later picture is conceived on a more monumental scale, it has a much greater range of values, it is far more effectively executed; but there is no fundamental difference in kind between the two.

The contrast with Renoir could hardly be more striking.[1] Starting his career under the influence of Courbet and Manet, he quickly

[1] For a detailed account of Renoir's development, see Barnes and de Mazia, "The Art of Renoir," pp. 47-160, Minton, Balch & Co., New York City, 1935.

assimilated the technique and characteristic effects of impressionism, added to them a fluid, rhythmic, expressive drawing all his
own, and in a short time painted pictures that were plastically more
varied, richer, more powerful, and especially more colorful than
any of Manet's, Monet's or Pissarro's. No sooner was this form
mastered than, in the late 1870's and early 1880's, he went on to
diversify his palette, vary his technique, intensify his light, and
give to his color more comprehensive plastic functions, both decorative and expressive. In the middle 1880's he developed a new
form which in many respects differed notably from that of his
previous work, and which marked his assimilation of the eighteenth
century French tradition. The delicacy and grace characteristic of
him from the start were endowed in these years with additional
picturesqueness and charm; a sculptural quality developed in his
drawing, modeling and textural effects; contours grew sharp, and
reminiscences of Italian frescoes and the classical tradition in art
made their appearance. In this period of active experimentation
and research, Renoir was exploring the traditions for new material;
the form thus developed was, for him, comparatively exotic, and
many aspects of it were subsequently discarded; but the added
resources remained as an essential part of his working capital, to
be utilized in all his later work.

In the 1890's, and still more in the years following 1900, Renoir
made his own, more completely than any other modern painter, the
qualities that set apart the Venetian tradition as the most important
in the whole history of painting. Discarding the sharp linear contours which had for a while been the instrument of his sculptural
effects, he drew everything with a constantly increasing fluidity.
To his grace and charm, the exquisite quality he had always pos-
sessed, he added the solidity, depth, dignity, and majesty characteristic of the Venetians at their best. More and more he eliminated
the inessential and adventitious; and coincidentally he made color
more and more completely the substance and integrating principle
of his form. No other painter ever excelled him in the use of color
to build up masses, draw space and organize composition. In his
latest pictures everything is color: actual line practically disappears,
light loses its separate identity and becomes a sparkle or glow of
suffused color, the constantly changing yet always harmonious
fabric of color binds together every area of the canvas.

Not only did Renoir show a capacity for growth that Cézanne
lacked almost entirely, but he was able to diversify his methods

and use them to draw out the significant character of any sort of material whatever. As we have so often observed, Cézanne's subjects are all conceived in much the same terms and his compositions are put together in the same general fashion. There are differences, of course, between the flesh in his figures and the pieces of fruit or napkins in his still-lifes, but the solidity, the weight, stands out with such intense conviction in both that the distinguishing qualities seem unimportant. Likewise with Cézanne's frequently recurring general types of composition: they are significantly varied by modifications of detail, but Renoir's inexhaustible ability to organize a picture about any one of a number of focal points, and to produce different schemes of organization in endless profusion, finds no parallel in them. In his figure-painting, Renoir was able to catch the pose, the gesture, the exact shade of facial expression which make human action and character convincing; except in his early work, and then often badly, Cézanne scarcely even attempted any such psychological characterization. His figures are dignified and real, but it is primarily as plastic or architectural units that they engage the observer's interest.

Cézanne's technical means are as limited in range as his pictorial effects. Pattern of brushstrokes and color-patches, flattened planes intersecting at definite angles to build up geometrical solid masses, general accentuation of line as a means of modeling and rendering perspective—these are the instruments on which he relies in all his characteristic pictures. As a result of his work in water color he was occasionally able to introduce a measure of fluidity and even of color-suffusion, but the rigid angular framework of the composition and the patterned technique are never really changed in essentials. Renoir was never compelled to rely on any single manner of execution: he could use very obvious and definitely patterned technique when he wished, or dispense with it altogether. Sharp line or loose line, linear perspective or aërial perspective, flattened planes or continuously rounded surfaces, together with textural effects of every sort, were all at his disposal. It was this infinitely varied command of plastic resources that enabled Renoir to achieve the art that conceals art, to make technique so completely instrumental to form, that we are unconscious of its existence except when, for purposes of analysis, we deliberately seek it out.

In the light of these differences between the two men, Cézanne's much greater influence upon his successors, and especially upon academic critics and painters, becomes readily comprehensible. Not only is his most characteristic effect, that of extreme dynamic power, overwhelming in its impact upon the observer's senses, but the means employed to secure it are comparatively few in number, obvious, and easy to stereotype. Hence the innumerable imitative pictures with patterning planes, blocklike volumes and arbitrary distortions; hence also the theories of "significant form," which have not the slightest foundation in modern psychology or scientific method, and which when applied reduce plastic form to decorative pattern. Those who see in distinction of form only idiosyncrasy of mannerism can find in Cézanne much to imitate, in Renoir, little or nothing. In neither, of course, can they see the qualities that constitute real greatness; Cézanne's color-power, especially, is entirely beyond them; but his general color-scheme and superficial peculiarities of technique can be reproduced in unlimited quantity. Renoir's form, complex, subtle, and infinitely varied in the manner of its execution, offers no comparable opportunity to the copyist or to the theorist with an axe to grind.

The foregoing comparison may have seemed unqualifiedly favorable to Renoir, and certainly his greater control of his medium, capacity for growth, and variety of effect are incontestable. Cézanne's relative lack of these advantages, however, does not compromise his standing as an artist of the highest rank. Lacking Renoir's natural endowment as a craftsman and his openness of mind toward new experience, Cézanne made of his limitations themselves a source of added strength. The struggle against immense odds to realize the effects of power and order in which his whole personality, conscious and subconscious, found its only natural expression, developed in him a degree of single-mindedness, of resolution, of fortitude, which immeasurably increased his sense of power itself. He achieved the full realization of his designs only on rare occasions, but when he did the result was of monumental quality which makes comparison futile and indeed impossible. There is no such thing as a choice between Renoir and Cézanne: far from competing with one another, they are both indispensable to a fully rounded contemporary esthetic experience. Both, in short, are so valuable as to be invaluable.

CHAPTER VII

THE INFLUENCE OF CEZANNE UPON CONTEMPORARY PAINTING

In the foregoing chapters an attempt has been made to present both the intrinsic esthetic content of Cézanne's form and its relation to the general traditions of art. Both aspects must be understood by anyone who wishes to grasp the significance of Cézanne's work, or indeed of any other artist's. His form itself, the record of his perceptions, feelings—ideas of his esthetic vision, in a word—was made possible in the first place by the traditions, in which were embodied the perceptions, feelings and ideas of his predecessors; the magnitude of his accomplishment can only be measured by the degree to which he succeeded in mastering these traditions, selecting and assimilating what was relevant to his own purposes, and transforming all that he had taken from them into a creation of his own, an expression of what only *he* could see, feel and experience.

A third aspect remains for consideration. The importance of any painter depends largely upon the value that his work has for those who come after him. Just as his predecessors, by leaving a record of their perceptions, enabled him to see vividly and penetratingly for himself, so his paintings provide an instrument for his successors, by which they in turn may broaden, sharpen and deepen their own vision. It is the crowning proof of Cézanne's greatness that he has furnished contemporary painters with so extraordinarily fruitful a means of insight, that there is scarcely one of these contemporaries, of any eminence, who is not deeply indebted to him—consciously or subconsciously—both for what he has had to say and for the means of saying it.

Cézanne's deservedly great reputation, unfortunately, has produced as a by-product a world-wide Cézanne-cult, largely factitious, which displays nothing but blindness to the most distinctive and important qualities in Cézanne's work. The attempt to divorce art from reality,[1] to stigmatize as merely imitative any interpretation of the world in which we live, to make distortion for its own sake—meaningless distortion—an end in itself, has constantly appealed for justification to Cézanne's alleged precept and practice. Nothing could have been more repugnant to Cézanne himself than this sort of fetishism, the antithesis of everything for which he stood in life as in art, and no account of his work and esthetic ideals would be complete which left the fundamental pretensions of the Cézanne-cult unexposed. This cult has succeeded in misleading students by volumes filled with errors in critical judgment—often buttressed by misinterpretations of Cézanne's own sayings—and has caused countless contemporary painters to make a fetish of the obvious and superficial aspects of Cézanne's design. It has been a blight upon its victims, misdirecting their energies and stultifying their powers; it has filled exhibitions with assemblages of clichés—patterns of Cézannesque planes, blocklike volumes and senseless distortions—as barrenly imitative as were the former popular re-hashes of Manet, Whistler or Monet. In this mimicry of surface-characteristics, everything that gave meaning to the original is lost. Any attempt to evaluate the heritage left by Cézanne must there-fore begin by excluding from consideration these academicians of today.

To make clear the fundamental difference between academic imitation and the legitimate employment of a tradition or of an individual's work, it is necessary to digress briefly into the psy-chology of perception and artistic creation.[2] Everyone alike, ordi-nary man as well as artist, is at first able to perceive, to see, only what has been called to his attention. Perception, like all other human activities, is at bottom a matter of habit, and our habits are from the beginning of our conscious lives stamped upon us by our environment. We see only what we have learned to see, and, however acute our physical senses, by far the larger part of what is happening all about us passes unnoticed. Even under the spur of practical necessity, it is difficult to take cognizance of what we have been accustomed to ignore, and in the world of esthetic per-ception, in which no material danger is involved in being oblivious

[1] Cf., John Dewey, "Art as Experience," pp. 93-94, Minton, Balch & Co., New York City, 1934.
[2] For a detailed study of the psychology of perception, see Barnes and de Mazia, "The Art of Renoir," pp. 10-20, Minton, Balch & Co., New York City, 1935.

to our surroundings, the vast majority of us make no attempt to enrich our perceptions, diversify them, or make them more coherent. To employ a distinction of John Dewey's, we "recognize" most things but do not "perceive" them: we identify them by some obvious trait or feature without ever achieving a detailed consciousness of the specific qualities and relations—the "form"—that lend them individuality, make them what they are.

What we can all verify by observation of our own experience in this respect, is no less true of the artist. The ordinary man pays attention to the visible aspects of his world casually, intermittently and unsystematically; the artist does so habitually and of set purpose; but he, no less than the layman, requires stimulus and guidance in the work of seeing, and he finds it in the traditions of art. To know only one tradition is to see things from one angle only, it is to be aware of one set of attributes and manner of organization to the exclusion of all other qualities and principles of order. Knowledge of a diversity of traditions frees the individual from slavish dependence upon any one of them and makes growth possible, though it does not make it certain. What distinguishes the artist from the mere craftsman is that, using the perceptions of other artists as his point of departure, he is able to perceive something for himself—not of course something previously undreamed of, but something which, in its concrete totality, has never presented itself to any other painter. The ensemble of purposes, observations, feelings, ideas, experiences of success and failure, which are developed by the interaction of organism and individuality, and which constitute personality, is never the same for any two individuals, and in consequence no two people ever see exactly the same things arranged in exactly the same way. The subjective, personal individuality of the artist, in other words, and the objective vision which he has made his own, the world which he has embodied in his work, are essentially correlative, two sides of the same fact. He would have a meager vision of the esthetically significant in the world if he had not had at his disposal the traditions, the recorded perceptions of other painters; but the authenticity of his art depends upon a genuinely creative use of these traditions—their use, not as prescriptive models, but as instruments for the discovery of a way of seeing which is his and only his.

The distinction may be made more definite by a reference to technique. To express himself, to go on record at all, the painter requires technical means, and it is often taken for granted that the technique is independent of what is expressed by it, as the skill of a bricklayer, for example, can be directed to the construction of an office building, a church, or a private house. No more disastrous error could be made. The wholeness, the integrity, of an artist's form depends upon a union of means and end so thoroughgoing that the two are inseparable; for purposes of reflective analysis they may be distinguished, but in a really integrated form each is so inherently a part of the other that its distinctive character is lost if it is isolated. The particular fusion of light and color found in the impressionists, for example, is not something which could be realized by any other technique, any more than the miniature effects of van Eyck, the extensive and precisely organized space-compositions of Claude le Lorrain or Poussin, or the chiaroscuro-designs of Rembrandt, could be rendered impressionistically. This is what is meant when it is said that the style is the man himself: that the distinction between means and end has disappeared, that every element and aspect in the painter's form is relevant to every other. Not only must the general means, color, light, line, and space, be harmoniously merged, but the actual execution apparent in such devices as perceptible brushwork, lines of perspective, flattened planes, and distortions in general, must be adjusted to the specific design and to that alone.

We are now in a position to define the academic or eclectic painter. When any technical means or specific esthetic effect is taken over from another painter unchanged, without reference to a new esthetic purpose or design, there is a loss of artistic integrity, and this loss is the essence of academicism. The test is the nature and degree of modification, and though no abstract formula can be laid down by which imitation, slavish or fraudulent, can be distinguished from intelligent adaptation, the difference, unmistakable to the trained observer, can be illustrated from every period in the history of painting. Titian's use of Giorgione's contributions, or El Greco's of Tintoretto's, or Velásquez' of the Venetian form in general, or Renoir's both of the work of his immediate predecessors and of the French eighteenth century and Venetian traditions, not to speak of Cézanne's own use of impressionism—in all these, creative re-interpretation and re-synthesis are present at a very high level. The painter has found real illumination in his sources, he has grasped the relation of technical means to artistic effect, and in the interest of his own specific purposes has converted the borrowed elements into an organic part of a new form. The same authenticity, if not the same magnitude of achievement, is found in such a man as Glackens, whose resemblance to Renoir arises from an actual similarity of temperament and community of interest; their forms are closely akin, but Glackens' is differentiated by a very personal type of drawing, and by detailed modifications in the use of all the plastic means which establish the definite individuality of his work.

The academic or eclectic painter, having no real artistic vision of his own, attempts, not an intelligent use of other men's methods, but an imitation of their gross effects. Lacking the experience and the spirit out of which creation springs, he can only take over their means unaltered, hoping thus to cover his nakedness with a borrowed investiture. If he follows a single other painter or tradition, his work may have a superficial unity, in that it is all patterned after the same model, but since no one can really see with another's eyes, he merely parrots his exemplar. If he is an eclectic, he may repeat the surface-effects of a number of traditions; the result, however, is not a synthesis but a patchwork, the unreality of which is obvious to every trained observer. The lack of wholeness, of integrity, in the imitator prevents him from grasping the form of the prototype in its entirety, and the resulting exaggeration of a single quality or aspect reduces the manufactured form to unreality. Thus Luini is a feeble echo of Leonardo da Vinci; Palma Vecchio, imitating Titian's fluid drawing, achieves only softness and flabbiness; Sebastiano del Piombo, singling out Tintoretto's drama of light and color as a model for mimicry, exaggerates it into melodrama and adds an equally melodramatic movement of line and represented action. The academic or eclectic painting, no matter how skilfully executed, is at bottom a counterfeit, and it cannot really be dressed up as anything else. It says nothing which has not been said before, and has no artistic *raison d'être*.

Derain and Emile Bernard, among those who followed Cézanne, may be taken as typical of the eclectics, Picasso and Matisse of the artists. The former see the obvious technique which for Cézanne was a means to an end, but they have no comprehension of its relation to his design, and therefore no sense of its possible relation to any other design; in consequence they imitate it in its entirety; in their work it lacks the whole complex set of relationships which in Cézanne himself made it the instrument of an extraordinarily penetrating and original insight into the objective world. It thus

becomes a piece of empty pretentiousness, a shadow without substance, a mere parody.

Neither Picasso nor Matisse, in contrast, profoundly as each
has been influenced by Cézanne, has painted a picture designed to
reproduce the specific quality of his. Nothing that either of them
has produced could possibly be confused with a Cézanne: their
paintings have an identity of their own, and express what Picasso
and Matisse, not Cézanne, saw and felt. As we shall see in the
discussion of their individual pictures, they have adapted relevant
parts of Cézanne's technique to forms of plastic organization
radically new. Though neither of them approaches him in artistic
stature, they have genuinely carried forward his own vision, enriched it, and made it a flexible instrument, capable of being used
in the exploration of new fields of experience. The creative use
of Cézanne's contributions, by them and by other artists of insight
and imagination, which has made his influence the most powerful
of modern times and been responsible for most of what is best
in contemporary painting, is the subject of the present chapter.

We may now proceed to consider those features of the work
of a few of the important modern and contemporary painters which
owe their origin to Cézanne's form, and point out how the derived
factors have been reworked and assimilated as integral parts of
new and individual forms.

Among the artists thus influenced was **Renoir,** who knew Cézanne intimately and extolled the strength and individuality of his
painting. In Renoir's hands the derivations from Cézanne, radically
changed and subtly employed, added enormously to both the expressive and the decorative values of a form already enriched by
the insight gleaned from many and diverse antecedent traditions.

Perhaps the earliest manifestations of direct and specific influence of Cézanne upon Renoir appear in the latter's "Fruit of
the Midi" (298) of 1881 and "Apples in Dish" (290) of 1883,
with their modeling and drawing by hatchings of color and their
accentuation of dynamic relations between three-dimensional volumes and spatial intervals. By 1884,[3] the earlier sporadic influences
of Cézanne upon Renoir had become cumulative, appearing fre-

[3] E.g., Renoir's "Children at Wargemont" (295); "Dovecote at Bellevue"
(297); "Girl in Field" (299); "Grape Gatherers Resting" (300); "Madame
Renoir" (302); "Madame Renoir at the Gate" (303); "Summer" (310);
"Three Pears" (311).

quently in such characteristic traits as patches of organized brush-work, increased solidity of color, hardness of texture, greater emphasis upon weight and three-dimensionality of volumes. The most important and lasting influence was upon Renoir's technique, especially his use of small groups of parallel brushstrokes organized in patches of color which function as planes in the drawing and modeling, and are the characteristic features of his dynamic space-compositions. The patches sometimes extend in different directions throughout the canvas; [4] at other times, though they are actually parallel, changes in color make them appear to extend in opposite directions. [5] Each patch is of a single general color throughout, but is varied by differences of tone in the constituent brushstrokes. These pictures have in common an accentuated color-pattern, and its distinctive effect is different from that of either the crisscross brushstrokes and shimmering surfaces of Renoir's painting of the middle seventies, [6] or the definite pattern of contrasting broad color-areas of the early eighties. [7] The technique in this color-pattern, derived from Cézanne's, is stamped indelibly with Renoir's own individuality by the way in which it is used in connection with color and texture of surface. In most cases it is associated with color-schemes in which either pastel or oriental color-effects play an important part. Indeed, Cézanne affected Renoir mainly by giving direction to tendencies which were already evident in the latter's work, such as the bright vivid color of the early eighties and the accentuated narrow brushstrokes of the mid-seventies; by 1884 these are organized in a definite individual form on which the influence of Cézanne is clearly apparent.

Other borrowings from Cézanne, especially other adaptations of his technique to new purposes, appear in many of Renoir's pictures. In "Three Pears" (311) of 1884, for example, the patches are organized in compact planes which model the pears as three-dimensional volumes closely resembling Cézanne's, but the patches are less rigid, independent contour-lines are absent, and the color-scheme is of Renoir's own oriental type. [8]

"Pasture along the Seine" (307), painted about 1890, repre-

---

[4] E.g., Renoir's "Girl in Field" (299).
[5] E.g., Renoir's "Summer" (310).
[6] Cf., e.g., Renoir's "Beautiful Season: Conversation" (293); "Beautiful Season: Promenade" (294); "Jeanne Samary" (301).
[7] Cf., e.g., Renoir's "Dance in the Country" (296).
[8] Cf., e.g., Cézanne's "Compotier, Pitcher and Fruit" (128).

sents perhaps Renoir's closest approach to the forcefulness, power and general form of Cézanne. The resemblance is increased by the technique of hatchings and pattern of patches and planes which build up trees and hills into weighty and definite masses. Brush-work and color-scheme are in the main those of Renoir's 1884 period, but the pastel colors in the sky, the oriental yellow over-tones in the distant hills, and the broad brushstrokes and pattern of patches have more positiveness than the earlier form, and the deep solid greens establish a forceful contrast with the pastel and oriental color-areas.

The foreground in Renoir's "Near Pont-Aven" (306), of about 1892, is rendered by a succession of broad ill-defined areas of contrasting colors in a pattern not unlike that of Cézanne's familiar patches.[9] Also as in Cézanne, the brushstrokes within the indi-vidual patches tend to run in a parallel direction, but Renoir's strokes are less perceptible and more varied in their length. Hence the strokes in one patch of color, not being so evenly aligned where they meet those in the adjacent patches, tend to merge with the latter and thus diminish the sharpness of the contrast in color, shape and direction. Renoir's handling of the pigment itself achieves a greater variety of color-effects than does Cézanne's: the brush-strokes in the center of his individual patches are heavily loaded with pigment and as the color extends toward and reaches the edges of the patch its substance diminishes until it becomes as thin as a wash or glaze; thus the color, naturally lowered in degree of intensity at the boundaries of the areas, flows more freely into the color of adjoining patches. In the central part of the sky, however, just above the uppermost distant small tree, Renoir almost dupli-cates the effect of one of Cézanne's patch-motifs, with its align-ment of parallel brushstrokes and intensification of color along one edge of the patch.

Renoir's "Mother and Baby" (304), of about 1886, recalls the effect of a Cézanne water color in the green-and-blue modulations of the skirt, which are shadows applied in transparent washes and organized in geometrical areas.

Cézanne's contributions are usually so thoroughly modified and so well adapted to Renoir's own designs that they are integral, indispensable elements in a highly individual form. Occasionally, however, they stand out as unassimilated and isolated, and the quality of the picture suffers accordingly. In "Madame Renoir"

---

[9] Cf., e.g., the foreground-plane in Cézanne's "Gardener" (130).

(302) of 1884, for example, the Cézannesque blue linear contour around part of the body and the long parallel brushstrokes grouped in patches, which ought to function as constructive planes, remain as relatively superficial patterns. The failure of the linear contours and of the patches and planes to enter into proper relationships leaves the volumes inadequately solid and three-dimensional, and prevents integration of color and form. What massiveness the torso has is attained speciously by layers of heavy impasto on the projecting parts.

Gauguin, a contemporary of Cézanne, was rumored to have antedated him in the use of several technical devices which Cézanne himself is usually regarded as having invented. Whatever the truth may be as to priority, the undeniable technical resemblances do not in any degree affect the immense differences in esthetic value of the two men's work. Both the resemblances and the differences may be illustrated by a brief comparison of two characteristic pictures.

The green area in Gauguin's "Haere Pape" (316), dated 1892, presents an appearance almost identical with that of the background in Cézanne's "Five Nudes" (74), painted in the late 1870's. In both pictures the technical means are mainly parallel brushstrokes, almost unvaried in their regularity, and forming an all-over pattern of striations. The unit in the Gauguin, however, is simply a patterned, semisolid, broad, flat area of color, in which the parallel brushstrokes serve merely to break the monotony of a flat surface. They do nothing to establish a recession or coming forward of constituent planes and masses; unlike the similar brushstrokes in the Cézanne, they play no part in the drawing or modeling or spatial location of three-dimensional volumes. Gauguin's trees, for example, seem like flat, cut-out shapes silhouetted against the contrasting color of the sky—one of the most specious and threadbare of all the devices for obtaining perspective.

This difference in employment of basically the same technique epitomizes the vast gap existing between decoration *per se* and decoration duly subordinated to full-bodied expression, to the rendering of essential reality. The internal patterns of brushwork in the Gauguin have no higher esthetic status than that of harmonious elements in a total decorative design of broad, exotic color-areas and bizarre static arabesques, with the screenlike effect of a few large planes compactly arranged in space. The pattern of brushstrokes in the Cézanne is equally decorative, but it serves also the vastly more important ends of drawing the volumes and planes, modeling them and setting them in space: while it imparts immediate sensuous appeal to the powerful dynamic movement, it actually builds up and organizes the masses themselves. Color in Gauguin remains likewise primarily a surface-decoration; in Cézanne, it not only forms the substance of solid masses and colorful space, but by its quality and relationships imparts to the technique functions and meanings nonexistent in Gauguin. The difference is that between the superficial and the vitally significant in any sphere of human experience.

Gauguin is not, however, an eclectic. His use of devices which Cézanne made significant by the ideas and feelings they were instrumental in expressing, was not designed to imitate Cézanne's work or make a parody of it. Gauguin used the devices constructively to create forms which speak eloquently in their own rights as decorations of a high order.

Van Gogh can hardly be regarded as having been directly influenced by Cézanne, even though the forms of the two men have certain technical features in common. Working during the same period, both men naturally made use of features current in the work of their contemporaries and immediate predecessors, especially of the technical innovations that resulted from Manet's and Monet's experiments with color, light and brushwork. Cézanne, as has been pointed out in detail in the preceding chapters, adapted these innovations to ends so radically new and different that the form which he developed had little in common with the raw material upon which he worked. Van Gogh, with the same material, also arrived at a very personal expression, but with no such creative capacity either in his use of the means or in the expressive content of the form as did Cézanne. A brief study of the difference between the two men in these respects will serve to illustrate further the fact that technique is of fundamental significance only when it is instrumental to the personal expression of definite ideas and profound feelings.

Van Gogh's "Man Smoking" (320) reveals the use of the same Daumier-Manet-Monet sources which Cézanne drew upon,[10] both men departing from these sources in developing an accentuated angular pattern in the settings. The pattern in van Gogh,

[10] Cf., e.g., Cézanne's "Provence Peasant" (151).

however, remains at the level of that in a screen or wall paper; in other words, it is not the pattern and spacing that set off the foreground-figure and link it compositionally with the background by kindred linear, color-, light-, and space-relationships, but the contrast between the bizarre bright colors of foreground and background. The outstanding characteristic of the organization as a whole is a pattern of bright, exotic, bizarrely shaped color-areas which is primarily a decorative illustration. Cézanne's treatment of similar elements converts them into integral parts of a comprehensive dynamic space-volume composition and radically recasts them to suit his purpose; van Gogh's shows little departure from the sources, and makes them function principally as accessories in a type of drawing and modeling close to Hals's, and in a decorative ensemble strongly reminiscent of Japanese prints. In short, the derivations are too obviously close to their originals, too feebly integrated, and hence too easily isolable, to be regarded as organic factors in a fundamentally new form.

Another point which van Gogh and Cézanne have in common is a frequent organization of brushwork such that the striated markings of the brush vary in different parts of the color-organization, with the patterns of brushstrokes contributing both to the feeling of movement and to the compositional unity of the picture. The difference between the results is that in Cézanne the movement and unifying function of the pattern involve the solid substance of planes and masses, which are actually constructed by the patterned strokes of solid color. In van Gogh, the effect is principally a matter of activity of surface.[11]

Van Gogh's line is akin to Cézanne's in so far as it is an actual broad line that emphasizes the shape of areas and contributes to the drawing, modeling and spacing of masses.[12] Again, however, there is a fundamental difference of function in the two cases: Cézanne's line is primarily constructive in the drawing, modeling and space-composition as a whole, while van Gogh's mainly determines the contour, shape and direction of color-areas. Van Gogh's line is often scarcely to be differentiated from his long, ribbonlike brushstrokes, so that it is more definitely a part of the ubiquitous pattern than an integral part of the form; like the technique, it thus suffers from overemphasis upon surface-effect at the expense

[11] Compare, e.g., Cézanne's "Well" (174) with van Gogh's "Factories" (317).

[12] E.g., van Gogh's "Flowerpiece and Fruit" (318).

of structural achievement. Often the linear contour of objects and areas is made of individual brushstrokes, so that the linear pattern and the pattern of technique actually coalesce. A similar condition occurs occasionally in Cézanne but its constructive purpose can always be discerned, while in van Gogh it is chiefly a more or less haphazard incident in a decorative pattern.

Another distinctive linear effect in van Gogh has certain affinities with one to be seen in Cézanne: linear contour achieved by aligned extremities of parallel sequential brushstrokes. Cézanne uses the device on a small scale in the linear edges of his quill-like patches and thereby secures such effects, incidental to larger compositional purposes, as definiteness of shape, solidity and spatial location of planes. The effects which van Gogh obtains by the use of the same device all tend toward a mixture of illustration and decoration, with expression chiefly taking the form of a revelation of van Gogh's own temperament, rather than of the essential nature of an object or situation. His work is very individual, and its characteristics, which as already indicated arise from an over-accentuation of certain of its elements at the expense of more important ones, result in a disbalanced form, symptomatic of the psychological disturbances that dogged his entire mature life. His decorative patterns of bright exotic color, his lively bizarre movement, and the strange picturesqueness of his design, all contribute to the sense of emotional excitement experienced by the observer in contemplating his work. His form, while legitimate as the expression of an unbalanced personality, is not of the highest esthetic order. Compared with Cézanne, he was a stylist whose assimilation and constructive use of the significant perceptions and practices of other artists was relatively superficial.

Picasso, who shares with Matisse the distinction of having been the principal source of the fundamental ideas and technique of most of the significant contemporary painting, owes more to Cézanne than to any other preceding artist. Never at any stage of his career did he imitate Cézanne's form, or use the derivations otherwise than as material to be reworked into his own designs. His originality in this respect can be understood only by a detailed study of his work of all periods, with specific attention to the particular elements or devices which he borrowed from Cézanne and recast into new plastic organizations.

Picasso's paintings of what is known as his "blue period," extending from about 1902 to 1907, show the most numerous and varied derivations from Cézanne as well as the widest range of authentically creative forms. The best of his work of this period represents an extraordinarily diverse, imaginative and ingenious fusion of various basic devices of Cézanne's with significant features of Piero della Francesca, El Greco, Manet, Toulouse-Lautrec, and many other painters. From Cézanne he adopted and adapted the rigid angular pattern, blocklike masses, color-patches forming planes, general pattern of planes to organize background and foreground in a single form, parallel individual brushstrokes, broad dark linear contours, dominantly blue color-scheme, and the division of background-setting into geometrical shapes. These borrowed features are worked into new contexts in many different ways. Planes, for example, are less numerous in Picasso and the space they occupy is shallower, so that the compositions compared with Cézanne's are flat. Moreover, while Picasso's angular pattern of planes plays a part in the drawing and modeling, its part tends to be more definitely decorative and illustrative than expressive: its participation in the construction of masses is secondary.[13] The same distinction between Picasso's primarily illustrative "blue" pictures and Cézanne's work appears in Picasso's employment of a type of distortions developed by Cézanne. Facial features, for example, are distorted in Cézanne into a bizarre pattern which contributes to the blocklike solidity and feeling of abstract power of the head, with scarcely an indication of the character of the sitter, while Picasso's blocklike solidity, achieved through modifications of Cézanne's brushstrokes, drawing and modeling, brings out the essentially illustrative aspects of the subject.

Other differences between Cézanne's and Picasso's types of compositional organization, arising from Picasso's modification of selected features in Cézanne's drawing, modeling, technique, and color, are illustrated by Picasso's "Baby in Blue" (348) and "Girl with Cigarette" (350). The latter is drawn and modeled by hatchings of color organized in planes which, instead of building up solid three-dimensional masses as in Cézanne, produce flattened volumes, pattern the surface and give a sense of movement and direction. A ghastly eerie tone of color, reminiscent of El Greco, and broad Manet-like brushstrokes fuse with the Cézannesque

[13] Compare, e.g., the folds of the table cloth in Cézanne's "Oranges and Bottle" (148) with the folds of the white garments in Picasso's "Composition" (349).

hatchings, contour-lines and planes to form a type of drawing, modeling and color-scheme individual to Picasso. In "Baby in Blue" (348) derivations from Cézanne and from other painters are merged into still another new and distinctive form. The block-like head, while strong and solid, conveys little sense of abstract power, it is conceived in harmony with the illustrative character of the entire design. The whole dress is executed in the long parallel brushstrokes of Cézanne's mid-seventies period, which, as in Cézanne, play the part of planes, but their primary function is that of surface-decoration, somewhat in the manner of van Gogh. Similar planelike brushstrokes in the white collar, working in conjunction with the quality of color and thickness of impasto, contribute to the producing of a Picasso version of the color-effects of both El Greco and Cézanne: here the quality of power is also present. Planes in the background are arranged in Cézanne-like patches, but they serve principally, not as instruments of dynamic space-composition, but as components in a decorative color-pattern.[14]

Cubism, like many other similar vagaries, would never have existed but for Cézanne; and the theories of art, fabricated to justify it and comparable schools and cults, have usually taken as their point of departure principles for which Cézanne's authority is claimed. The intersection of the angular planes of varied geometrical shapes, and the broad contour lines, which are outstanding features in the framework of Cézanne's mature paintings, form striking patterns that have a unique esthetic appeal over and above their function as elements in a fully expressive form. It was this effect of pattern which intrigued young painters of the first decade of the present century and was one of two source-materials utilized by them in the experimentation which resulted in many types of abstract painting, including cubism. The other source was African Negro sculpture, which at this period began to be recognized as a distinctive, highly expressive art-form. These strains of influence merged readily because of their close affinity in a number of basic features—the presence of accentuated contours and planes, bizarre shapes of patterns, projecting masses, abrupt recession of space. Picasso, one of the chief pioneers in this new field, produced between 1907 and 1909 a series of pictures in which the two sets of traits appear, sometimes in about equal proportions, sometimes with one set or the other predominating.

[14] See also following discussion on "Cubism."

His still-life "Grouped Objects" (351), for example, shows a Cézannesque composition of color-planes and modeling by patches, successfully united with the angular blocklike projections and sharp recessions characteristic of African Negro sculpture. The objects, while bearing sufficient representative detail to be identifiable, are very much simplified and distorted, with accentuation of the compositional framework of lines, planes, masses, and spatial intervals. This picture represents abstract painting in its incipiency, clearly displaying the marks of its origin in Cézanne and African Negro sculpture. It anticipates the type of abstract painting which practically eliminates representative characterization of objects, while organizing their framework of lines, planes and spatial relations in a design which owes its esthetic significance to the organization of nonrepresentative constituents.

A comparative study of Cézanne's mature work, of African sculpture, and of the fully arrived cubism of Picasso and Braque, confirms the essential identity between many of the plastic constituents and animating motives of the source-materials, and the technique and ideas which governed the abstract painters in their selection and treatment of the borrowed features. The blocklike sculptural forms of accentuated massiveness and ponderosity, common to the African Negro sculpture and Cézanne, are dismembered by the cubists, and the component planes and contours are so simplified, distorted and reconstructed that they produce a dynamic rhythm of static units, in a composition predominantly angular and rigid even when curvilinear units are present.

There can be no graver error, however, than to assume that the cubists, in building on what are indubitably basic elements in Cézanne's form, either attain to its esthetic essence or produce pictures of great intrinsic importance. In dissecting out the pattern that underlies Cézanne's compositional framework, they reduce his design to a skeleton that never takes on the flesh and blood of a living body. His form in its integrity represents the response of an actual personality to an actual world: his planes and patches of brushwork are what they are because of their relation to all the other elements in the design and to the objective reality presented in it. It is the whole ensemble of qualities, pervading his form, that give it life and reality: color that lends weight and solidity to volumes, line that has depth and force, planes that have substance, space in which masses move and encounter one another with thrust and counterthrust, brushwork which is felt as the actual constructive means of all these effects. In cubistic painting,

the isolation of pattern and loss of objective reference result in
a general collapse of expression: in place of the dynamic rhythm,
the equilibrium of moving forces, the overwhelming reality of a
still-life, a landscape or a group of figures, we have only an abstract
design of lines, shapes and color-areas, suspended in a vacuum
and totally incapable of conveying any real sense of the concrete
world in which we live.

The qualities of objects and situations, as Cézanne depicts them,
produce so violent an impact upon our senses that they are felt
with an intensity unknown in our ordinary perception of nature,
and we may seem to be experiencing dynamic movement, sculpturesque solidity, the infinity of space, power, in a word, independently of the things in which they are embodied. In reality, of
course, the power is in no literal sense abstract: it is always the
power residing in some actual object, some figure or mountain,
and the magnitude of its conception and execution cannot as a
matter of fact detach it from the concrete world which ultimately
makes all experience possible and gives it whatever meaning it
can have. The effect in such cases seems greater than the cause,
taken by itself, could warrant; but the cause is always there, and
Cézanne secures his effects by heightening its force, not by creating them out of a void.

So-called abstract painting, in contrast, has no such foundation in human experience. The elements selected by the cubists
from Cézanne's form are so excessively attenuated, their points of
contact with actual perception are so slight, that they lack recognizable identity and bear no relation to those universal interests
which, however generalized and held in solution, underlie all our
feelings and activities. In this respect the cubists proceeded to the
opposite extreme from Derain and Bernard; instead of taking
over too much of Cézanne's form, they take too little; but they sin
equally against the integrity of experience. In divorcing Cézanne's
patches of color, planes, lines, and distortions both from their
function of giving richer meaning to concrete situations and from
their source in Cézanne's personality, they deprive the pattern
itself of all value as a means of insight, and destroy its human
appeal, while from the strictly plastic point of view they leave it
without any deeply unifying principle of integration. The dismembered planes, which in Cézanne function as means for building up masses and organizing space, become in the cubists separate
units out of which the composition is constructed, but they have
little or no intrinsic relation to color, and their movement consists

mainly of a collision of lines and shapes with one another. It has almost nothing in common with the forceful dynamic rhythm of solid color-volumes in deep space which is the corner stone of Cézanne's form, the equilibrium of opposing energies which endows his compositions with both their monumental character and their sense of profound repose.

The difference, to sum up, is that Cézanne's form embodies a harmonious interaction of all the basic plastic elements, unified by the pervasive activity of color, while in cubistic paintings part of the form is overaccentuated and elaborated in an organization in which color has little or no unifying function. Pattern, in Cézanne an instrument strictly subordinated to the expression of values inherent in the real world, becomes in cubism the entire esthetic content, and this degradation of form leaves cubistic painting with no claim to any status higher than that of decoration.

In spite of its limited intrinsic significance, abstract painting is important historically in that it generated ideas and technical devices which many of the most influential contemporary painters have utilized in novel and authentically expressive pictures. Matisse, Picasso, Pascin, Modigliani, de la Fresnaye, and many others have reinstated in quasi cubistic patterned compositions, vastly more of the essential plastic values of painting, and of the human values residing in the world of nature and man, than were ever revealed by abstract painting itself.

Matisse has made perhaps more varied and consistent use of Cézanne's contributions than any other contemporary painter, adapting them with eminent success to the predominantly decorative purposes of his own designs. The importance of this transformation lies in the fact that he has carried the tradition of Cézanne into quite another direction than that of the original, and has developed a form from which much of what is new and significant in contemporary painting draws its inspiration.

Matisse's early compositional arrangements of subject-matter are very frequently based upon Cézanne's, but the less structural color and more ornamental line, light and space in Matisse result in ensembles primarily decorative, in comparison with Cézanne's monumental and deeply expressive form.[15]

Of like origin is Matisse's common method, in his work of the

[15] E.g., Matisse's "Blue Still-Life" (323); "Collioure" (326); "Composition with Melon" (327); "Country House" (328); "Oranges" (337); "Peaches" (339); "Sideboard" (344).

early 1900's, of modeling by hatchings and planes of color, but his simplification of the planes and diminution of their number, combined with less structural color, make his objects less round, less solid and less weighty.[16] Occasionally, the hatchings and planes, rendered with relatively thin pigment, are modified by elements of drawing taken from Manet and Renoir.[17] In another adaptation of Cézanne's modeling, the planes are relatively isolated areas of light and shadow, little more than units in a decorative pattern.[18]

The technical variations introduced by Matisse into Cézanne's method of modeling alter the appearance of both the individual objects and the total design. The objects lack the weight, mass and solidity which Cézanne attained by piling the hatchings of color on top of one another: both the number of hatchings and their perceptibility are diminished in Matisse, the colors are brighter, and the contrast in tone between individual hatchings is emphasized. The result is that objects become primarily series of colored areas, elements in a decorative pattern, each object having a degree of solidity commensurate in plastic value with the color-units, linear patterns, patches of colored light and brushstrokes, all of which are treated in harmony with an all-embracing decorative form.[19]

The widely different degrees of three-dimensional quality and the variations in execution by planes and hatchings, in individual pictures, are determined by Matisse's particular design. For example, a jug in a still-life may be as solid and three-dimensional as one in a Cézanne, and in consequence form a dramatic contrast with adjacent flat planes of color.[20] Modeling by planes may be modified by long broad brushstrokes which simulate the effect of hatchings;[21] the planes may be so arranged as to form part of a complex linear design;[22] or they may be used in conjunction with mosaiclike patches of color.[23] In general, Matisse's conversion of

[16] E.g., "Blue Still-Life" (323); "Composition with Melon" (327).
[17] E.g., Matisse's "Moroccan Tray" (335).
[18] E.g., "Girl on Balcony" (331).
[19] Compare, e.g., Matisse's planes, which model the figure and bushes, and organize the composition, in "Seated Nude" (343) with Cézanne's "Five Nudes" (74). In Matisse the planes function primarily as contrasting strips of color, and the general Cézanne feeling has become part of an exotic symphony of color-contrasts.
[20] E.g., "Sideboard" (344).
[21] E.g., "Blue Still-Life" (323); "Peaches" (339).
[22] E.g., "Red Madras Headdress" (341).
[23] E.g., "Woman with Hat" (347).

Cézanne's planes to elements primarily decorative in function necessitates a reduction in the part played by them in modeling, and an increase of their activity as elements in linear patterns and color-contrasts.[24] The line itself when used in modeling is often more ragged than Cézanne's, and its decorative emphasis is less reminiscent of him than of the Byzantines and the Egypto-Romans.[25]

Cézanne's compartmental pattern, made up of patches of color and light, is utilized by Matisse, but with so many innovations that the differences between the two outweigh the similarities.[26] Matisse's patches are less numerous, his broad areas more numerous; nevertheless, his pictures are more definitely a patchwork because of his more vivid color-contrasts and his more pronouncedly linear drawing. The patches are primarily shaped color-areas; in Cézanne, of course, they function chiefly as planes of structural color that build up solid volumes. To say this is to say again that the decorative function is paramount in Matisse and subsidiary in Cézanne.

Levitation of objects, frequently seen in Cézanne's still-lifes,[27] is employed also by Matisse but for different purposes. The accentuated interval between a chair and a figure apparently seated on it, but actually unsupported, may form a dramatic contrast with a large area of subtly rendered unoccupied space;[28] or a bunch of flowers may be levitated to fit into a spatial version of Matisse's oft-repeated merging of objects and background in a decorative ensemble.[29] Another type of spatial distortion frequent in Cézanne and later used by Matisse is the detachment of floral decorations from the background of a screen, drapery or wall paper, by which they are made to function as volumes suspended in space.[30]

Cézanne's familiar tree trunks drawn by two or three parallel

[24] E.g., "Bathers at the Seashore" (322); "Blue Still-Life" (323); "Boy with Butterfly Net" (325); "Collioure" (326); "Composition with Melon" (327); "Girl Reading" (332); "Houses at Fenouillet" (334).
[25] E.g., Matisse's "Red Madras Headdress" (341); "Woman with Hat" (347).
[26] Compare, e.g., Matisse's "Collioure" (326) or "Country House" (328) with Cézanne's "Valley of the Arc" (109).
[27] E.g., "Jug and Fruit" (123).
[28] E.g., Matisse's "Woman on High Stool" (346).
[29] E.g., "Odalisque with Magnolias" (336).
[30] E.g., Matisse's "Moroccan Tray" (335)—Cf. Cézanne's "Girl at Piano" (19); "Oranges and Bottle" (148). Tintoretto's "Venetian Senator" (239) illustrates an old master's use of the device.

broad strips of color are the foundation of Matisse's more decorative tree trunks, which are executed in strips of brighter and
more daring color, more vividly contrasted and relatively deficient
in solid structural quality.[31] Here, as usual in Matisse's work, the
strips of color are rhythmic duplications of numerous other line-
and-color elements.

The only feature in Matisse's color-design that can be ascribed
to Cézanne is an occasional approach to the latter's surface-
quality, attained by subtle merging of light with color to produce
nuances of various intermingled tones. When this resemblance is
present, Matisse's color is sometimes structural to a considerable
degree and quite near in tone to his predecessor's;[32] at other
times the general appearance of the surface is like Cézanne's but
the color remains relatively superficial;[33] in still other cases the
Cézannesque surface is tempered with an effect derived from
Daumier, but the result lacks the depth and solidity found in both
its sources.[34] Even in those of Matisse's early paintings which
strongly suggest the immature work of Cézanne, Matisse's primarily decorative interest results in an appreciable plastic difference between the two forms.[35]

Matisse's relation to Cézanne may be illustrated by a few specific examples. "Collioure" (326) shows the following derivations
from Cézanne, appropriately modified: the broad linear contour
of areas or objects; the linear effect of the general framework;
the rigidity of the linear pattern even in arabesques; the broad
brushstrokes, single or in groups, which function as patches and
planes; the general compositional distribution of the subject-matter; and the clean-cut punctuation of space. The final result is
different from Cézanne's because Matisse's color is not structural
in the sense that Cézanne's is; the spatial rhythms lack power and
positiveness; the shapes of the planes and their color are more
pronounced than their substance. In short, all the derived features
are coördinated in a color-organization that owes its appeal to the

[31] E.g., Matisse's "Collioure" (326); "Fontainebleau: Entrance to the
Forest" (330)—Cf. Cézanne's "Plaza, Auvers-sur-Oise" (87).
[32] E.g., Matisse's "Blue Still-Life" (323); "Peaches" (339).
[33] E.g., "Boy with Butterfly Net" (325); "Rocks of the Valley of the
Loup" (342).
[34] E.g., Matisse's "Goldfish" (333); "Oranges" (337); "Painter in his
Studio" (338).
[35] E.g., Matisse's "Academy Figure" (321).

sensuous quality of varied colors arranged in a bizarre and striking pattern.

"Flowers in Pitcher" (329) shows another sort of adaptation from Cézanne. Lines of perspective are related to planes in space; patches in the background convert it into a space-composition continuing that of the principal units in the foreground; planes are piled up to render the roundness and solidity of the pitcher; broad lines of contour draw solid objects and determine their position in space; the general space-organization of the masses and planes likewise follows Cézanne's. It is, however, the particular colors of the areas and of the lines, and their pattern of contrasts, which give to the picture its distinctive character as a radiating spiderlike composition of contrasting color-units. Everything taken from Cézanne, in other words, has been assimilated and made an integral part of a characteristic Matisse form.

As Matisse developed, the methods and devices borrowed from Cézanne are simplified, generalized and merged with increasing number of features from other traditions; for example, with Chinese, Persian and Manet characteristics in "Two Figures Reclining in Landscape" (345); with aspects of African and Hindu sculpture in "Reclining Nude" (340); with Renoir's influence in "Moroccan Tray" (335); with Chinese and Japanese traits in "Blue Villa" (324).

In general, Cézanne's simplifications are carried further by Matisse, pattern functions in two rather than in three dimensions, and in consequence it is shapes rather than masses that play the most important plastic part in the design.

Pascin drew freely upon Cézanne's contributions, although his work as a whole shows a greater resemblance to that of Tintoretto, El Greco, Rubens, and Renoir. The Cézanne traits, most perceptible in Pascin's drawing and modeling, appear in simplification productive of facets and wedges that construct volumes; changes of color and tone that give rise to changes in the direction and the location of the color-facets; brushstrokes which are active both individually and as groups or patches; compositional pattern of color-patches enriched by tonal modulations within the patches; broad dark contour-lines of color used to reënforce the modeling and spatial location of volumes; systematic employment of planes to construct three-dimensional masses, render receding space, and form a pronounced surface-pattern of patches in which there is an uninterrupted sequence of color-modulations. From Cézanne is derived also Pascin's distortion of representative detail—for example, in facial features, perspective of objects, planes and surfaces generally—to enhance design; that is, to establish a plastic compositional continuity of rhythmic color-sequences in planes and patches, that model and set volumes in space from foreground to background. As a result, Pascin's figures, like Cézanne's, show little tendency to psychological characterization: heads, for example, are conceived primarily as units in a plastic design, and their facial features are distorted to accord with this general purpose.

Pascin's employment of these devices is always stamped with his own individuality: not only are the derived lines, planes, patches, and brushwork changed in detail, but they function differently in the construction of another type of design. Pascin's major interest, unlike Cézanne's, was in illustration, and his use of color, line, light, and space is controlled by the problem of giving plastic embodiment to the local character of scenes and the individuality, the particular attitudes and movements, of figures. In the solution of the problem Cézanne's means are revised and reconstructed with great ingenuity and imagination as well as extraordinary technical finesse.

Pascin's brushstrokes, less positive in shape than Cézanne's, display a fluid, swirling character. His color is also more fluid; it is lighter in tone and in weight, and is essentially delicate and often pearly. His impasto is thinner, frequently transparent, and it has the liquid, flowing quality of water color. More fluid also, and lighter-toned, is his light, with the light-and-dark element more emphasized than in Cézanne; the result is that the light-pattern is more active in giving character to the design. The light-units often have a floating quality, as in the Chinese and in Renoir. Pascin's line of contour, compared with Cézanne's, is more curvilinear, loose and undulating, often made up of a series of broken curves or scallops, and it is thus admirably adapted to conveying the feeling of active, rhythmic, somewhat swirling movement, both in figures and in the composition as a whole. The swirl of the line is paralleled or otherwise taken up by the numerous areas, bands, patches of color, light and shade, so that the swirl becomes a basic expressive and decorative motif.

The planes and patches of color in Pascin's work are less definitely marked off from each other than in Cézanne's and are less sharply contrasted in direction. Their edges are more diffuse, more vaguely defined, so that they float off into adjacent areas and planes. This treatment takes away the rigidity of pattern characteristic of Cézanne and makes Pascin's less pronounced pattern expressive of graceful, delicate lightness and fluidity. A similar thoroughgoing transformation appears in Pascin's modeling. He combines patches like Cézanne's with the parallel bands of Rubens, and adds a device of his own, consisting of related light and shadow, with the shadow on the crest of the volume and flanked on each side by a band or area of light. The planes which build up the masses are organized differently from those in Cézanne's modeling. The latter are compact, and they coalesce to produce an internal solidity of substance; with Pascin, in contrast, the emphasis is shifted from internal solidity to actual movement of objects. This method creates an appealing rhythmic movement of surface color-patches, radically different from Cézanne's weighty, static, monumental effects.

These variations in the use of patches and planes in drawing and modeling result inevitably in a type of composition that departs widely from Cézanne's, notwithstanding the presence of basically similar elements in each. Space is less abruptly punctuated and is filled with an atmosphere of color that tempers the drama of the mass-composition. Textures are not solid and weighty as in Cézanne, and are qualitatively more differentiated from each other. The volumes have a pulsating movement through space, but it is a gentle, fluid movement, the antithesis of Cézanne's throb of full-bodied ponderous masses.

The vogue of cubism from about 1910 to 1920 had its effect on Pascin, but the cubistic features with which he experimented did not alter in essence the use which he made of Cézanne's contributions. The chief result was an accentuated compositional pattern of color-patches with more pronounced linear features and sharp angles, which he adopted, with skilful modifications, as a framework for his characteristic illustrative and decorative form.

Pascin's "Seated Figure" (362) illustrates his use of derivations from Cézanne, combined with other traditional features, before the advent of cubism. The unit of still-life at the upper left reveals the influence of Cézanne's technique, drawing, color-form and general feeling, but the picture as a whole is so tempered with delicacy, lightness and a tendency to swirling movement that it is as reminiscent of Renoir as it is of Cézanne. In his later "Southern Scene" (363), Pascin shows an effective adaptation of cubistic practices: the framework is an accentuated Cézann- esque all-over pattern of angles, rectangles, triangles and other geometrical shapes, with infinitely more varied and plastically active color than that in actual cubistic painting. The components of the all-embracing pattern of shapes function as a series of color-planes which draw and model figures, house and trees, locate the masses in clean-cut space, produce a sense of very active movement, and contribute enormously to the expressive and decorative values of the composition.

Soutine's paintings, although they seem so individual, even so bizarre, owe much of their very originality and bizarreness to his use of basic features in Cézanne's form. He emphasizes, by means of a pattern of broad color-areas, the location, direction and shape of the main plane occupied by each of the units together with their intersection at contrasting angles. This emphasis involves, as in Cézanne, simplification of representative detail, positiveness of shapes, flattening of rounded surfaces by means of facets or planes, pronounced linear contour of color, accentuation of linear perspective, and surface-pattern of technique.

A more direct and specific derivation from Cézanne appears in Soutine's grouping of parallel or crisscross brushstrokes into se- ries of angular patches, which, by their relationships of color, light-and-dark, and shape, establish sequences of contrasting small units throughout the surface of the canvas. This produces an all-over compositional color-pattern of patches or planes placed in definitely contrasting directions. Within each of these areas, patches or planes, the internal patterning of the brushwork cre- ates a subsidiary set of dynamic color-units in planes, which do not, in Soutine's best work any more than in Cézanne's, disrupt the oneness of the larger compositional area to which they belong. Soutine's emphasis and bizarre use of these planes result at times in the apparent dislocation of parts of masses which is character- istic of African sculpture, and also in the actual separation of component parts prevalent in cubistic paintings, but in basic effect Soutine's planes remain close to their source in Cézanne.

Soutine's technique owes several other of its characteristics or functions to Cézanne's. His brushwork, like Cézanne's, is posi- tive, direct and forceful, and therefore in itself expressive; and its pattern contributes to compositional unity as well as to the drama of contrasts and to the total plastic movement. The thickness of Soutine's impasto, like that in some of Cézanne's early work, imparts a feeling of ruggedness and solidity to textures and color-surfaces. The general color-schemes or quality of color in the two men have little in common. Soutine's color, *per se,* is more luscious and unctuous; it is more varied and is used in more obviously contrasting areas. It is the sensuous quality of Soutine's color rather than, as in Cézanne, its substance and solidity which makes it stand out, a quality intensified by the texture of the rugged, juicy pigment. Soutine's surfaces are especially rich in color-chords produced not only as in Cézanne, by juxtaposed and overlapping brushstrokes, but by differently colored, irregularly broken layers of thick pigment—a technique individual to Soutine. The sensuous appeal of sparkling glow and rich surface of color in Soutine partly compensates for the comparative absence in his work of Cézanne's substantial color-solidity and many-sided color-composition.

At its best, Soutine's color gives an adequate degree of substance to volumes, and, together with an accentuated pattern of brushwork similar to that in Cézanne's work of the middle seventies, yields a quasi Cézannesque effect of structural solidity. This is accomplished mainly by patches of contrasting color placed back of each other in different spatial positions which draw and model volumes, and define their location in space by virtue of relations in color and tone. The method is basically Cézanne's, but Soutine's manner of execution is different, as are the effects obtained. His areas are larger and more varied in color, the brushstrokes are more obvious and more diversified, and the pigment, applied in another manner, yields different surface-qualities. The masses lack the convincing solidity of Cézanne's and the spaces are not so well defined or interrelated to produce a dynamic movement of volumes. Compared with Cézanne's, Soutine's houses, for example, are usually like shells, his trees two-dimensional, and the rhythm of planes is confined to shallow space.

Another fundamental difference between the forms of Soutine and Cézanne lies in the character and plastic purpose of the compositional pattern of planes and lines. Definite angles and straight lines have become, in Soutine, sweeps to about the same degree that curvilinear objects are rigid in Cézanne. The individual brushstrokes impart by their quivering, swerving, sweeping, swaying movement, a similar activity to areas, lines and contorted curves, even when the pattern retains some of the rigid angularity of Cézanne's. It is this sort of all-pervasive movement, in conjunction with sharp contrasts of weighty bright color, that gives to Soutine's best work its expression of powerful drama, or stormy turmoil, the antithesis of Cézanne's power, which results from strong forces brought into equilibrium and expressive of repose. Soutine's is tense, poignant drama, felt as the spontaneous outburst of deep feeling, a full-bodied exclamation uttered on the spur of the moment. Cézanne's drama and power are pervaded by peace and substantiality; they are felt to be the result of deep reflection and sustained labor, unruffled by violent emotion or the impulse to precipitate action.

Soutine's adaptations from Cézanne are never imitative, academic or mechanical. His form has never attained the artistic status of Cézanne's, and the very spontaneity and exuberance which explain much of its value and charm, are responsible also for its often fragmentary, disorganized character. It is, nevertheless, a proof of innate genius that by a legitimate reinterpretation of Cézanne's technical devices and the expressive power of his form, Soutine succeeded in embodying in his paintings a corresponding dramatic power which is nevertheless diametrically opposed to Cézanne's in its specific character. The power and drama in Soutine, however, are derived as much from other great traditional sources—Tintoretto, El Greco, Rembrandt, Goya, Daumier, Egyptian and African sculpture—as they are from Cézanne.

Maurice Prendergast used many elements of Cézanne's form, but modified and adapted them in a manner so individual to himself and merged them so subtly with other traditional features, that they become recognizable only upon analysis. His drawing and modeling by small superposed dabs of color are in principle similar to Cézanne's, but show wider variation in color, shape, size, and decorative value of the individual strokes; these are much less definitely shaped, more like irregular dabs or blobs of color than Cézanne's. They are less compactly placed and fused together, so that what is emphasized is more their individual character than the continuity of the color-area as a whole. This technique, in conjunction with a vibrating surface-quality of color and light derived from the impressionists, produces effects reminiscent of Seurat and Monet, together with a Cézannesque intrinsic structural solidity of color, all of which are greatly enhanced by a highly individual gamut of very varied, bright, delicate, cheerful, sparkling colors.

The dabs of color yield a greater diversity of patterns than do Cézanne's brushstrokes, and are more flexible, adapted to a wider range of different designs, so that the technique has on the whole more freedom, liveliness and decorative value than Cézanne's. The successive strokes of color that make up the pattern of overlapping patches coalesce into a series of receding planes, which build up volumes and define spatial intervals as they do in Cézanne. The constituent planes, however, are actually fewer in Prendergast's masses and less accentuated, with the result that figures are usually flattened and trees, especially when placed in compact space, appear as parts of a screenlike pattern, with little three-dimensional extension.

The compartments in Prendergast's color-patterns have neither the angularity of Cézanne's nor the multitude of lines running in many directions, although Prendergast also uses freely a broad contour-line of color. His line in general is less rigid, more varied in color, shape and size. Because of its more positive color-content and its tendency to a curvilinear arabesque, it functions more definitely as part of the all-over scintillating pattern of color and light than as an agent in spacing and the construction of solid masses. Prendergast, in other words, shifts the emphasis of the line from the primarily expressive to the decorative, in accordance with the general character of his design. The same is true of his use of planes: the series of receding planes which make up his compositions, and are derived from Cézanne, are more simplified, more contrasted in color, technique and pattern, and are organized as a more definitely decorative compositional framework of distinct color-planes or patches. In both men, the planes are compositionally continuous from foreground to background, but in Prendergast the fewer patches or planes seem to be more numerous and form more emphatic individual units of color-pattern.

This more assertive contrast of color-patches in Prendergast is an important factor in the general liveliness and active movement of his form, while the movement of his main compositional planes is further increased by the multiplicity of small strokes that make up the planes, and especially by the bright, cheerful, fresh, greatly varied and well-illuminated color, which imparts a rich sparkling glow to the rhythmic movement of the entire composition. The effect as a whole partakes both of the static rhythmic movement of Cézanne's organization and of the fluid classic grace of the work of Giorgione, Raphael and Poussin. The movement, adapted to basically illustrative and decorative ends, is truly plastic because it is born legitimately of the interaction of all the factors that enter into the organization. The drawing is very personal, and is effected by epigrammatic use of line, light and color, all finely co-ordinated, with very expressive distortions—elongated bodies and small heads—reminiscent of the Byzantines.

Another feature of Cézanne's form which Prendergast adapts to a different purpose is a compositional pattern of horizontal bands. In Cézanne these bands are always designed to give the effect of recession in deep space, while in Prendergast they make up a color-patterned framework against which is played a theme of contrasting color-patches, generally arranged vertically. This derivation, like the others mentioned above, takes on new meanings by its union with plastic elements from other traditions, to which are added a wealth of transferred values nonexistent in Cézanne. Prendergast's space-compositions render a friezelike or panoramic sequence of rhythms, sometimes involving the gentle movement of solid color-volumes in deep space, at other times a compact series of glowing color-units that rival the finest of old mosaics in their texture and patterned surface.

Prendergast's form has none of Cézanne's austerity or monumental strength and power. His reaction to the world involves an entirely different set of values: it is fundamentally a naïve enjoyment of out-of-door scenes, with people doing spontaneously the common things of everyday life. His form expresses quiet activity and drama, the joy of life lived naturally and unsophisticatedly. It renders the spirit of place and the essentials of figures and objects in delicate, decorative, animated color-rhythms, and imparts to them the same sort of charm that pervades the best of primitives.

Modigliani used elements from Cézanne successfully in the construction of a personal form based principally upon characteristics found in Florentine painting and African sculpture. His debt to Cézanne is most obvious in the surface-quality and texture of his paint, the structural color of his masses, and the pattern of planes in those of his pictures done under the influence of cubism. In his "Cypress Trees and House" (360), the variation of light in the color, working in conjunction with vaguely defined brushwork, yields surface-effects, texture and massiveness of volumes close to those of Cézanne. The ill-defined brushwork in the wall in this picture and the subtle contrasts of light and dark form a composition of internal planes, the prototype of which is the succession of planes of shadow in the background-wall of Cézanne's "Card Players and Girl" (141): the planes in "Cypress Trees and House," however, are only suggested and the solidity of the volume is less pronounced than in Cézanne.

The solidity of surface and texture in Modigliani's rendering of flesh recalls Cézanne's,[36] but the thin continuous graceful line of contour and the compartmental color, derived from the Florentines, together with distortions patently modeled on African sculpture, also combine to produce Modigliani's characteristic form.

Cézanne's influence appears in a different context in Modigliani's experiments with cubistic devices and motifs. His "Beatrice" (359), for example, shows an all-over pattern of interpenetrating angular shapes engrafted upon his more typical form. This picture reveals also, particularly in the upper right corner, his Cézannesque treatment of surfaces by vaguely defined planes of different colors, which through their contrast of light and dark yield an effect similar to that derived by Cézanne from Daumier. In this, a solid area of relatively uniform color—a wall—is transformed into a succession of vaguely defined, semivoluminous units in deep space.

Demuth, like Picasso and Pascin, combines decoration and illustration in a highly effective design based on elements in Cézanne's form. His early work, nearly always in water color, depicts interior scenes in which circus performers, cabarets, the stage, and flowerpieces appear. It is a series of compositions of delicate, well-defined planes of contrasting color which draw and model the units and set them in space. These color-planes, in contrast to Cézanne's, are so selected and related to each other that the essentials of subject-matter, and of active and poised movement, are brought out with a skill and force comparable to Degas's or Toulouse-Lautrec's at their best.

Demuth also utilizes Cézanne's water-color practice of accentuating the line of junction between his planes and his color-

[36] E.g., Modigliani's "Woman in White" (361).

areas so that a sort of hinge is formed. As in Cézanne, the color is rarely uniform, but is varied within each area by tonal modifications or by contrasting colors which are themselves planes and are patterned by light and shade. Demuth accomplishes these effects by a technique different from Cézanne's: the latter uses individual brushstrokes or washes of color, juxtaposed or overlapping; Demuth's washes are broader, more varied in shape, more fluid, and less definitely outlined. His extensively modulated tones, and much of the transparency, delicacy and fluidity of his color, are obtained by his very skilful blotting and blobbing of the washes.[37]

Between 1913 and 1922, Demuth worked mainly with the methods of cubism, relying upon Cézannesque color-planes as his principal instrument, and eliminating most of the representative details of his subject-matter. In these pictures, planes are definitely shaped and set in sharply contrasting spatial relations and directions to form a very accentuated patterned framework dominated by angular shapes. They differ from typical cubistic pictures in that the color-planes are varied by tonal modulations similar to those in Cézanne's water colors, and they interpenetrate much as the planes do in Cézanne's still-lifes. Frequently, Demuth varies his Cézanne-cubist form by injecting into its rhythm of interpenetrating angular planes an intertwining arabesque movement of various units, thereby giving a Chinese quality to the expression.[38] Even in its cubistic period, Demuth's work is pervaded with much of the delicacy, lightness and charm so characteristic of his early and more illustrative pictures.

Utrillo attains to his characteristic qualities of surface and texture by use of planes like Cézanne's, which, however, are executed by a different technique and have new incidental by-effects. His substantial, deeply structural masses are built up of color-planes formed by dividing up the surface into small color-units of irregular shape and vague contour. The tonal contrasts establish a series of receding planes, which penetrate into the structural depths of a volume—a wall for example—build up its solid massiveness, and pattern the surface with a series of color-chords sometimes as rich, glowing and varied as in the late paintings of Renoir. Not infrequently the distance between these planes

[37] E.g., "Bicycle Riders" (354); "Nana" (356); "Negro Dancing" (357).
[38] E.g., "Houses Seen through Trees" (355).

is so pronounced that the effect is not unlike that of Cézanne's flattened, semivoluminous planes employed in backgrounds to establish a compositional linkage with the accentuated space-volume units in the foreground.[39] Utrillo's planes are smaller and more irregularly shaped, the impasto is more unctuous and the color brighter and more varied, than in Cézanne. The surface and texture of the paint, deriving its solidity and richness from Daumier and Cézanne, is decoratively richer than theirs because of a profusion of multicolored chords which contain contour-lines and internal planes of varied colors that sometimes produce the effect of a rich landscape with vaguely defined trees, sky and buildings.[40] This method of drawing, modeling and increasing the decorative and expressive content of subject-matter by making parts of it the vehicle for a transfer of values intrinsic to other fields of human experience, is highly individual to Utrillo. It is accomplished by technical devices basically Cézannesque, his usual reorganization of which, especially in his early work of the "white period," produces a form as delicate and lyrical as Corot's at his best. In accomplishing this, Utrillo resorts to no means actually imitative of Corot's, but constructs a new form by a synthesis of the features taken over from Cézanne with the brushstrokes and color-light effects of the impressionists.

How profoundly Cézanne has influenced the artists of our time and determined the course of contemporary painting, may be judged from the foregoing account of what a number of individual painters owe to him. Our account has been designed to illustrate, not to exhaust, the subject. Many other artists besides those discussed have utilized Cézanne's contributions in arriving at authentically expressive forms of their own. Among them are de la Fresnaye, Marin, Klee, the Pintos (Angelo, Biagio and Salvatore), Settanni, Raoul Dufy, Lurçat, Maurer, Gritchenko, de Segonzac, Miró, and such German expressionists as Hofer and Kokoshka. It would carry the present volume far beyond its intended scope to discuss in detail the debt of each of these artists to Cézanne, or the extent to which they have advanced the tradition established by him. Employment of the method set forth in this chapter will enable the student to observe in other artists' work the

[39] Compare, e.g., the walls in Utrillo's "Church with Red Roof and White Walls" (358) with the background in Cézanne's "Oranges and Bottle" (148).
[40] E.g., "Church with Red Roof and White Walls" (358).

specific elements adopted from Cézanne, as well as the extent to which these have been transformed into means of individual expression. It will be found that in many cases the significant features were taken not directly from Cézanne but indirectly from the forms of other contemporaries who have used Cézanne's insight as a means for sharpening and deepening their own perceptions. In these cases, whatever transformation the essential features may have undergone in the course of their adaptation to new purposes, they have not lost the marks of their origin. The difference between the work of the authentic artists and that of the legion of painters who have imitated Cézanne's surface-characteristics, is that in the painters who are also artists the source-material, whether derived directly or indirectly, has been no more than the point of departure for the expressions of ideas and feelings that bear the stamp of individuality.

ILLUSTRATIONS

Judgment of Paris (2)

147

Artist's Sister (3)

Head of Man (6)

Achille Emperaire (9)

Artist's Father (7)

Antony Valabrègue (10)   Analysis, page 311

Christ in Limbo (11)   Analysis, page 311

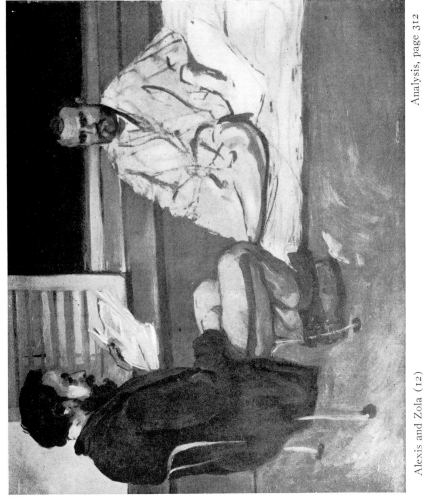

Alexis and Zola (12)

155

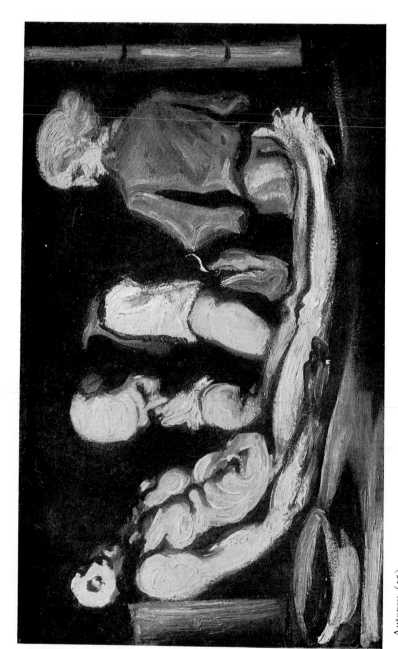

Autopsy (15)

Girl at Piano (19)

Analysis, page 309

Donkey Thieves (18)

158

Analysis, page 312

Red Roofs (35)

159

Picnic (21)

Black Clock (14)

Analysis, page 312

Green Jar and Pewter Pitcher (27)

163

Two Men and Two Women (25)

Idyl (26)

Head of Emperaire (28)

Four Women (31)

Boyer (30)   Analysis, page 313

Presumed Portrait of Valabrègue (42)   Analysis, page 315

Two Strollers (37)   Analysis, page 313

Man Putting on Coat (56)   Analysis, page 317

Railroad Cut (22)

Suicide's House (45)

Avenue of Jas de Bouffan (41)

Quay on the Seine (59)

175

River and Hills (48)

Mount Ste. Victoire and Valley (57)

Modern Olympia (33)

New Olympia (34)

Analysis, page 314

179

Eternal Feminine (62)

Temptation of St. Anthony (60)

Combat of Love (49)

Analysis, page 328

Four Bathers (75)

Cupid's Arrow (53)

Analysis, page 316

184

Leda and the Swan (68)

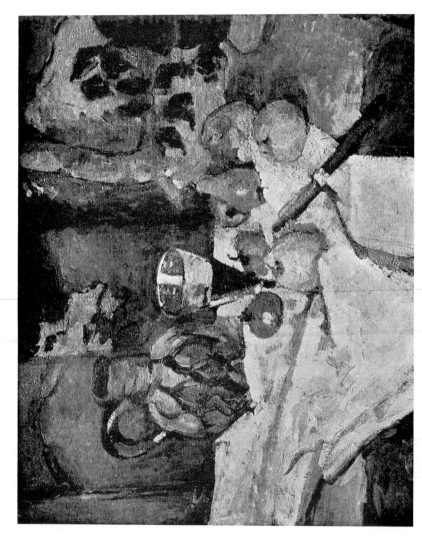

Jug, Wineglass and Fruit (46)

Banquet Table (50)

Plate with Grapes and Peach (58)

Plums and Pears (79)

Fruit and Tapestry (55)

Compotier, Glass, Apples and Knife (64)

Well Driller (40)

Choquet in Armchair (52)

Head of Victor Choquet (61)   Analysis, page 323

Head of Choquet (71)   Analysis, page 338

Ile-de-France (77)

196

Bridge at Créteil (104)

Analysis, page 354

197

Bathers at Rest (63)

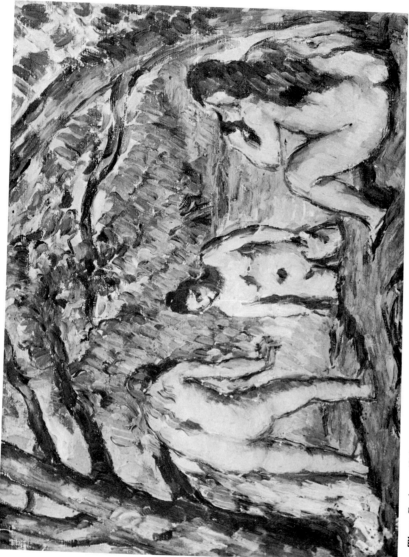

Analysis, page 333

Three Bathers (82)

Five Nudes (74)

Men Bathing (164)

Analysis, page 332

Analysis, page 339

Luncheon in the Open (78)

Pears on Chair (69)

Analysis, page 330

Self-Portrait on Pink Background (81)   Analysis, page 339

Self-Portrait in Front of Window (80)   Analysis, page 338

Interior with Nude (83)

Girl with Bird-Cage (97)

Self-Portrait with Bowler Hat (99)   Analysis, page 343

Madame Cézanne with Striped Skirt (72)   Analysis, page 338

Plaza, Auvers-sur-Oise (87)

Normandy Farm (114)

Analysis, page 388

Mountains in Provence (85)

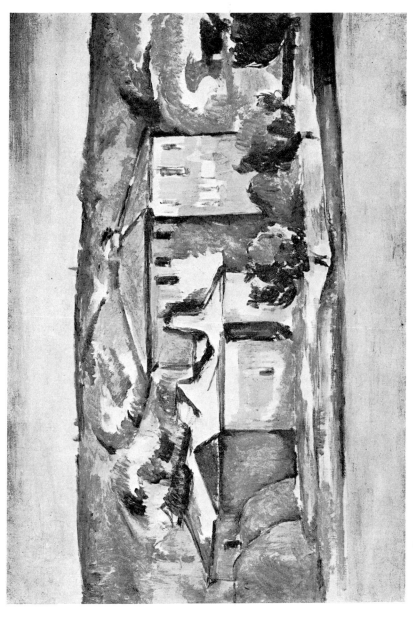

Country Home (91)

213

Red Apples (84)

Analysis, page 340

Four Peaches (129)

Analysis, page 373

Self-Portrait with Palette (88)

Madame Cézanne in Red, Holding
 Handkerchief (133)

Analysis, page 373

217

Spring House (89)   Analysis, page 342

Potted Plants (116)

Provence Landscape (138)

Analysis, page 372

221

Gardanne (92)

Analysis, page 343

Sugar Bowl, Pitcher and Fruit (117)

222

Fruit (163)

Analysis, page 390

Yellow House (102)

Farm of Jas de Bouffan (96)

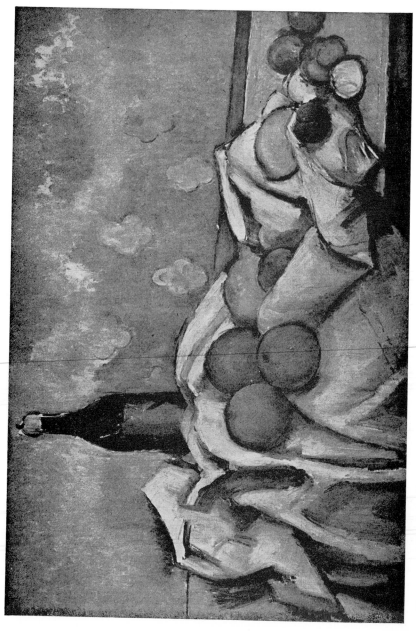

Oranges and Bottle (148)

Table, Napkin and Fruit (172)

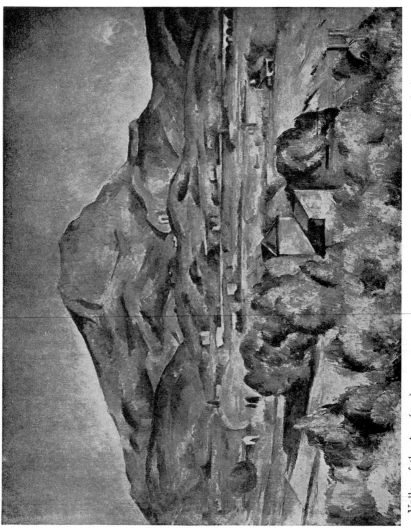

Valley of the Arc (109)

Analysis, page 355

228

Red Earth (III)

Analysis, page 357

Woman with Green Hat (103)   Analysis, page 348

Woman with Shawl (118)   Analysis, page 361

Nude Seated on Bank (86)

Gardener (130)   Analysis, page 380

Approach to Jas de Bouffan (112)

Large Oak (132)

Harlequin (105)   Analysis, page 354

Man in Room (136)

Big Trees (160)   Analysis, page 388

Mardi-Gras (106)   Analysis, page 353

Pine Tree at Montbriant (115)

Well (174)

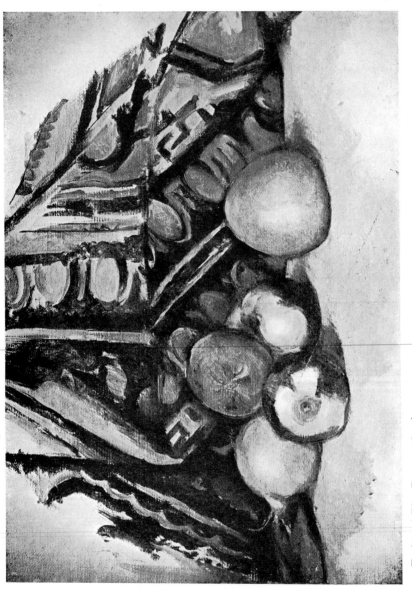

Fruit and Blue Drapery (120)

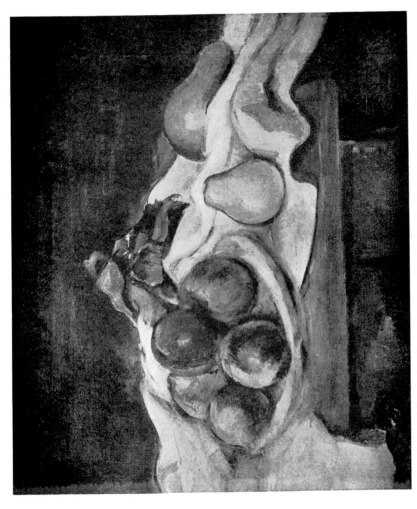

Peaches and Pears (137)

Plain, Trees and Hills (150)

Tile-Roof House in Landscape (139)

245

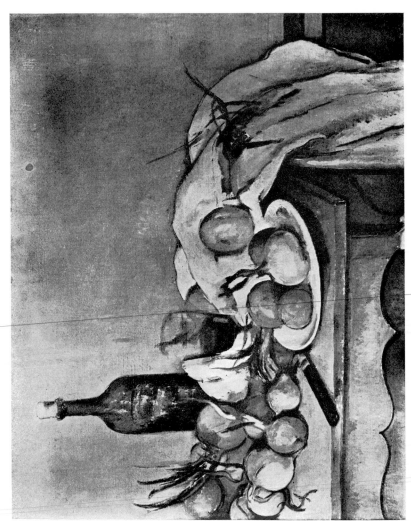

Onions and Bottle (167)

Analysis, page 389

Apples and Oranges (159)

House and Wall (147)

House on Hillside (131)

Woman and Coffee Pot (140)   Analysis, page 382

Madame Cézanne in Red, Holding Roses (134)   Analysis, page 381

Self-Portrait on Blue Background (108)   Analysis, page 360

Gustave Geffroy (144)   Analysis, page 385

Rocks and Trees (179)

Bibemus Quarry (155)

Peasant in Blue Blouse (149)   Analysis, page 383

Boy in Red Vest (119)

Provence Peasant (151)   Analysis, page 383

Man and Skull (142)   Analysis, page 368

Quarry at Le Tholonet (168)   Analysis, page 388

Viaduct (152)   Analysis, page 347

Madame Cézanne in Yellow Armchair (135) Analysis, page 373

Ambroise Vollard (158)   Analysis, page 390

Mount Ste. Victoire through Trees (166)

Village Church (185)

Rocks at Bibemus (170)

Flowers (162)

Ginger Jar and Fruit (181)

Drinker (177)

Two Men Playing Cards (143)

Card Players (125)

Analysis, page 364

271

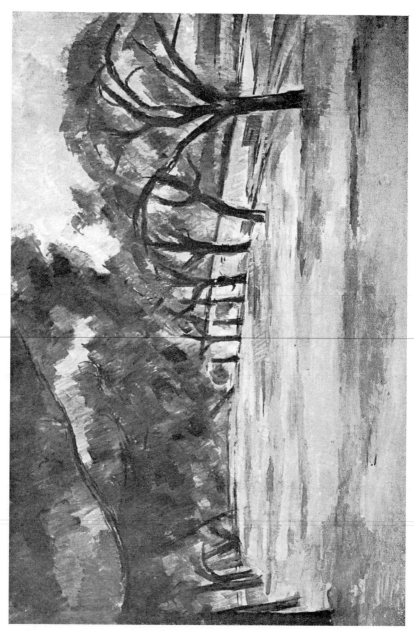

Road at Marines (153)

Mount Ste. Victoire with Pine Tree (124)

Analysis, page 363

273

Gray Jug and Fruit (122)

274

Skull and Fruit (187)

Card Players and Girl (141)

Analysis, page 365

Eight Women Bathing (161)

Analysis, page 390

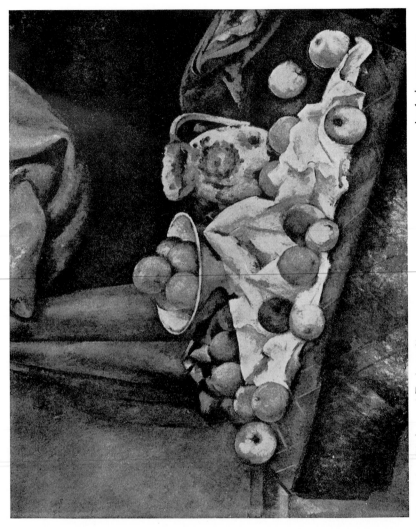

Compotier, Pitcher and Fruit (128)

Two Pitchers and Fruit (173)

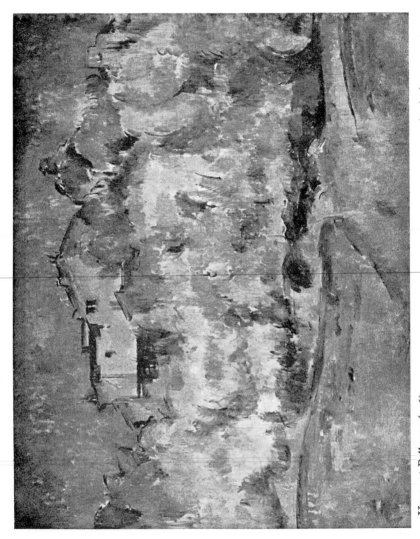

House at Bellevue (126)

Analysis, page 347

Mount Ste. Victoire Seen from the Chemin des Lauves (189)

281

Mount Ste. Victoire with Two Houses (183)

Analysis, page 347

Corner of Quarry (176)

Large Bathers (190)

Analysis, page 391

Group of Bathers (182)

285

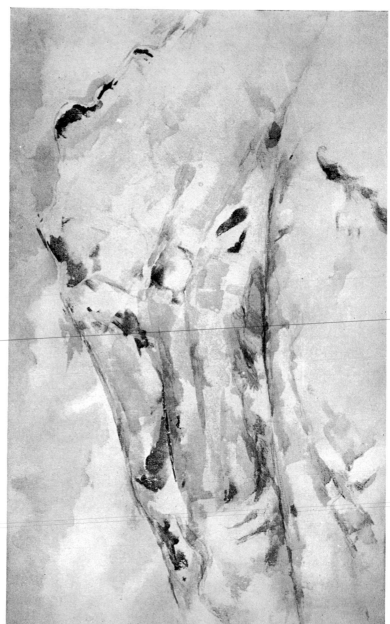

Peak of Ste. Victoire (202)

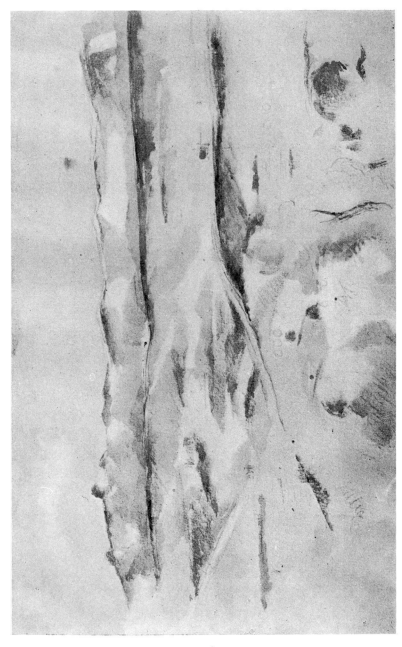

Mountain Range (198)

Group of Houses (194)

Bathers in Landscape (206)

Trees (204)

Smoker (203)

Bathers at Rest (63) (detail)

Plate with Grapes and Peach (58) (detail)

Oranges and Bottle (148) (detail)

Valley of the Arc (109) (detail)

Leda and the Swan (68) (detail)

River and Hills (48) (detail)

Bibemus Quarry (155) (detail)

Rocks and Trees (179) (detail)

Nudes in Landscape (191) (detail)

Mount Ste. Victoire and Valley (57) (detail)

296

Fruit and Tapestry (55) (detail)

Table, Napkin and Fruit (172) (detail)

Gardener (130) (detail b)

Gardener (130) (detail a)

298

Red Earth (111) (detail)

Well (174) (detail)

Provence Peasant (151) (detail)

Ginger Jar and Fruit (181) (detail)

Three Apples (65)   Analysis,
page 329

Ginger Jar and Fruit (181) (detail)

Group of Bathers (182) (detail)

Five Nudes (74) (detail)

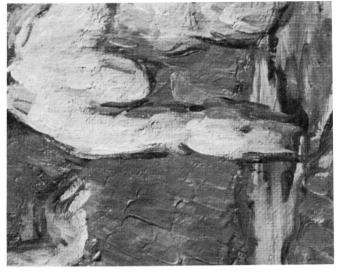

Triumph of St. Michael (263)—Delacroix   Five Nudes (74)—Cézanne

The above two details illustrate similarities and differences in the drawing and modeling of Delacroix and Cézanne.

Nudes in Landscape (191) (detail)

APPENDIX

APPENDIX

INTRODUCTION

THE foregoing discussion of Cézanne's form, technique and traditional derivations has stated conclusions without, as a rule, examining in detail the particular pictures on which the conclusions ultimately rest. In this appendix, therefore, Cézanne's form will be analyzed in its individual exemplifications, and the specific adaptations of his technique and color to problems of drawing, modeling, spatial organization, and composition will be pointed out. Because of the generic similarity of Cézanne's forms, most of the paintings will be considered only with reference to points of form or technique which they outstandingly illustrate; a number of his more important works, however, will also be analyzed comprehensively. The sequence of the analyses is roughly chronological.

ANALYSES

JUDGMENT OF PARIS (2) of the early 1860's.[1] The striking feature of this picture, supposedly painted almost at the start of Cézanne's career, is the bright colorful ensemble—orange and blue sky and light flesh color. The subject-matter has a classic feeling reminiscent of Rubens, Titian and Poussin, although with a different technique and much looser drawing than in any of these predecessors. Ill-defined brushstrokes slightly pattern the surface of the paint; the figures, modeled by contrasts of light and dark (the darks being chiefly tones of brown) form a set of a few planes placed at different locations, at a short distance from the foreground. The picture as a whole is essentially Venetian in character with strongly marked influences of Rubens and Delacroix.

DONKEY THIEVES (18) of the late 1860's.[2] At first glance this early Cézanne might readily pass for a Daumier. The similarity resides in the general dramatic organization of strongly opposed light and dark color-areas, and the combination of expressive con-

[1] Illustration, p. 147.　　　　[2] Illustration, p. 158.

tour and broadly patterned modeling which serves to draw figures in representative movement and to render the essence of a dramatic narrative. This similarity is closest in the dark figure dramatically silhouetted against the light background near the tree at the right;[3] in the red, blue and black used in the modeling; and in the dramatic movement of the compactly grouped figures in the lower left corner.[4] In these latter figures, however, distortions typical of Cézanne's early period[5] definitely distinguish the drawing from Daumier's. The figures, in general, are modeled as a series of globular masses, the brightly lighted areas of which contrast vividly with shadows that often deepen to an actual black. The paint is applied in broad blobs, with no clearly defined individual brushstrokes, so that the pattern of the main units is constituted by the globular masses themselves.

A succession of receding curvilinear planes, in sharp light-and-dark contrast, form the foreground of the picture; these planes extend from immediately to the left and just back of the directly vertical broad tree trunk, which emphasizes the first plane of the composition, at the extreme right. At the center, the area of deep blue water is a focal color-note, behind which a series of parallel bands continue the recession of space. The organization as a whole is based on a highly dramatic alternation of light and dark areas, which embrace the swirling and rectilinear planes just mentioned. Although the contrasts are supported by color, they are, like the sweeping motifs in the land, rocks and trees, rather obvious, and the effects are specious. Contrast of flat areas, such as the trees and ground, with the accentuatedly solid and three-dimensional figures and donkey, contributes further drama, but ineffective rendering of spatial relations[6] make the contribution only partly successful.

The picture illustrates Cézanne's inferiority to Daumier in Daumier's own field: Cézanne achieves a certain naïve expressiveness, but the drawing and modeling instrumental to it are mechanical in comparison with Daumier's varied and infinitely sensitive plastic drawing.[7]

[3] Cf., e.g., Daumier's "Man on Rope" (266).
[4] Cf., e.g., Daumier's "Wrestlers" (269).
[5] Cf., e.g., Cézanne's "Reading at Zola's" (23); "Idyl" (26); "Luncheon in the Open" (78).
[6] E.g., in the forward-coming portion of ground seen between the legs of the man at the extreme left.
[7] Cf., e.g., Daumier's "Hypochondriac" (265).

READING AT ZOLA'S (23) of the late 1860's.[8] The general characteristics of this picture may be briefly summed up as follows: drama of light-and-dark contrasts; movement of pattern due to swirling bands of color; picturesque distortions in the drawing of the figures and in the rendering of space; absence of actual contour-lines; modeling by parallel bands of light and dark; tendency to overaccentuation of highlighted areas; and deficient internal illumination of color. Its general traditional foundation is the form of the old masters, particularly Tintoretto, El Greco and Rubens; there is also a vague suggestion of the Le Nains in the occurrence of plastic drama in the expression of a tranquil interior scene. Space is the least successfully used element; while it is fairly adequate on the whole and adds by its distortions to the picturesqueness of the composition, it does not sufficiently differentiate the figure at the left from its setting, and the units in the background from each other; the floor, moreover, appears like a floating, levitated carpet rather than a solid plane upon which volumes are set. Disturbances and difficulties in the handling of space which Cézanne seldom entirely surmounted appear here in their early crudity.

This picture, like "Donkey Thieves" (18), illustrates also what may be the germ of a familiar device of Cézanne's mature form; that is, the accentuation of receding space by its definite demarcation from a compositional plane in the foreground: the drapery at the left is plastically analogous in this respect to the various table cloths, table fronts, trees, rocks, etc., in his later typical compositions.

GIRL AT PIANO (19), of the late 1860's,[9] one of the strongest and best pictures of Cézanne's pre-1870 period, ranks in plastic quality, forcefulness, vitality, and individuality with some of the finest Venetian paintings, the outstanding achievements of seventeenth century Dutch painters of interior scenes, of Ribera and Zurbarán at their best, of the Le Nains, and of Courbet and Manet —to all of which it is in some measure indebted. The varied influences are pervasive, and they are so organically merged that their effects, while clearly recognizable, are not separable from each other in the new units in which Cézanne has combined them. The dramatic light-and-dark contrasts, for instance, partake of the

[8] Illustration, p. 154.
[9] Illustration, p. 157.

characteristics of both the Spanish and the Dutch tradition, and, in their varied plastic functions, they recall also effects familiar in Tintoretto, the Le Nains and Manet. Drawing and modeling, in the girl at the piano, are derived basically from both Courbet and Manet; in the figure on the couch, plastic traits reminiscent of Ribera and Zurbarán are given an individual rendering mainly by color, simplifications and technique akin to Manet's, the effects of which predominate in the drawing and execution of the garments. Cézanne's use of these traditional features results in a plastic form more solid and vigorous than that of his predecessors, largely because of the color which is pervasively structural, well illuminated, and plastically effective in its contrasts and rhythms. The dark colors have a deep, warm internal glow, and the whites have that rich quality of old ivory sometimes present in the work of Giorgione and Titian.[10]

Anticipation of several specific traits of Cézanne's later work are recognizable: the modeling by light-and-dark contrasts forecasts his familiar use of planes; bare canvas, in the painting of the piano, already functions as color; the decorative motifs on the armchair and wall are detached from the ground of their fabric, and are used, as so frequently in his later work, to form subsidiary space-compositions of planes and masses;[11] on the wall, the units of the pattern stand out like solid planelike volumes of carved wood, and their distinction in space from each other and from the wall is made more emphatic by the use of a broad outline of light— a device which Cézanne often employed in his mature work to emphasize spacing.

The high quality of the plastic integration appears in the fact that a feeling of quiet drama, of repose in the atmosphere of a domestic interior, emerges from a union of plastic elements which individually are characterized by vivid drama of light and dark color, widely varied contrast of pattern, and an active interplay between rigid angular figures and objects and curvilinear decorative motifs. Matisse probably owes to this picture some of his characteristic pattern-effects and contrasts of rectilinear and curvilinear rhythms.

[10] Cf., e.g., Giorgione's "Sleeping Venus" (228) or Titian's "Venus with Dog" (231).
[11] Cf., e.g., "Jug, Wineglass and Fruit" (46); "Fruit and Tapestry" (55); "Man and Skull" (142); "Oranges and Bottle" (148). Compare with Tintoretto's use of a similar device in "Venetian Senator" (239).

CHRIST IN LIMBO (11) of c. 1868.[12] A black-and-white reproduction of a painting attributed to Sebastiano del Piombo (232) was used as a model for this picture, but because of the accentuated contrasts of black-and-white effect, and the broad, dramatic sweeping pattern, Cézanne achieves an effect more Spanish than Italian, and more powerful than the original.

ANTONY VALABREGUE (10) of c. 1868.[13] This powerful portrait represents a successful and very personal interpretation of traits derived from Hals, Courbet and Manet. There is also a suggestion of Delacroix in the color of the flesh, particularly in the hands. The pigment is very heavy throughout, and the technique is obvious; the paint is applied in some areas by the brush, in others by the palette knife. The strokes as a whole recall those of Hals rather than of Manet: they are small for the most part, with raised edges that create an indented surface and also form a striking and effective pattern. The rich, deep, unctuous color, especially in the hands and face, together with the brushwork, produces an effect not unlike that in Soutine's early painting.

Line in general is not accentuated, even as contour, and it plays little part in the modeling, which is done chiefly by contrast of light and shadow.

The background lacks Cézanne's characteristic modulations that create space by giving the effect of a receding succession of plastic units, and it remains, as in much of Hals's work, clearly separable from the figure. This imperfect compositional integration appears also in the drawing of the head: it makes the mass seem to extend forward without at the same time going backward and making connection with the space of the setting. Above the forehead, the hair seems not to project but to sink back, so that the face has the effect of a mask set in front of a bunch of wool, an effect heightened by the texture of the ceramiclike flesh. In his typical later work, Cézanne piles up paint on shadows, leaving lights and highlights relatively thinly painted or even areas of bare canvas; in this and other early pictures,[14] the reverse procedure is followed, and the thinly painted shadows or dark areas, especially when they approach an actual black, sink into the canvas.

Here, the defect in question, an example of Cézanne's early difficulty in the use of color to realize solidity and define spatial rela-

[12] Illustration, p. 153.   [14] E.g., "Uncle Dominique" (5).
[13] Illustration, p. 152.

tions, is destructive of continuity between the hair and forehead, and between the mustache and face, and leaves these areas of the picture in a state of relative disorganization.

ALEXIS AND ZOLA (12) of 1868-1870.[15] Cézanne's individuality at an early stage is shown here in his creative use of the forms of Courbet and Manet. Composition, color and drawing, on the whole, are Courbet's, but the qualities derived by Courbet from Velásquez are accentuated; the simplifications and generalized brushwork are akin to Manet's, particularly in his sketches. Cézanne's subtle but unmistakable departures from the original sources may be noted in, for example, the pattern of color-patches in the face of the man on the left, and in the more forceful general expression.[16] The characterization of each figure is strong, drawing is expressive, color and light are in general well harmonized, and the picture embodies the feeling of repose intrinsic to the scene.

GREEN JAR AND PEWTER PITCHER (27), of c. 1870,[17] is interesting chiefly because of its close adherence to the Velásquez-Manet form. The prevalence of the Spanish motif of light-and-dark contrast brings the effect close to that of an early Velásquez,[18] but because of Courbet's and Manet's influence the color, particularly the whites, is richer, better illuminated and more deeply structural. Manet's influence is perceptible also in the generalized broad drawing, in the technical execution, in the compositional organization, and in the characteristic deep slate-gray tone of the background.[19]

RED ROOFS (35) of the early 1870's.[20] The dramatic effects of Cézanne's characteristic early sweeping rhythms are heightened in this landscape by the contrast between the relatively light color of the snow and roofs and the heavy, dark color of the sky and trees. This accentuated light-and-dark motif exemplifies Cézanne's

---

[15] Illustration, p. 155.
[16] Compare with Courbet's "Proudhon and his Children" (271) and Manet's "Luncheon on the Grass" (280).
[17] Illustration, p. 163.
[18] Cf., e.g., Velásquez' "Meeting of Tipplers" (256).
[19] Cf., e.g., Manet's "Boy with Fife" (275); "Georges Clémenceau" (278) or "White Peonies" (283).
[20] Illustration, p. 159.

debt to the seventeenth century Dutch tradition, upon which he has engrafted more definite patterns and contrasts of directions, the solidity of Venetian color, the color-drama and color-movement of Tintoretto (and, to a less extent, of Rubens), the matter-of-factness of Courbet, and the tonal relationships of Daumier. The technique is derived from Hals and Manet, but emphasis upon individual brushstrokes and their pattern is reduced. Lines of contour, broken in continuity, surround nearly all the units, often as independent black lines that appear sunken below the surface of the object which they define, or as curvilinear yellow brushstrokes, which form a scalloped edge around the masses of foliage in the trees. The pervasively muted color, like that of slate, is only slightly relieved by the red of the roofs: it lacks internal illumination and fails to carry conviction in certain areas of the ground. In spite of the general color-deficiencies, the sense of depth and solidity is well realized in the trees, and the total effect is powerful. It anticipates many characteristics of Derain, Vlaminck and Rouault.

TWO STROLLERS (37) of the early 1870's.[21] Courbet's form, in this picture, is only slightly changed despite Cézanne's more angular drawing and somewhat more appealing color-scheme. Contrasts of light and dark and of linear directions are the fundamental means of expression. The execution is heavy and mechanistic.

BOYER (30) of the early 1870's.[22] The use in this portrait of an orange-salmon color in the flesh to temper the Hals-Courbet-Daumier-Manet tradition forecasts Cézanne's abundant use of that color, particularly in landscapes, after he came under the direct influence of Pissarro. Here, however, the orange and the other colors lack luster or internal glow, and the pigment has the waxy surface characteristic of Courbet, a defect which recurs intermittently in Cézanne's work at various periods of his career.[23] Drawing and modeling are essentially Manet-esque, with an active pattern of expressive brushstrokes in the face, a "lost-and-found"

[21] Illustration, p. 170.
[22] Illustration, p. 168.
[23] E.g., "Madame Cézanne with Striped Blouse" (98); "Geranium and Apples" (121); "Madame Cézanne in Red, Holding Roses" (134); "Madame Cézanne in Yellow Armchair" (135); "Onions and Bottle" (167).

outline of black or gray shadow around the hat,[24] and the rendering of the coat simplified to such an extent that a single line upon a broad, practically uniform, color-area draws the essentials of coat, body and arm.[25] An interesting feature is the effect of planes receding in space in the background on the right; this may be the result of Cézanne's repaintings of the area, but the effect undoubtedly resembles that achieved by one of his later intentionally used devices, the employment of roughly parallel bands of shadow, placed outside the volume, to transform uniform areas of walls, tables, doors, etc., into cognate plastic participants in motifs of space-composition.[26]

MODERN OLYMPIA (33) of the early 1870's.[27] The most interesting feature of this picture is the evidence of Delacroix's influence, in the represented movement and in the general conception; of Courbet's, particularly in the drawing of the man; and of Velásquez', in certain color-relationships that include the wine-red tone. The familiar diamond-motif serves as a framework to the organization. The color is dull, and the tricky contrasts of light and dark are obviously relied upon to obtain effects that should be secured by color.

NEW OLYMPIA (34) of the early 1870's.[28] Subject-matter, practically identical with that in the picture just discussed (33), is here rendered through the medium of a delicate Delacroix-Fragonard motif, strongly affected by Manet's type of drawing. Compositional movement and balance are established by rather obvious contrasts in the directions of the main units. The free and varied impressionistic brushwork adds additional activity to the organization, and a series of dark areas—the negress, the nude's hair, the book, the dog, the hat—very effectively punctuate the generally light and delicate color-ensemble. The rhythms, the patterns and the color, however, are scarcely more than surface-effects.

[24] Cf., e.g., the outline in Manet's "Dead Christ with Angels" (276).
[25] Cf., e.g., Manet's "Woman in Landscape" (284).
[26] E.g., "Man in Room" (136); "Woman and Coffee Pot" (140); "Card Players and Girl" (141); "Drinker" (177).
[27] Illustration, p. 178.
[28] Illustration, p. 179.

PRESUMED PORTRAIT OF VALABREGUE (42), of c. 1871,[29] is a powerful rendering of character and a striking example of Cézanne's progress toward his distinctive form. It shows the influence of Courbet, and more particularly of Manet. The color-effects, more luminous, glowing and structural than Manet's, are realized without Cézanne's early use of thick impasto. The strongly accentuated pattern of brushstrokes, much closer to Manet's than to Hals's, which lends an intense plastic activity to the face, makes a contrast with the relatively unpatterned, but still Manet-like, painting of the coat and vest. There are no independent contour-lines, except where some of the edges are scalloped by single curvilinear brushstrokes. The hair and face are imperfectly unified, but there is no such actual break between them as that noted in "Antony Valabrègue" (10), so that the head as a whole is a more successfully realized single volume. Perhaps the most serious defect is that the pronounced pattern of the brushwork in the face interferes somewhat with the textural unity of the flesh. The superposed strokes in the collar at the left, with their abrupt changes of tone, and also the brushstrokes in the flesh, clearly anticipate Cézanne's subsequent technical use of planes in drawing, modeling and composition.

JUG, WINEGLASS AND FRUIT (46) of c. 1873-1874.[30] Standing apart in its color-scheme and manner of organization and execution from the other Cézannes of the period, this picture is also one of the most original and individual works of his entire career. The color-scheme, with its dominant interplay of grays and salmon-pinks, combines a pronounced rhythmic pattern of quasi curvilinear areas with a delicate yet rugged texture of pigment, in a composite effect reminiscent at one and the same time of oriental art—such as Chinese and Japanese paintings—the still-lifes of Chardin, and the eighteenth century French tradition in general. The background accounts for much of the distinctive character of the total form: oriental feeling and decorative color and pattern, concentrated in the screen or tapestry, reach the maximum degree of emphasis in the right half of the background, in which the predominating Chinese quality is productive of effects later made familiar by the work of Matisse.

The principal agent of unification between background and fore-

[29] Illustration, p. 169.
[30] Illustration, p. 186.

ground is the large pitcher on the left, the Chinese-like pattern of which echoes and counterbalances the pattern of the background and thus establishes compositional relationship between the two parts of the picture. This same pattern also helps to draw and model the pitcher and endows it with unusually rich and active rhythms. In the right third of the canvas the composition consists of a continuous flow of plastic units which succeed each other rhythmically from the lower right corner of the foreground, through the pinkish area of the table and the three pieces of fruit, upward and backward to the decorative motifs of the background-tapestry. These decorative motifs appear detached from the ground of the fabric and thus transform this portion of the setting into a very eloquent composition of volumes and planes in two- and three-dimensional space, the transferred values of which are those of a landscape seen against a distant sky. Distortions in other sections of the background introduce a set of values transferred from oriental art, and the rhythmic interflow of all these color-units is uninterrupted throughout the entire picture.

Technique and quality of pigment contribute much to the character of the painting: the impasto is as thick as in "Compotier, Glass, Apples and Knife" (64), but there is no such systematic use or grouping of the brushstrokes as in the latter picture; the brushwork is perceptible but irregular, and is so organically merged with the color and the Chardinesque surface and texture of the paint that its pattern is an integral part of the form.

As so frequently in Cézanne, even in his best work, the color is not uniformly successful. In the upper part of the pear, for instance, defective color-relations make the surface appear to shrink inward as though into a hole, and similarly in the red fruit to the right of the glass, the parts of the volume that ought to project appear to recede. Color, nevertheless, functions extraordinarily well on the whole, and from a distance the ensemble, though it lacks sparkle, has the richness of a basket of multicolored jewels. Gauguin, Matisse and Lurçat owe much of their characteristic work to this type of picture.[31]

CUPID'S ARROW (53) of the middle 1870's.[32] In color-quality and in general plastic organization, this small and simple

[31] E.g., Gauguin's "Flowerpiece" (315); Matisse's "Blue Still-Life" (323); Lurçat's "Rocks and Water" (364).
[32] Illustration, p. 184.

composition is outstandingly fine and rare for its period. The combined influences of the French eighteenth century painters, of Delacroix and of Constable are embodied in a new form in which color, thoroughly illuminated, is pervasively expressive and decorative. The pattern of the brushwork subtly animates the color-areas, and by its organic relationship to the drawing and modeling of the volumes it effectively reënforces the rhythmic movement of the main units. A great part of the charm of the color-organization is due to the very successful use of red, which punctuates and enlivens the general ivory-green-blue ensemble.

MAN PUTTING ON COAT (56) of the middle 1870's.[33] In the text, this picture has been noted as representing a transitional stage between Cézanne's early period and his maturity, in that emphasis has been transferred in a measure from represented to plastic activity, and that the brushwork shows a definite tendency to functional organization. Instances of the latter tendency are to be found in the bush at the lower left, the tree at the upper left, and the uppermost part of the sky, in all of which a number of adjacent strokes have in common a general color, shape, size, and direction, and thus begin to coalesce into a homogeneous group or single patch, a definite plane related in deep space to the surrounding areas.

Apart from this specifically instrumental use of technique, the drawing is more expressive; compositional unity between figure and setting is relatively more complete than in Cézanne's earlier form. The positions of the man's figure, arms, coat, and sleeve establish a gentle rhythmic sweep which is echoed and balanced in various parts of the setting: in the trunk of the tree on the right, in the slant of the cliff, and in the counterbalancing curve of the small tree at the upper left. Compositional integration is also enforced by one of Cézanne's familiar devices, the network of linear directions that virtually bind together, in two- or three-dimensional space, units otherwise separated from one another. The fact that these linear effects are interrupted and redirected at intervals and on other planes emphasizes their compositional activity. The upward lower sweep of the tree on the right, for instance, leads the eye across areas of blue space to the dark sleeve of the man's coat and the upper right outline of the tree at the upper left of the setting. The small bush immediately back

[33] Illustration, p. 171.

and to the left of the man's shoulder may likewise be conceived as the starting point of a compositional linear direction, sweeping upward along the arm and hand of the figure and part of the sleeve of the coat, and continued by the vertical area outlining the large mass of foliage just above the elbow of the sleeve. This elbow punctuates also the quasi horizontal linear direction that extends through space to tie together the lower outlines of the foliage on the right, of the small tree on the left, and of the triangular shadow above and back of the small tree. Running parallel to this is the linear direction of the horizon, which is carried across the canvas by the waist of the figure and the patches of green and of tan on the cliff at the left. Again, the band of shadow along the edge of the cliff involves in its downward slant the man's face and part of the shaded area of his body, and counterbalances the diagonal rhythm that sweeps upward from the bushes at the lower left along the man's arm to the mass of foliage at the upper right.

This unification of parts achieves a compositional movement which, as a whole, is much less disjointed and representational than in the earlier form; that is to say, more plastic, more expressive; but because of the incomplete structural quality of the color this movement is as yet not deeply ingrained in the substance of things. The cliff, for example, and the feet, legs and eyes of the figure have little internal solidity of volume to support their shape, and in consequence the rhythmic organization remains a matter largely of surface-pattern, and the compositional movement is confined to particular areas rather than embracing the design as a whole.

FRUIT AND TAPESTRY (55), of the middle 1870's,[34] offers good material for a comparative study of Cézanne's modeling. This modeling, as we have seen in the text, depends to a considerable extent upon the pattern made by brushstrokes, fused into color-patches that constitute planes of varying definiteness in shape. Line is of great importance in it, but the line is not independent of the technique: it is sometimes an actual narrow strip of color, often showing an alignment of individual brushstrokes; sometimes it is the meeting place of color-patches; sometimes it is a sequence of elements of technique or spots of light or color, in which many

[34] Illustration, p. 190.

interruptions may occur without preventing the eye from following a definite direction, or the imagination from filling in the gaps. These means of modeling are not combined in accordance with any definite formula in, Cézanne. Unlike Leonardo, for example, who invariably resorted to continuous change in degree of illumination to round out his volumes, Cézanne at his best varies his means to secure an exact adjustment of method to individual purpose or problem in each unit modeled; the result is often a very great variety of effects even in an individual picture. This variety of effect combined with an underlying unity of principle is very well illustrated in "Fruit and Tapestry," the units of which reveal wide differences in technical detail, and at the same time have in common a construction that is nonimitative, fundamentally plastic, and individual to Cézanne.

Cézanne's methods are exemplified in this picture by two sets of objects, the pieces of fruit, which are fully rounded three-dimensional volumes, and the plate and leaves, which, though also convincingly solid, are of much flatter shape. In spite of this difference, which involves a somewhat different handling of means, the principles of construction are revealed by analysis to be fundamentally the same in both sets.

In the green peach on the right, the brushstrokes are merged into patches of contrasting color and tone, so shaped and related as to constitute two comparatively well-defined patterns. One is made up of a series of concentric strips, of which the smallest is closest to the eye, and the series grows larger as it recedes into distance, until it terminates in the heavy linear contour or outer edge of the peach itself. These strips, which function as planes, are so compactly placed that they overlap at the edges, and the lines thus produced create the patterned effect of the surface; their gradual recession as they grow larger, marking as it does the movement of the surface away from the observer, establishes the spatial organization of the volume as a whole. Their compact placing, the fact that no unoccupied space appears between them, gives to the volume a continuous solid surface, and the structural quality of the color together with the density of the pigment reenforces and accentuates the effect of solid, weighty massiveness.[35]

The second pattern arises out of the first. The concentric strips, while maintaining their essential continuity, show variations in

---

[35] It produces also a one-piece character in the volume which is more typical of Cézanne's still-lifes than of his landscapes.

color and tone, as well as minor spatial interruptions; and these modifications, especially the changes in color and tone, are organized into another set of linear sequences radiating out from the point of the volume nearest the eye and forming a general hub-and-spokes pattern. These sequences have the function of lines of perspective, carrying the eye backward into deep space and thus adding their effect to that of the concentric strips, thereby emphasizing the rotundity of the volume as seen from the front. This, of course, is the latitude-longitude arrangement referred to in the text; [36] by means of it Cézanne gives to his areas of solid color, his light-dark contrasts and his characteristic technique of superposed patches a conjoint function in building up the material of each mass and organizing it in deep space. Each area on the surface, almost each spot, belongs to both patterns and enters into both sets of relationships.

This method of modeling enables Cézanne to introduce plastic effects impossible for more conventional painters. In the piece of fruit just studied, for example, the highest spot of illumination is to the left of the area nearest the spectator, and it appears to be both on the surface of the volume and at the same time depressed beneath it. This distortion, an instance of the sunken light which appears in so many of his pictures, introduces into the body of the peach a subtle yet picturesque element of space-composition, an internal rhythm of receding planes of which the foremost is the yellowish-green patch at the center of the volume, and the most remote the highlighted area which serves as a distant focus of illumination.

In the organization of the red and yellow peach to the left of the piece of fruit just discussed, the same principles are employed, but with modifications entailed by use of the quill-motif. Close together in the middle of the volume appear two spots, one red and the other blue, both of which are applied in the quill-form, with the specific character of the motif determined by the exigencies of modeling. To adapt it to this end, Cézanne makes of both spots two relatively detached or superposed planes. In spite of the fact that they are darker than adjacent areas, they are enabled by their positive color to play the part of highlights, and to render the effect of spatial projection in that area of the volume. A second adaptation appears in the alignment of the ribs of the two quills, which makes them approximately continuous along the latitudinal

[36] See p. 70.

or equatorial line from left to right; the direction of the quills themselves—the barbs—in contrast, lies along the meridian lines which represent the bulge of the peach as its surface rises toward the eye and sinks away again. In this piece of fruit, as in that previously discussed, the most highly illuminated area falls on the receding part of the volume and thus produces the distortion of sunken light.

In the dented peach at the back, the two sets of lines are accentuated in different degree, with emphasis falling strongly upon the longitudinal. These radiate from a pole or nodal point close to the top of the volume. The latitudinal lines are scarcely more than suggested; they appear chiefly in a few partial strips that duplicate internally the upper outline of the peach, and in a heavier line, produced by the junction of light and dark areas, which similarly parallels the lower contour.

Still another correlation of the two patterns appears in the pear on the plate. The pole in this is a dark spot near the bottom, and the longitudinal lines radiating from it are comparatively broad strips or alignments of parallel patches. These are modulated in varying degrees of light and dark, and it is the sequence of these modulations, extending at right angles across the meridians, that form the latitudinal lines placed in a more or less concentric arrangement around the dark nodal point. Since, however, the alternation of light and dark in the first set of lines does not take place simultaneously in all, a light spot in one is often adjacent to a dark spot on the lines to the right and left, with the result that the latitudinal lines also display a constant rhythm of light and dark color. The two sets of lines bring out, as usual, the projections and recessions of the volume in the directions in which they lie, and thus reënforce the general functions of color and tone in modeling.

All these pieces of fruit, but especially the pear, show also evidences of another type of modeling referred to in the text, the junction of patches, stripes and bands in comparatively sharp lines and at definite angles. Conjoined with the general tendency to flatness in the planes, this angular character makes the surface seem faceted, as though it had been carved out with an adze. The result is not only a more pronounced sense of solidity, but the introduction of a great number of lines of perspective, which make clear and emphatic the direction in which every area of the surface is placed, together with its relation to adjacent areas. In this respect the modeling reflects the general character of Cézanne's form, its tendency to abruptness, ruggedness, even harshness—the qualities that make for power rather than grace.

In the red and yellow peach nearest the background, neither set of lines is more than indicated, and the indications must be interpreted by the help of the more accentuated pattern in the other pieces of fruit. What really does the modeling in this peach is the color, a dark spot of red at the upper right, an area of intense red on the left, and one of vivid yellow at the extreme left outer edge. These are solid and structural, and it is primarily the relations of color and light that organize the unit in three principal parallel planes, the yellow plane, the red plane superposed upon it, and the dark red plane superposed upon the second and functioning as the high spot. The slightness, the sketchiness of the linear patterns reduces the voluminousness of this peach, but its color-intensity and the vivid contrast between light and dark color make it one of the focal points in the color-organization as a whole. Because of its lessened three-dimensional character it is also well qualified to serve as the compositional bridge between the other weightier pieces of fruit and the still flatter leaflike decorations in the background.

In the plate and leaves the same utilization of pattern for the rendering of solidity and perspective appears, though naturally the space involved is shallower. In part of the plate, especially on the left, the drawing and modeling are done by a series of concentric parallel bands, beginning with the broad heavy contour-line on the outside, and continuing through alternate lines of light and shadow which gradually grow broader until the broadest of all lies against the edge of the pear. These bands belong to the general latitudinal category, and because there is little or no suggestion of the corresponding meridional lines the plate as a whole has a much more definite extension in two dimensions than in three.

In the first and darkest leaf above the table on the left, a pattern of strips and elongated areas accentuate the longitudinal axis of the leaf as a whole, and thus reënforces the compositional function of the leaf, which is to carry the rhythm of the table over into the more curvilinear pattern of the background. In the leaf just above and to the rear of the first, the pattern of brushstrokes and areas of color, light and shadow has also a set of transverse bands, in which light and shadow are accentuated. The relations of the two patterns, together with the tonal modifications, make this leaf slightly more three-dimensional than the first. In the leaf above this, a rhythm of short strips, starting from the scalloped edge, repeats internally both the curvilinear and the longitudinal aspects of the volume as a whole; a second pattern, very faint but visible upon close inspection, is formed by parallel tonal modifications running crosswise from the scalloped edge to the opposite ill-defined contour.

In the leaf which shoots up obliquely toward the upper right, both types of pattern play an active part in the modeling. One set of strips or long brushstrokes lies in the direction of the longer axis; within these strips patches of color, light and dark are so related in tone and general shape to adjacent patches in the parallel strips that a second series of sequences or lines of perspective proceeds across the width of the leaf. In spite of breaks in continuity, these transverse lines of perspective, operating in conjunction with the accentuated longitudinal rib, make of this leaf a wedge-shaped mass which echoes in a lesser degree the voluminousness of the pieces of fruit in the foreground.

The foregoing account illustrates the fact mentioned in the text that, while Cézanne's technical methods are limited in range, the multitude of variations within the limited field result in a great variety of effects, which compensate for the restricted general range. This analysis also illustrates that to appreciate Cézanne's methods and ideas, a detailed study of his variations in technique is indispensable.

QUAY ON THE SEINE (59), of the middle 1870's,[37] is as close to Pissarro as possible without being slavishly imitative.

HEAD OF VICTOR CHOQUET (61) of c. 1876.[38] Traits to be noted are: a Hals-like technique, novel color-distortions,[39] deficient internal illumination, and a richly varied color-gamut which anticipates that of Cézanne's later work. The flesh, with its reds and yellows, recalls Delacroix's, from which it is distinguished by an accentuated pattern of short, rather broad brushstrokes. The surface of the painting has the quality of ceramics and resembles that of Soutine's early work: the impasto is heavy and is applied wholly by the brush, with each brushstroke a solid mass of color. Definite contour-lines are almost entirely absent and the awkward-

[37] Illustration, p. 175.
[38] Illustration, p. 194.
[39] E.g., blue hair highlighted in gray-blue; greenish-blue tones in the flesh.

ness of execution prevalent at this period of Cézanne's career is very little in evidence.

ETERNAL FEMININE (62) of c. 1876-1877.[40] The composition is focused about a diamond-shaped formation extending upward and backward—a large whitish area which has the effect of a tent, at the center of which is placed a nude. The contrast between this tentlike area and the surrounding darker-hued figures and objects, of yellow, red and deep blue, provides a colorful version of the familiar light-dark motif.

Goya, Daumier, Forain, and Toulouse-Lautrec are the traditional sources most in evidence in the drawing, while the vivid contrast of light and dark areas is reminiscent of Tintoretto and El Greco. The planelike volumes are compactly placed in a rapidly ascending general compositional plane which terminates at the upper part of the background in two parallel horizontal bands. The great animation of the whole picture is due to the linear character of the drawing and modeling, the occurrence of multiple contour-lines, and more especially to the profusion of short and narrow parallel brushstrokes running in practically the same oblique direction throughout the canvas. Many contrasting lines of direction produce a series of compositional thrusts and counterthrusts, but the resulting movement, vivacious as it is, remains more illustrative than plastic. The impasto is thin, the color has little carrying power, the drawing and modeling have a sketchy appearance, and the surface-pattern has merely the decorative effect of tapestry.

BATHERS AT REST (63) was painted in 1877,[41] the year in which Cézanne participated in the exhibition of the impressionists, and at a period of his growth when he was saturated with the spirit of the time. It displays with great clarity the influence of Courbet and Pissarro, and in spite of the crudity of its execution it shows also how thoroughly Cézanne had already conceived his own distinctive form of design, with its fidelity to essentials, its compositional unity and its characteristic power. The details of subject-matter are as definitely as Courbet's a part of the real world, but what is emphasized in them is not their particular textural quality, and still less their momentary degree of illumination, but their solid structure, especially as this is given by color and by the relation of the details to the other units, in a compre-

[40] Illustration, p. 180.
[41] Illustration, p. 198.

hensive plastic ensemble. The dark green bank in the right foreground, for example, though sufficiently convincing as an entity, is of such shape and color that part of its rôle is to enter into compositional relations with other rhythmic accents of dark green—for example, the large tree on the extreme left, the green tree in the left center, the arabesque tree on the extreme right, and the shadowed area on the right of the hat in the immediate foreground—all of which unite in a roughly circular movement in deep space. Numerous other color-rhythms are similarly intertwined throughout the picture.

The color-scheme of blue, orange-yellow and green, each color diversified into many individual shades, is derived from Pissarro; but constantly recurring contrasts of light and dark impart a dramatic quality lacking in that painter. This quality is powerfully accentuated by the pronounced and bizarre pattern that arises from the character and definiteness of the shapes of the individual color-areas. The units belonging to each color-theme are fundamentally interlinked by their color-rhythms, while in shape and degree of voluminousness they are related to units of the other color-themes. The green rocky bank in the right foreground, for example, and the mass of green foliage on the extreme left, though they are contrasted in color and degree of illumination to the clouds in the sky, are united with the latter by their configuration and the degree of their massiveness; and this sort of union extends throughout the whole composition, which is a synthesis of heavy volumes interacting in deep space. This same foreground-bank is linked by its trapezoidal shape to the angular pattern which radiates out through the adjacent bended knee and other parts of the man's body, the water and the land, thence to similar triangular and trapezoidal shapes in the other areas of the picture; and this is the basic color-pattern of the composition. Again, the ascending contour of the bank in question is the beginning of a movement which, extending upward and backward to include the Japanese-arabesque tree on the right and the clouds beyond, makes a wide sweep to the extreme left, and is there, in the small area of smoky color, prolonged into infinity. All the units in this movement are further harmonized by the similar accentuation of the planes used in their modeling.

The compositional movement, a balance of centrifugal and centripetal forces, is described in general terms in the text,[42] but a number of illustrations and further details may be added here.

[42] See p. 91.

The canvas as a whole is divided horizontally into three broad planes—Cézanne's usual sandwich-arrangement—but the movement of the principal masses which extends through all three is so definitely the major theme of the design that the divisions are really only differentiations of a single continuous setting. This movement is stabilized partly by its total circular or elliptical form, but also by specific relationships which aid in keeping individual objects in equilibrium with one another. For example, the standing figure in the foreground is flanked on either side by figures so placed that they seem to diverge or withdraw from it, thus interrupting the continuous circulation of masses and imparting an added interest. The figure on the right, however, is brought back into the general in-going rhythm of the movement by the relation of its head to the canopylike tree above, which swings definitely upward and leftward; a similar office is performed for the reclining figure on the left by the relation of its arm to the curve of the small standing figure in the middle distance, which in turn is linked with the mountain and clouds. By such continuities of direction, as well as by immediate color-rhythms, relations of pattern and particular devices, the apparently simple circular arrangement of masses is transformed into a complex system of compositional relationships, the subdivisions of which are revealed by analysis to be quasi independent space-compositions in their own right. Because of this complexity any unit may be selected as focal, and the composition as a whole orientated about it. This is true of any well-organized picture by a painter of the first rank; what is distinctive here is the bizarreness of the shapes and directions of the masses as they are deployed through space, a bizarreness which lends to the effect as a whole an extraordinary, almost a unique, degree of picturesque quality.

Cézanne's relations to the general traditions of painting and to his immediate predecessors, over and above those to Courbet and Pissarro already noted, are strikingly illustrated by this picture. The space-composition is Venetian in general, and the movement and drama recall those of Tintoretto and El Greco, with Cézanne's characteristic modifications in the form of more definitely defined volumes, clear-cut spatial intervals and a plastic instead of a representational rendering of movement. The dramatic contrast of light and color in the sky, in comparison, for example, with the corresponding flash of light against a dark background in El Greco's "Mocked Christ" (244), is made more powerful by the greater weight of the masses used in conjunction with it. The space-composition has the clarity of the Florentines', or of Poussin's, though Cézanne's ruggedness, passing frequently into crudeness, and his rigidity and angularity, perceptible even when contours are actually curved, dispel any suggestion of Poussin's delicate, fluid grace and suavity. Both Cézanne's general resemblance to Michelangelo and the difference between the two are also well illustrated. The sense of power is present in the intensity of color in the sky, and in the massiveness of the volumes, and the feeling of sculpture is no less unmistakable. A more specific kinship appears in the drawing of the figure on the right, which recalls the classic feeling of some of Michelangelo's figures in "Last Judgment" (227), but Michelangelo's anatomical accentuations are replaced in all the figures here by the inherent solidity of the color itself. Moreover, the sculptural quality is not Greek but Egyptian and Negro, with much of the sheer bulk and weight, the unyielding massiveness, of the cliffs and mountains sculptured by nature itself. All these points of distinction may be made in an even greater degree with reference to Cézanne's relation to Signorelli, reminiscences of whom also appear in this picture.[43]

Cézanne's general resemblance to Carpaccio in point of definite demarcation of spatial intervals and volumes is equally demonstrable, although architectural detail is entirely absent. The abrupt contrast between masses in size, in shape and in direction of placing, characteristic of Carpaccio, occurs also in this, as in all Cézanne's work, but it is reënforced in a much higher degree than in Carpaccio by solid, structural color, and the entire form is a more closely-knit fabric of plastic relationships.[44]

What makes this picture so definitely an embodiment of Cézanne's individual form is the high degree in which the individual masses are sculpturally conceived, and the architectonic ordering of the ensemble. The central figure, for example, has the character of a caryatid supporting a great weight; and not only are the units of the composition integrally related to one another, but the interrelation recurs on several levels, with a whole set of details on one level forming a single unit in a more comprehensive synthesis. The effect is not only architectonic but monumental, not unlike that of the ruins of Glastonbury Abbey, in which the particular

[43] Compare, e.g., the figure standing in the foreground with the figures in Signorelli's "Paradise" (222).
[44] Cf., e.g., Carpaccio's "Saint Ursula Leaving her Father" (225).

masses, forceful as they are individually, exhibit their full pictorial power only when they are seen in conjunction with the earth and sky.

No picture illustrates better than this the inherent power of Cézanne's form, for in none is the inadequacy of execution to conception more painfully apparent. Not only is the pigment often clumsily handled, but the color-relations are in places so ineffective that the actual result is obviously incongruous with that intended. Solidity is secured in many of the masses by a piling up of pigment to such an extent that the surface of the canvas has almost the physical configuration of a bas-relief, and the color-relations are sometimes, as in the green portion of the landscape seen between the arm and body of the central figure, so defective that areas seem to project when they ought to recede. Similarly, in the blue area of water, between the rocky bank and the legs of the figure on the extreme right, spatial continuity is seriously compromised by defective color-relations; and again, in the meeting place between sky and mountain, in spite of the fine painting within each area, the differentiation between the two is so unsuccessful that their order in space remains confused. So overwhelming, however, is the effect of the composition as a whole that these defects are felt to be altogether trivial, incapable of detracting from the rugged power in which the epic quality of the design resides.[45]

COMBAT OF LOVE (49) of 1875-1878.[46] A feeling of active movement in the figures and other masses, and of color-drama strongly akin to Tintoretto's and El Greco's, differentiates this picture from Cézanne's other figure-compositions of the late seventies. The Tintoretto-El Greco motif—particularly noticeable in the figure of the man on the left[47]—though closely adhered to in essentials, is so harmoniously placed in and related to a Cézannesque ensemble that it becomes an organic element in Cézanne's own design.

The extremely animated movement recalls Cézanne's earlier Delacroix-esque work, but with the great difference that in "Combat of Love" the movement has passed out of the realm of illustration and into that of direct plastic activity. The technique consists

45 "Nudes" (207) is a later lithograph of the same subject-matter.
46 Illustration, p. 182.
47 Compare, e.g., the drawing of the man at the left with that of the Infant in El Greco's "Vision of St. Hyacinth" (246) and of the figures in Tintoretto's "Paradise" (236).

of parallel strokes slanting in the same direction throughout large areas, much as in a number of Cézanne figure-compositions,[48] still-lifes [49] and landscapes [50] of about the same period. The ease and freedom of the technique and the successful relationship between contour-lines and highlights obtain a convincing degree of solidity without recourse to thick lumps of paint. The success of the organization is due largely to a rhythmic balance of forceful contrasts: a basic similarity of shape occurs in practically all the main color-areas—figures, clouds, sky, foliage, and units of space; and the large masses in the setting, the clouds and trees, move backward and forward against the distant sky, in unison with the thrusts and counterthrusts of the figures. All the masses enter into a complex interplay of forces or tensions, which despite the general lack of color-luminosity gives to the picture a vivid sense of plastic drama.

COMPOTIER, GLASS, APPLES AND KNIFE (64) of c. 1877.[51] The all-over pattern of parallel oblique brushstrokes is heavy, pasty and mechanical, the color dull and leaden, and in none of the units is there an adequate fusion of light and color in the drawing. Such solidity as there is depends chiefly on thick impasto, light-and-dark color-contrasts, and heavy contour-lines of accumulated paint.

THREE APPLES (65) of c. 1877.[52] The unifying continuous weft of slanting parallel brushstrokes counteracts only in part the breaks occasioned by faulty color-relations in several areas of the painting. For example, in the apple in the foreground, the area of shadow appears disjointed from its adjacent color-area; in the color-relations between the two other pieces of fruit the contrast between the dark red and the bright yellow tends toward a disrupting clash; in all three volumes, modeling is achieved speciously by a piling up of the paint as the color reaches the highlighted area, so that this area is a series of superposed patches, and at the same time the outline, the furthest boundary of the volume, is actually sunken,

[48] E.g., "Temptation of St. Anthony" (60) ; "Leda and the Swan" (68) ; "Five Nudes" (74).
[49] E.g., "Compotier, Glass, Apples and Knife" (64) ; "Three Apples" (65) ; "Pears on Chair" (69).
[50] E.g., "Estaque" (66).
[51] Illustration, p. 191.
[52] Illustration, p. 301.

that is, physically below the level of the paint that covers the projecting part of the mass. The rendering of space is more specious than convincing: the cast shadows are sharply set off by adjacent areas of lighter color, and form a pattern of bands which extend upward and backward like lines of perspective.

PEARS ON CHAIR (69) of 1877-1882.[53] In this still-life the technique of parallel slanting brushstrokes produces an element of contrast in the surface-pattern: in the red pear, the brushwork tends to generalization in broad areas or patches which results in a smooth, unbroken, one-piece effect; in the upright pear at the top, the pattern of the constituent patches and brushstrokes is so pronounced that the resulting planes create a subsidiary compact space-composition within the modeling of the volume; in the chair, especially in the foreground, the individual brushstrokes are so contrasted in color and tone, and so pronounced in shape, that they form an accentuated pattern of small patches, in which single brushstrokes of dark color seem to be superposed, almost levitated, upon the lighter-colored ground.

On the whole, the modeling by hatchings and patches does not build up fully convincing volumes, but a measure of three-dimensional character is obtained by an accentuated dark contour-line, which in some cases is partly detached from the volume and functions more directly as an element in the general pattern than in the rendering of solidity. In the pear in the foreground, the lack of luminosity in the large area of red flattens the volume and detracts from the color-quality of the ensemble. The masses are light rather than weighty, and a sense of lightness extends to the whole composition; nevertheless the volumes and spatial intervals are distinct, and their rhythmic organization is as successful as the organization in most of Cézanne's work of this period.

FIVE NUDES (74) of the late 1870's.[54] The technique is characteristic of the period: [55] slanting brushstrokes, short, broad, flat, and individually accentuated, run parallel to each other over large areas of the canvas. They combine the effect of Cézanne's earlier technique, in which the brushstrokes are individually pronounced

[53] Illustration, p. 203.
[54] Illustration, p. 200.
[55] Cf., e.g., "Compotier, Glass, Apples and Knife" (64); "Three Apples" (65); "Fruit Dish" (67); "Pears on Chair" (69); "Red Apples" (84).

and active,[56] with that of his organization of parallel brushstrokes in small groups and patches, which he begins to use systematically in the mid-seventies.[57] As in many of his other pictures painted in the late seventies and early eighties, the brushwork forms a pronounced all-over pattern which tends to give a uniform tapestry-like texture to the entire surface, but the means employed to thus unify the contrasting areas savor of speciousness. In spite of this almost mechanical pattern of the brushwork, the masses in "Five Nudes" have the monumental solidity of volumes sculptured in high relief, and their interrelations in space are dynamic and powerful.

Much of the solidity in the figures is derived from Cézanne's adaptation of a type of drawing and modeling characteristic of Delacroix: the pattern of brushwork, which models the volume by means of distinct color-patches or bands, works in close conjunction with a similar pattern of strokes that makes up the sectioned contour, and it is rhythmically extended beyond the contour of the volume into a series of subsidiary contour-bands or area-lines. Into Delacroix's method—derived in turn from Rubens—Cézanne has injected a more concrete sense of vigor, forcefulness and power: the area-lines, bands, patches, brushstrokes, have none of the flamboyant curvilinear character of Delacroix's; their size, direction, location, color, and tone are controlled by Cézanne's design of sculpturesque masses; the strokes are more rigid; and the color is more varied with more accentuated contrasts, it is firmer and more solidly three-dimensional, and it has a much greater degree of internal luminosity.[58]

This picture is another instance of Cézanne's early realization of a fully personal form of expression. The general design, the color-scheme, the drawing, the modeling, and the technique are all basically the same as in his later work. The composition, likewise, illustrates a number of his familiar devices, such as the three-banded setting, the pyramid or tentlike formation, the accordion-pleat rhythm of the vertical masses, and the circular—hub-and-spokes—grouping of volumes in deep space. The in-and-out movement of the masses takes the form of a kind of planetary revolution around the pivotal sitting figure, and the varied in-

[56] E.g., "Man Putting on Coat" (56).
[57] E.g., "Mount Ste. Victoire and Valley" (57).
[58] Compare, e.g., the drawing of the figure seated in the center in Cézanne's "Five Nudes" (74) with that of the reclining central figure in Delacroix's "Triumph of St. Michael" (263). See details illustrated, p. 303.

clinations of the volumes give to this revolution an extraordinarily vivid intensity; with this the almost vertical, relatively continuous, screenlike background forms a striking contrast. This movement springs not only from the relations of the figures, their slant toward one another, but also from the linear directions of their subsidiary parts, and the continuation of these into the setting. The left arm and the head of the figure at the upper right, for example, lead the observer's eye in a leftward-upward direction to the line at the top of the hill, which is continued by the extended arm of the central figure, the extremity of which enters into rhythmic relations with the head, arm and hand of the figure on the left. Also, the pivotal figure is set at a lower level within the area of space established by the other four, as though in the apex of an inverted cone or funnel, and its relations to the other figures establish a version of the hub-and-spokes compositional motif. The shape of this funnel has a decided tendency to angularity, almost to squareness. As the heads of the figures—the focal units—are linked to one another, they form triangles and parallelograms in different planes which are repeated over and over throughout the compositional pattern in varying degrees of accentuation; examples of this are the total arch made by the two trees and their foliage, the shieldlike cloth surrounding the figure at the left and the slanting plane which links the heads of the figures.

The relatively uniform large green area and the mechanical pattern of brushwork are minor drawbacks, which in the best of Cézanne's later work [59] are replaced by more varied color and technique, with individual constituents of the pattern discharging more organic, varied and specific functions.[60]

FIVE NUDES (74) of the late 1870's; [61] THREE BATHERS (82) of the late 1870's; [62] MEN BATHING (164) of the late 1890's.[63] These three groups of figures with landscape-setting exemplify Cézanne's ability to use essentially the same elements in a series of compositions basically very similar in form, and to achieve in each a fully individualized organization. All of his paintings, it is true, lie within a comparatively narrow range of effects; as we have seen in the text, they are conceived in substantially the same terms whatever the subject-matter, and both the principles of order

[59] Cf., e.g., "Men Bathing" (164).
[60] See also comparative study which follows.
[61] Illustration, p. 200.
[62] Illustration, p. 199.
[63] Illustration, p. 201.

and the technical means of execution are similarly restricted; but because of the exceptionally close resemblance between these three compositions they provide a very striking illustration of Cézanne's resourcefulness and imaginative scope within his own compass.

In all three pictures the color-scheme is the familiar blue-green-ivory ensemble, with the blue and green forming the broad areas in the setting against which the ivory figures are placed. There are differences in actual shade, of course, and the color-quality, like the command of medium, is finest in "Men Bathing"; but these differences are of minor importance in the present analysis: the significant distinction is in the compositional function discharged by the color-scheme in each picture. In "Five Nudes" the main blue and green areas of the landscape tend to unite in a single upright screenlike setting immediately back of the figures, almost like the background in a bas-relief; in "Three Bathers" the parts of the setting are so distributed and interrelated that even independently of the figures the effect of deep space is strongly accentuated. In "Men Bathing" the broad areas of green and blue form planes at angles to each other, establishing an expanse of space which encloses the figures, and behind them, in the blue area of the background, conveys a sense of depth prolonged into infinity. In "Three Bathers," in contrast, the recession of space back of the figures is interrupted by volumes of foliage, with the areas of blue at the sides yielding an effect of distinctly more limited spatial depth. In addition, the means by which the space here is carried back are less those of color-quality and modulation by light than of lines of perspective formed by the trees and bushes on either side and the shadows cast by the figures in the foreground.

Another point of similarity is that in all three pictures the immediate foreground is composed of the usual directly receding horizontal plane, through which extend lines of perspective formed by cast shadows, by actual lines, or by the alignment of successive units. But in "Three Bathers" this foreground is part of a more extensive plane receding continuously to the end of a vistalike space. In "Five Nudes" the recession of the foreground is only sufficient to balance that of the upper part of the setting, made up of trees and sky, and to detach and bring forward the two figures in the foreground corners; an active agent in the process is the banded pattern of this plane. However, this foreground plane is so related to the large green area that constitutes the main portion of the background that it is primarily part of a continuous one-

piece setting embracing foreground, middleground and background
in which the combined effect of recession and rising contributes to
the accentuatedly contrasting slant of the figures. The variation
of this plan in "Three Bathers" is the continuous succession of
clean-cut spatial intervals from the foreground, between the figures, into deep distance; in "Five Nudes" these intervals are com-
pressed both laterally and in the third dimension, as they would
be with figures in an interior or with objects in a still-life. In
"Men Bathing" the receding foreground-plane is confined to a
small triangular area about the path, and its plastic function is different: by its relation to the oblique planes of the banks right and
left, it creates a cone or funnel of space in which the figures are
placed at clean-cut intervals; at the same time its horizontal position emphasizes by contrast the uprightness of the figures.

Another basic similarity in all three pictures is that the beat of
the main volumes takes place in the foreground and is predominantly vertical, but with the following variations in each version:
in "Men Bathing" the beat is made more striking by contrast with
the depth of practically unoccupied space in the background; in
"Three Bathers" the beat is continued, though in diminished degree, by the sequence of trees and bushes through the vista; in
"Five Nudes" it is relatively more spread out, but is confined in
a shallower space, almost as though the figures were part of a
frieze.

In each design, the figures and the masses in the setting are
more or less symmetrically distributed about a central focus, and
the compositional plan is based upon relations of triangles, pyramids, cones, diamond-patterns, circles, enframing-motifs, and continuities of linear direction, which are varied in the degree of
their accentuation in each picture. In "Men Bathing" the masses
are more definitely vertical, and the beats in space are formed by
a lateral sequence of elongated upright volumes, spatial intervals,
and parts of volumes; the brushstrokes in large areas are also
placed in a generally upright direction. The rhythm of this sequence is accentuated by an alternating rise and fall in the length
of the component parts, from the short one at the extreme right
to, in succession, a longer, a shorter, a longer, and a shorter, until
the series is concluded in the long tree and part of the bank
at the extreme left. Additional variation is introduced by the fact
that the shorter figures start at their base from a level higher up
in the canvas, and end at the top at a level lower down, than do

the taller figures, so that the relation of the heads to one another, and also of the feet, produces a series of triangular areas above and below, the apexes of which are alternately forward and backward in their relations to each other in space. This arrangement of masses and spatial intervals exemplifies the in-and-out rhythm of upright units which, in the text, we have termed the accordion-pleat motif.

The general scheme of composition in "Five Nudes" is similar to that in "Men Bathing" both in lateral rhythm and in rise and fall in the length of the upright units. The tree at the right extends to the very top of the picture; the next upright unit, a composite of two figures immediately left of the tree, extends further downward at the base but stops at a greater distance from the top; the third or central unit, also a composite of two figures, but prolonged at the top by small tree trunks, is again on approximately the same level as the first; and this alternation continues with the fourth unit, a single figure far to the left, and the fifth, the tree at the extreme left. But a variation in the angle at which these volumes are set appears in each picture. In "Five Nudes," those on the sides are slanted toward the center, while in "Men Bathing" the directions throughout are preponderantly vertical. The following diagram gives a schematic indication of both the resemblances and the differences between the two accordion-pleat compositional groupings.

"MEN BATHING"   "FIVE NUDES"

It will be seen that the additional stresses set up by the tilt of the figures in "Five Nudes" give to the composition a more dynamic character; on the other hand, the units in "Men Bathing" are smaller and more broken up into parts, so that the movement is more rapid or agitated, less tranquil. In "Five Nudes" the single figures are broader masses, and the repeated coalescence of two figures into a single unit of pattern produces an effect of increased simplification.

In "Three Bathers" there is again a rising and falling lateral sequence of upright volumes interlinked by lines of direction that convey an effect of perspective and introduce an accordion-pleat in-and-out movement in deep space; but a decided element of curvature in all the figures and trees makes them less definitely upright, and tends to emphasize the movement laterally and in deep space rather than up and down. The smaller number of units and their broader rendering reënforce the wide, receding expanse of open space and give to the composition its distinctive identity.

The in-and-out movement in "Three Bathers" is comparatively simple, and the organization of planes and volumes in deep space tends to be circular. The three figures in the foreground are grouped to enclose a large bowl-shaped volume of deep space, and the enclosure-motif is repeated in an arch formed by the trees, with the tree on the left duplicating and reënforcing the inward-going curve of the adjacent figure, that on the right counterbalancing the outward slant of the figure immediately in front of it. The space in this picture, unlike that in "Five Nudes," is, as we have already seen, continuous from the foreground into deep distance, and the arrangement of bushes and foliage, with the branches of the trees felt as projecting definitely inward, carries the enframing-motif to the rear as well as laterally. So constant is the repetition of this encircling motif that each of the main volumes is either enclosed in its own roughly bowl-shaped expanse of space or related to others in an enclosing volume-formation.

The enframing-motif in "Five Nudes" is formed by the sharply ascending and rigid trees at each side, which, balancing the zigzag upward movement of the figures, rise obliquely with little or no change in direction until they approach the top, where a slight inward bend appears as they join the transverse band of foliage and sky. This band balances the horizontal plane of the foreground; and the total frame so formed brings the actively moving figures into equilibrium, though in several of the enframing units there is sufficient curvilinear emphasis to impart to them a slight tendency toward the circular movement of the rest of the composition. In accordance with the general high-relief treatment, the enframing effect of the trees is predominantly lateral, with depth indicated rather than definitely rendered.

The general sense of volumes enclosing space, and space enclosing volumes, recurs in "Men Bathing" in the triangular area lying back of the central standing figure and enframed by the sitting figure on the left, by the figure at the right in the extreme rear, and by the standing central figure itself. The last is set in a kind of avenue of space, and it also determines one angle of a second triangular area of space, which extends the first in the direction of the foreground, and is bounded by the middle figure, by the figure in the extreme rear, and the large upright figure on the extreme right. Taken together, the two triangles produce the effect of a zigzag arrangement of two contiguous pyramids of space. The enclosing effect in this picture is produced by the figures themselves in relation to the shaft of space between them; it does not arise, as it does in "Five Nudes," from converging angular directions, or, as it does in "Three Bathers," from converging curves, but primarily from the contrasting directions of the main planes in which each figure is set. This contrast appears also in the other two pictures, but its part is secondary in "Three Bathers," and in "Five Nudes" it appears only as a slight modification of the generally parallel placing of the planes. Furthermore, the frame in "Men Bathing," in accordance with the general space-volume character of the design, has many breaks in continuity: there is no duplication of similar volumes right and left, for example, and the masses of foliage at the top are too ill-defined, too much like floating volumes, to form an unbroken arch. On the left a vertical band composed of part of a tree trunk and part of a bank corresponds to the tree in the other two pictures; on the right this rôle is taken by the vertical section of the bushes on the bank and the small figure close to the edge of the canvas; the upper connection across the canvas receives its archlike character largely from the accentuated color-spots made by the heads of the figures. This curving linear sequence of color-punctuations is carried down on both sides by the outlines of the figures themselves, and completed by the heads of the two partially seen figures on the right, the feet of the standing central figure, and the slanting edge of the bank at the left, so that the entire sequence becomes an oval version of the diamond-motif.

In these three pictures, in brief, Cézanne, employing much the same elements in accord with the same general principles, produces in each a distinctively individual effect. In "Three Bathers" the simple, broad, slow rhythms have a ponderous beat; in "Five Nudes" they are also heavy, but more animated, and entirely different in their disposition in space; in "Men Bathing" the movement is more complex, agitated, kaleidoscopic. Moreover, the sculptural feeling, common to all three, tends toward that of the high-relief in "Five Nudes" and of completely detached volumes in the other two; in "Men Bathing" there is an additional lightness and grace reminiscent of Phidias and Praxiteles.

HEAD OF CHOQUET (71) of 1878-1880.[64] The most striking features of this picture are the thick paint and the pronounced surface-pattern of almost square patches which model the face, hair and beard. Distortions in the drawing of the arm and hand and in the masklike face are not successful from the plastic standpoint: the face is not incorporated in the mass of the head, and between the simplified flattened arm and hand and the rest of the picture, much more solidly modeled, there is a contrast so extreme that it passes into discrepancy and conflict.

MADAME CEZANNE WITH STRIPED SKIRT (72) of c. 1878-1880.[65] Thick impasto and lumpy ridges of paint on contours reveal Cézanne's usual struggle to control his medium, but the even thickness of the paint over most of the surface and the orderly organization of the planes, which make up both the figure and the background, bear witness to a marked improvement in technical execution as well as to an individual, highly expressive integration of the plastic means. Color is more varied, of greater internal illumination, and better related than in most of his earlier work. These advances result in more expressive drawing, more solid structural modeling, and a finer general color-organization. The difference between this portrait and one of about ten years later is that the planes here are not so variedly and successfully used in the drawing, modeling and compositional organization.[66]

SELF-PORTRAIT IN FRONT OF WINDOW (80) of the late 1870's.[67] This portrait offers evidence of Cézanne's lack of mastery of his medium, and of his partial reversion to devices of his immature form. The modeling, for instance, has advanced little beyond the tricky contrast of light and dark patches characteristic of "Uncle Dominique" (5) and other paintings of the same type. The figure, likewise, with its strongly highlighted and patterned face, is spatially set off by overaccentuated contrast from the background which is dull and almost uniform in color, without internal illumination; and an additional means of differentiation, the broad

[64] Illustration, p. 195.
[65] Illustration, p. 209.
[66] Cf., e.g., "Woman with Green Hat" (103).
[67] Illustration, p. 205.

band of color with multiple parallel brushstrokes, is no less specious.

LUNCHEON IN THE OPEN (78) of the late 1870's.[68] The composition owes its appealing sense of liveliness both to the Tintorettoesque hub-and-spokes organization, and to the accentuated pattern resulting from attenuated volumes and an extensive use of small units of bare canvas in the drawing. There are also reminiscences of the *fête-galante* type of painting of Lancret, Watteau and Pater.

SELF-PORTRAIT ON PINK BACKGROUND (81) of the late 1870's.[69] The outstanding features of this portrait are the good characterization of the figure, the dominance in the color-scheme of a rosy terra cotta background patterned by broad irregularly shaped areas, the active pattern of brushstrokes which models the head, and the pervasive egg-shell quality which suggests Domenico Veneziano and Boucher. This feeling of fragility, unusual in Cézanne, occurs also in his "Self-Portrait with Palette" (88) of the early 1880's. Spatial relationships between figure and background are not entirely successful: the deep rose area to the left of the man's neck, for instance, tends to project from the rest of the setting; the color of the background in general lacks luster, and the dark and light areas by which it is patterned are neither well enough defined as planes nor ordered in receding space with sufficient distinctness to give to the setting a degree of plastic organization commensurate with that of the figure. Similar problems recur constantly in Cézanne and as a rule are more successfully solved.[70] In this picture the decorative character of the color-scheme outweighs the functioning of color-relations as compositional factors.

HILL OF LE GALET AT PONTOISE (76) of the late 1870's. The familiar Pissarro derivations are here transformed by Cézanne's characteristic pattern of numerous short brushstrokes, parallel throughout large areas and mostly slanting. The accentuated technique fails, however, to function adequately in the draw-

[68] Illustration, p. 202.
[69] Illustration, p. 204.
[70] Cf., e.g., "Woman with Green Hat" (103); "Woman and Coffee Pot" (140); "Card Players and Girl" (141); "Oranges and Bottle" (148).

ing and modeling, with the result that space-composition is blurred and confused, and plastic expression is sacrificed to the shallow effect of a lively decorative pattern. Contributing factors to this deficiency are dull colors, indifferent color-relationships, mechanically used color-scheme (greens and oranges alternate monotonously, with practically no effect of variation), and Cézanne's constantly recurring inability to coördinate color and light. The discord between color and light prevails in the entire lower third of the canvas: inadequate illumination of the greens, slate-grays and brownish tans causes them to appear leaden, and sets off in disrupting contrast the highlighted spots on the path. Better fusion of light and color establishes a relatively continuous flow of color in the upper part of the composition; but even there, a few color-patches are so inadequately illuminated that they appear as sunken holes, and the clashes of color-relationship in the lower part of the landscape remain unredeemed by any harmony in the background. The incongruity in color-quality between the upper and lower sections of the landscape thus remains unattenuated and flagrant.

RED APPLES (84) of c. 1880-1882.[71] A pervasive color-quality so delicate as to recall Renoir's, and a series of color-planes and volumes related in space with very unusual subtlety, combine to give great distinction to this picture and to place it among Cézanne's successful work. The familiar all-over pattern of parallel slanting brushstrokes unites with color to produce an unobtrusive sense of movement and life. The individual brushstrokes and their groupings, in organic conjunction with their relationships of color and tone, subdivide each volume and area into a number of color-planes; and these, without destroying the identity of the units as volumes and spatially related planes, create a subtle, uninterrupted, rhythmic, back-and-forth movement of color-units from the very front of the picture to the infinite distance in the background.

The three main areas or bands of the setting—the front of the chest, the top of the chest, and the wall above—are arranged in a steplike formation of three large planes. The horizontal-oblique central plane supports the most positive rhythms of the entire space-composition, and seems levitated above the lower vertical plane (the front of the chest) because of the unusual accentua-

[71] Illustration, p. 214.

tion, in the latter, of planes of delicate color that depict space at various depths within the plane of a single vertical area which they collectively constitute. The upper section or plane of the setting, the wall, although perhaps less obviously transformed into a space-composition of directly receding planes, is animated by the extraordinarily effective and delicate motif of space-composition created by the foliage and stem of the decorative plant. This unit, a masterstroke of compositional ingenuity, performs manifold and vital functions. Besides playing the rôle of a decorative wall-motif which echoes in the background the pattern of the fruit, chest-hasp and foreground-planes, it expands delicately into subtle three-dimensional space, and thus contributes to the pervasive delicacy of the entire space-composition; moreover, by the position and direction of its constituents in relation to the group of still-life objects and to the hasp and planes in the immediate foreground, it helps bring all the contrasting main units within the equilibrium of a pyramidal or diamond-shaped organization, and this effectively counterbalances and completes compositionally the lateral rhythms of the fruit, the plate, and the three parallel main bands of the setting.

The total form has a delicacy and floating quality pertaining more to water color than to oil painting, a characteristic which distinguishes also some of Cézanne's successful work of his late period,[72] and which is achieved intermittently throughout his career.[73]

MOUNTAINS IN PROVENCE (85) of the early 1880's.[74] Expressively and decoratively, this landscape illustrates Cézanne's enriched version of Pissarro's form: the structural quality and internal glow of color are greater, drawing is more generalized, and the accentuation of contour or shape of the color-areas gives a more lively, almost a mosaiclike, all-over pattern of contrasting patches. A rhythm of contrasting tensions in the pattern makes of the composition a swirl of angular color-areas which forecasts, in this respect, "Bibemus Quarry" (155) of 1898. In contrast to the later picture, the oblongs and squares are here less distinctly color-planes in space than contrasting color-areas in an all-over compo-

[72] E.g., "Red Earth" (111); "Pine Tree at Montbriant" (115); "Well" (174); "Rocks and Trees" (179).
[73] E.g., "Banquet Table" (50); "Interior with Nude" (83).
[74] Illustration, p. 212.

sitional pattern. The ensemble has a forceful individuality: it is alive and very appealing, even though the slate-blue on the mountain and in areas of shadow lower down in the canvas lacks the glowing luminosity of the other colors.

SPRING HOUSE (89) of c. 1882.[75] In this, as often in Cézanne, a compositional contrast-theme is strongly supported by rhythms of technique. The main units are sharply differentiated from one another in the direction of their constituent planes and brushstrokes. The areas of the general pattern tend to be rectilinear in shape, even when, as with the trees, the objects depicted have normally curving edges. The general effect of the pattern is that of an irregular checkerboard, and the prevailing squareness of the large and small areas, planes and patches is extended to the individual brushstrokes, as well as to the numerous areas of bare canvas which function as light.

The command of the medium, especially the use of color to give the effect of space, is very uneven. In the upper middle and right of the picture, the sky, which should recede, actually projects in front of the trees—a defect caused by the leaden tone of the blue; in the foreground, on the contrary, in the house, millstone and trees, the color-relations by which space is organized are highly successful.

VIEW OF ESTAQUE (101) of the middle 1880's. Pissarro's influence is here so thoroughly assimilated and transformed that it has become an integral yet subsidiary element in the Cézanne form. Most of the units display a good adjustment of color and light, and the distant mountains on the left, in particular, owe much of their delicacy, convincing reality and striking though subtle drama to a superb fusion of color and light. The heavy blue of the water, however, intrinsically weak in quality and poorly related to the other units in the ensemble, disrupts the continuity requisite to a fully satisfying and harmonious color-composition.[76]

The contrast between the area of the water and the foreground-landscape is further emphasized by the relative absence of brushstrokes in the blue area, and the greater perceptibility of their pattern in the foreground. The large expanse of blue is vaguely

[75] Illustration, p. 218.
[76] Cf. "Bay of Marseilles Seen from Estaque" (90) for similar lack of color-quality in the leaden blue of the water.

modulated by ill-defined islandlike patches not unlike the green foreground in "Mount Ste. Victoire and Valley" (57), while a considerable part of the landscape proper is executed, like the mid-distant hills and mountains in the latter picture, by individually accentuated parallel brushstrokes in compact alignment, interspersed with some spots of bare canvas. The color, however, is not nearly so rich and jewel-like as in "Mount Ste. Victoire and Valley," and the technique itself is mechanical and monotonous.

SELF-PORTRAIT WITH BOWLER HAT (99) of the middle 1880's.[77] The pigment is thick and pasty, highlights appear sunken below the level of the surface which they illuminate, and the general effect of the picture is flashy.

MADAME CEZANNE WITH STRIPED BLOUSE (98) of the middle 1880's. This is one of Cézanne's conspicuous failures to achieve an expressive personal form. Paint instead of color is felt to be the substance of the drawing and modeling, and the form as a whole has all the characteristics of a bad Courbet: literal depiction of facial expression, fiberless drawing, dry color, and painty and waxy surface. The color-contrast between the figure and the background, and the pattern of bands in the blouse, give to the picture a superficial attractiveness.

GARDANNE (92) of c. 1885.[78] The basic theme of this picture, as noted in the text, is one of movement of planes receding and rising, steplike, to a peak in the middle distance, with numerous contrasts vigorously reënforced by the brushwork. The approach to the main part of the design is the familiar directly receding foreground-plane, composed here of numerous variously modulated green and tan patches, the general boundaries of which form a series of horizontal lines or bands, placed one above the other and conveying the effect of recessive movement. The brushstrokes, horizontal on the right, vertical on the left, contribute to this movement, as does a pronounced narrow band, a wall or fence, which divides the general foreground-section into a pair of converging roughly triangular areas.[79] Starting in the middle of the

[77] Illustration, p. 208.
[78] Illustration, p. 221.
[79] Cf. Cézanne's variations upon this device in, e.g., "River and Hills" (48), "Mount Ste. Victoire and Valley" (57), "Plaza, Auvers-sur-Oise" (87), "Near Gardanne" (93), "Red Earth" (111), "Gardener" (130).

immediate foreground, this band recedes obliquely toward the left
until it meets the wall around the houses; this wall, starting at
the lower left of the picture, extends in turn to the right and backward to its point of junction, near the shed or one-story house,
with a third line formed by the confluence of this shed and the
bushes and wall on the right.

These three linear elements—fence, wall, and bushes-and-wall—
working in conjunction with the pattern of green and tan patches
and bands mentioned above, emphasize the perspective of the foreground-plane as a whole, behind which the planes, volumes, brushstrokes, and pattern of line, color, and of light and shadow, all unite
in a sharply accentuated ascending rhythm of compact and solid
plastic units. The movement upward is varied, but not fundamentally altered, by the backward slant of the roofs; the total effect
is that of a flight of stairs, which rises as a whole in spite of the
horizontal position of individual steps.

In the two large houses on the left of the composition and in
the four adjoining trees, the uprightness of the masses is accentuated by the constituent planes, pattern and technique: vertical
brushstrokes are used in practically all of these units, and vertical
oblongs are formed by the patches of light and dark in the trees,
and by the windows, doors, chimneys, and portions of walls in the
buildings.

The same vertical motif appears in the general shape of the mass
of trees on the right and in its pattern of light and dark; but the
brushstrokes in these trees, like the hills in the upper right background, are placed at a slant, and thus counterbalance the contrasting slope of the large roofs at the extreme left of the composition.
Throughout the main part of the design, especially in the ascending houses, perspective is attained partly by broad contour-lines of
color, partly by linear effects arising from the intersection of areas
or planes, and in general also by the brushstrokes themselves,
which are parallel within each area and which repeat in their direction that of the area as a whole.

In the sky the brushstrokes slant from lower left to upper right,
and thus lie directly across the predominant compositional movement in the rest of the painting; they thus further develop the
contrast-theme and at the same time stabilize the movement of the
pattern and planes. The sky as a whole, placed at an angle to the
plane of the foreground, forms with the latter a kind of horizon-

tal niche, within which lie compactly the strikingly solid, vertical, blocklike masses which make up the main motif of the design.

Two additional relationships in the technique contribute further to the ordering of the composition—that between the pattern of brushstrokes in the sky and the dramatic light-dark pattern in the trees and houses, and that between the more or less mottled color of the sky and the similarly mottled color of the foreground.

The conjoined effect of the multiple compositional rhythms leads the eye through the foreground, diagonally upward and backward to a point on the left of the center of the composition, from which point the direction shifts and passes through a series of steps, upward to the peak of the pyramid of buildings, and to the right, to the focal point of illuminated deep distance in the sky. Besides balancing this compositional movement, the rhythms create also a series of subsidiary relationships among which occur the familiar pyramidal motif and diamond formation. The composition as a whole may also be considered as a single large step, with the foreground-plane as the first tread, the wall-like mass of upright large houses, at the left, and wall and trees, at the right, as the riser, and the roofs of the central group of houses, in which perspective is accentuated, the second tread.

The execution is extremely uneven. In the trees, for example, especially the two on the left, the highlighted and the darkest areas are practically juxtaposed without any tonal transition between the two; the result is that light appears overaccentuated and in consequence relatively isolated, much in the manner of the melodramatic light-shadow effects of Cézanne's early period.[80]

The quality of the color varies widely in different areas. In the sky, especially at the left, it is decidedly poor, not exactly leaden but certainly opaque; in the right one-third of the picture, however, from the foreground-wall and -bushes to the top, it is superbly used to exercise all its plastic functions, even though around the triangular roof below the large trees, the attainment of space is too obviously dependent on accentuated contour-line. The picture is a good example of a condition frequently encountered in Cézanne's mature work: in the same painting, superbly rendered parts coexist with gross defects of color and execution, and yet the form as a whole is expressive of a power and strength seldom found in the more evenly balanced work of other artists of the first rank.

[80] Cf., e.g., "Plate with Grapes and Peach" (58).

BLUE VASE (94) of c. 1885-1887. Color, on the whole, is bright and appealing in its relationships, but the surface is waxy and the drawing literal rather than expressive. The flowers are not much more than a colorful version of a Corot-Manet form, and the plate is perhaps the most successful unit in the picture.

SUGAR BOWL, PITCHER AND FRUIT (117) of the late 1880's.[81] The bright, internally illuminated colors add much to the bizarre composition of picturesquely related, sharply contrasting vertical, horizontal and oblique units. The long lateral extension of the vertical front-plane of the table, and the deep-blue band extending diagonally across the upper part of the picture, are brought into equilibrium by the contrasting vertical positions of the sugar bowl, the milk pitcher and the table pedestal at the upper right. This compositional rhythm of contrasts in the main objects is echoed, with variations in color, size and degree of emphasis, in the pieces of fruit and in the patterning of the folds of the table cloth. The color is adequately structural, the pigment is thin and relatively smooth in texture, and the picture as a whole is a fine and typical instance of Cézanne's mature expression, realized delicately instead of in the more familiar ponderous form.

PINE TREE AT MONTBRIANT (115) of the late 1880's, HOUSE AT BELLEVUE (126) of c. 1890-1892, VIADUCT (152) of the middle 1890's, and MOUNT STE. VICTOIRE WITH TWO HOUSES (183) of the early 1900's, are all supreme triumphs of landscape-rendering, each with its own distinctive character of expression and style of technical execution. The color in each is well lighted and the contrasts are harmoniously blended.

"Pine Tree at Montbriant" (115) is remarkable in several of its characteristics:[82] its pervasive lightness and delicacy, which takes the form of a very unusual lacy quality in the striated sketchily drawn trees; its successfully functional use of bare canvas; and its subtle rendering of deep space reminiscent of Perugino in the relations of the small lacy trees. The flood of sunlight, the thin impasto and the many small areas of bare canvas that function as color, space, line, and light, and even take the shape of long brushstrokes, impart a pronounced water-color effect to the whole

[81] Illustration, p. 222.
[82] Illustration, p. 240.

painting. The large foreground-tree emphasizes, by its definite location, the space receding through its striated area of foliage and
expanding on the left in a contrasting, vast, unobstructed vista
of distant landscape, relatively unpatterned by individual brushstrokes. The lightness and delicacy are reminiscent of Renoir.

In "House at Bellevue" (126),[83] superb color functions effectively both in the construction of masses and in the rendering of
space. The objects, however, function more as planes than as
masses, and the general character of the painting is that of a
water color, with even less solidity than Cézanne gets in his best
aquarelles. The composition is of the sandwich-type, and the
bright orange and green foreground is relatively uniform and quiet.
The middleground is highly animated by contrasts in the size,
shape and direction of its constituents; its light-green trees are
rendered in broad planes, with few scalloping contour-lines and
much bare canvas functioning as light between the clumps of
cloudlike masses of foliage. The background of white houses is
again relatively uniform, but in the sky the pattern of brushstrokes, small patches and spots of bare canvas echoes the movement of the middleground.

"Viaduct" (152) [84] is highly patterned with patches of rather
broad brushstrokes, and its impasto is heavy. While color is, in
general, extraordinarily juicy, some of the areas in the trees and
in the mountain lack adequate internal illumination and appear to
sink in. The space-composition is of a type familiar in Cézanne:
one side of the picture conveys essentially the feeling of deep distance, while the other consists of series of compact planes with
subtle indication of space-intervals. The composition resembles
that in Cézanne's "Well" (174) [85] especially in the screenlike use
of foreground-objects and the contrast between dense masses of
foliage and broad units of space, but the spacing in "Viaduct" is
not quite so subtle nor so completely successful.

"Mount Ste. Victoire with Two Houses" (183) [86] is flooded
with sunlight, and its exceptionally bright and effulgent color-
ensemble, which approaches the richness of autumn foliage, conveys a vivid sense of the atmosphere of the *Midi*. A feeling of
delicacy pervades the entire picture: it is lightly painted, with

[83] Illustration, p. 280.
[84] Illustration, p. 261.
[85] Cf. also Cézanne's "House and Wall" (147).
[86] Illustration, p. 282.

thin even pigment and much bare canvas functioning as color and light; the trees are drawn as broadly generalized color-masses; linear contours around trees and mountains are considerably broken in continuity. Technique is unobtrusive, and so also is the pattern of patches: the color-areas are loosely divided, and within each patch of brushstrokes the color shows only minor variations. The only instance of pronounced technique appears in the use of the sharp-edged quill-motif. The gentle swirl of the masses and the pervasively delicate blending of color and light in the series of loose Chinese-like islands give to the color-areas a floating rather than sharp quality, and result in a degree of delicacy unusual for Cézanne.

WOMAN WITH GREEN HAT (103) of 1888.[87] The general form of this picture and the qualities which establish its outstanding position in Cézanne's work are set forth in the text;[88] the present discussion will be concerned with a more detailed account of the employment of the plastic means.

The dominant blue-gray of the color-scheme is subtly and attractively varied by the pinks, greens and tans in the flesh and the unusual purplish-brown in the chair and in the band on the wall. The contrasts are unified by several means: by rhythmic echoes, in each area, of the color which gives the keynote to adjacent areas; by similarity in internal patterns, either of light or brushstrokes; and by resemblances in the shapes of areas as a whole. The bands of the chair-frame, for example, are in general contour duplicated by the more or less bandlike pattern of light and shade in the greenish upholstery of the chair, as well as by various similarly shaped areas in the sleeve, waist and wall. The most important agent in the unity, however, is the pervasively high quality of the contrasting colors themselves, and their organic fusion with light. The integration of color and light is perfect throughout the canvas, and the variations in the degree of light are so precisely correlated with the compositional importance of the areas illuminated that the coördination yields pronounced and convincing drama; that is, the most vivid and glowing color is found in the focal points of the design—the hands and face—and it lends to these units a striking effect of depth, richness and power.

A peculiar adaptation of sunken light appears in the hat: two

[87] Illustration, p. 230.
[88] See pp. 82-85.

patches of light placed on the front of the brim give to it an internal composition of rhythmic planes, which duplicate some of the planes on the lap, and also suggest the volume of the head underneath the hat.

The fusion of color and technique, so organic that technique has gone into solution and appears as a distinguishable element only if explicitly sought out, is attested by the fact that contrasts in pattern are felt primarily as contrasts not of shape but of color and light. Even with the highly patterned hands and lap, the plastic purpose involved in the accentuation is establishment of a contrast with the more evenly painted areas, and in this contrast the color-and-light relationships are fundamental. When deliberately isolated for separate examination, the pattern of the technique throughout the picture reveals as many constituent elements as that in any other Cézanne, but no mechanical repetition of similarly shaped units; its distinction is that it is richer, more varied, subtle and continuous than in any of Cézanne's other portraits. The variety of the technique is shown by the adaptation to figure-painting, especially in the face, of brushstrokes akin to the hatchings employed in landscapes, but adjusted with perfect precision to the specific characteristics of features and flesh. So also with the typical Cézannesque modification of the Hals-Manet technique in the drawing and modeling of the head: it renders both the sculpturesque and the masklike traits found singly in "Provence Peasant" (151) and "Woman with Shawl" (118); and the fusion of technique with a color more structural than in either of the other pictures makes of the head a solid volume of overwhelming reality.

The torso shares with that in "Woman with Shawl" a quivering pattern of brushstrokes, color-modulations and sunken light. In "Woman with Shawl" the function of this pattern is primarily to render the textural surface-quality, with solidity adequate but secondary; in the present picture it is the solidity that is emphasized, and the pattern, so generalized as to preclude any precise realistic representation, is subsidiary to a broad organization of planes that give to the body the effect of a massive column of stone.

The main planes of the figure are five in number: the first includes the hat and face; the second extends from the shoulders over the chest; the third recedes from that line to the waist; the fourth includes the lap; and the four together embrace the front of the figure. The fifth main plane, corresponding to the deep-blue shadow between the woman's left arm and her chest, gives three-dimensional extension to the side of the body, as the other three do to the front. Both the boundaries of these planes and the sequence of elements within them give rise to lines of perspective, by which the spatial relations are compositionally ordered. The folds of the bodice, for example, form a subsidiary space-composition of planes at the same time that their color and pattern build up the solid mass of the torso itself; in this the folds play a part similar to that of the corresponding details in "Provence Peasant" (151), but because of the greater structural quality of the color in "Woman with Green Hat" they do so much more effectively, conveying a sense of the underlying substance which is scarcely felt in the other picture.

The book in "Provence Peasant" and the lap in "Woman with Green Hat" alike serve as a receding horizontal plane which throws into stronger relief the contrasting movement of masses, but the book is a comparatively facile and obvious device, not nearly so well integrated with the rest of the figure in a continuous dynamic sequence as is the lap in "Woman with Green Hat." In both pictures, the placing of the figure at such an angle to the background that it both projects from it and slants to one side also adds to the drama, but the relation of vertical, horizontal and oblique directions is more subtly achieved in "Woman with Green Hat." Indeed, it is only after a point-by-point comparison with "Provence Peasant," itself one of Cézanne's very important plastic achievements, that the superlative quality of "Woman with Green Hat" becomes fully apparent.

In the vertical in-and-out movement of the composition, an important part is played by the position of the planes of the hands in relation to the direction of the planes constituting the body, and also by the slight tilt of the head and hat which gives to the movement an additional picturesque zigzag effect. At right angles to this rising in-and-out rhythm, extends a transverse movement passing from the plane of the wall at the left, forward and at an angle to this wall, to the shoulders and upper part of the torso, thence at another angle through the plane of the chair, and finally back to the plane of the wall at the right.

The zigzag character of the rhythms throughout the figure is largely due to the linear pattern, which is angular and rigid, but so completely subordinated that it is the effect, never the means, which impresses the observer. Indeed, the integration of line in the total form is as complete as that of the technique in general. Line, used as an actual narrow or broad band of color, light or shadow, to model and give spatial position, is everywhere an integral part of the object itself, even when, as along the inside contour of the woman's right arm, a narrow strip of the lighter color of the background can be seen between the line of contour itself and the object to which it belongs. This contour-band, in addition to playing its part in drawing and modeling, enters, together with the parallel color-bands of light and shadow on the arm, into a network of linear connections which, like the tentacles of an octopus, intertwine and interweave the figure, chair and background into a comprehensive compositional rhythmic structure in deep space. The line of shadow around the chin, compared with that in "Provence Peasant" (151), is part of the chin, of the neck and of the intervening space as well; not, as in the other picture, a comparatively superposed means of separation.

The upper outer contour of the right arm is distinguished from the background by a line of light which has, on a smaller scale, the same function as the accentuated light back of the head in "Woman with Shawl" (118), but it is not emphasized to the point of overaccentuation, and its integration in the general light-pattern prevents it from being felt as factitious. This light-pattern, used in conjunction with strips of color, extends along the folds of material within the bodice and skirt and along the contour and internal pattern of the other arm; it is active through the upholstery and frame of the chair, and is prolonged, with gradual diminution, to the pattern in the background made up of slanting bands of modulated color. The function of these lines and strips of light varies from area to area: they set off the woman's right shoulder from the background; they assist in converting the folds of the bodice into planes in the space-composition; they contribute to the modeling of the chair; and they are an additional means of differentiating the subtly moving bandlike planes in the background.

The compositional use of line is also highly varied. Broad streaks in the lap at the right repeat the pattern made by the thumb and index finger; they also, in conjunction with the shadow outlining the hands on the left and continued by the line of the cuff and the line at the waist, make of the lap a roughly circular, platelike horizontal-oblique plane upon which the hands rest like the objects in a still-life. This entire unit balances that constituted by the brim and crown of the hat. The hands themselves are united with the

arms and face in one of Cézanne's characteristic diamond-forma-
tions, which is made more definite by repetition of the focal light
in the hands and face. The bend of the elbows emphasizes the projecting position of the body as a whole, and the relation of the
woman's arms to the arms of the chair further accentuates the
general in-and-out movement, forming at the same time an additional undulating movement of elongated volumes. Both the body
as a whole and the chair as a whole actively participate in other
ways also in the general compositional movement. On the right,
the outer side of the chair roughly parallels the plane of shadow
between the chest and left arm; the plane of the back of the chair
is tilted at a slight angle to the direction of the shoulders; the distorted front part of the arm of the chair at the left projects forward toward the right. This boxlike chair, in brief, repeats in the
direction of its parts and in its various aspects the units of the
figure which it encloses.

The background is treated in Cézanne's usual manner, but with
many variations in detail. Its general function is to set off the foreground by contrast, but it also contains elements of contrast within
itself, and these are successfully harmonized. Each of the two
sides of the background is a plane, one of which is slightly to the
rear of the other; both are executed in a pattern of brushwork
of substantially identical color, though with differences of tone to
which the brushwork lends a quivering effect. The community of
color-quality, color-modulations and quiver of pattern unifies the
two sides, as do also the set of slanting bands and areas which,
paralleling the slant of the figure, move across the canvas and are
brought into equilibrium by contrasting horizontal bands in the
background and the quasi vertical partition in the wall.

The unification of the figure with the background as a whole is
also accomplished by Cézanne's characteristic means. The general
outline of the hat, head and shoulders is duplicated by a bandlike
color-motif which links the planes of the head with those in the
solid mass of the wall; but the linkage, unlike that in "Woman
with Shawl" (118), is unobtrusive and really effective. Many of
the general lines or directions of the parts of the figure are carried
over into the setting: the lower outline of the right forearm, for
example, is continued into the background at the left by a series of
changes of tone in that part of the setting that create an upward
receding linear effect, above which the alignment of broad, sharp-
edged quill-patches carries the linear slant upward to the right;

on the portion of the wall at the right a subtle series of color-modulations in the form of planes, bands and lines bridge the gap between hat and chair without sacrificing the identity of the intervening space.

The use of space also follows Cézanne's familiar methods. A well-defined unit of space immediately back of the head sets off and accentuates the voluminousness of the head itself. Conversion of the solid mass of the background-wall into a movement of planes and quasi volumes, one of Cézanne's habitual practices, shows the same precise subordination of means to designed end. Solidity and depth of space are at their maximum in the figure itself, from which they decrease continuously as the compositional movement proceeds outward, and at each point the pattern of planes and volumes has exactly the degree of emphasis required by its place in the diminuendo as a whole. Each color-unit retains its individual identity as a part of the solid chair and wall, but none is ever so emphatic as to attract independent attention to itself and enter into competition with the figure. The sculptural quality, the strength, the color-power of the figure are thus, in appropriate manner and degree, communicated to every part of the entire composition. In perhaps no other of his pictures are all the means so perfectly coördinated to obtain a form fully expressive of qualities unique to Cézanne.

MARDI-GRAS (106) of c. 1888-1890.[89] The first impression of strength is dissipated by analysis of the means by which the effect is obtained: indeed, the great reputation of this picture testifies only to the commonness of the confusion between striking effect and intrinsic plastic strength. The color is leaden, and the ubiquitous grainy contours are the mark of Cézanne's failure, after repeated efforts, to obtain the relationships of color and tone necessary for proper spacing of planes and masses. This is conspicuously apparent in the harlequin's right arm, badly differentiated from the background: thick layers of paint in the area between the arm and the body form a mass of pigment projecting beyond the level of the adjacent colors. In the drapery at the upper right, the thick grainy contour similarly fails to establish the necessary spatial distinction between the drapery itself and the wall back of it.

The picture abounds in specious devices: the contour-band, for

89 Illustration, p. 239.

example, or area of light around the figure of the harlequin, by which space is achieved there, is so accentuated that it falls into the category of illegitimate tricks. Moreover, devices characteristic of Cézanne's best work are rendered ineffective by labored execution; instances of this are the pattern of angular patches of contrasting color on the floor, and the contrasting color-areas in the modeling of the faces and rendering of texture in the garments and draperies. The net result of these shortcomings is that the illustrative motif of the subject-matter lacks adequate plastic integration: it is overemphasized and relatively dissociated from the means of execution. In short, Cézanne's drawing, modeling and pattern are here scarcely more than a formula put at the service of illustration and narrative.

HARLEQUIN (105) of c. 1888-1890.[90] In this, in antithesis to "Mardi-Gras" (106), illustration is perfectly merged in a plastic form of the highest order, approaching the best achievements of Cézanne's career. It resembles "Woman with Green Hat" (103) closely in general color-effect, in patterning of the background by unaccentuated patches of brushstrokes, in the execution of the textiles, and in the pervasively organic merging of color with light and of technique with form. The impasto is slightly heavier than in "Woman with Green Hat," the modeling of the face by planes of color is perhaps not quite so subtle, and there is greater reliance upon an area of light around the figure to set it in space. Strange distortions of the face—pointed chin, muzzlelike jowl, absence of mouth—do not compromise the value of the design as a delineation of essential character, since every unit of the picture, like the form as a whole, is an organic fusion of significant plastic factors. The outstanding feature of the drawing is the grace and wonderful poised movement of the figure—a very rare if not unique achievement for Cézanne. In drawing, expression and general feeling Picasso's "harlequin" series very likely owe much to this picture and also to "Mardi-Gras" (106).[91]

BRIDGE AT CRETEIL (104) of c. 1888-1890.[92] The photographic realism of this landscape—for example, the practically lit-

[90] Illustration, p. 236.
[91] Picasso's "Harlequins" (352) is a more successful plastic illustration than "Mardi-Gras" (106). Compared with Cézanne's "Harlequin" (105), the Picasso contains a different set of plastic and traditional values, but is incomparably inferior in vigor and power.
[92] Illustration, p. 197.

eral reflections in the water—and the specious contrasts of light and dark mark this painting as one of Cézanne's numerous attempts to paint a Salon picture. It shows both how much better a painter he was than the official exhibitors, and also how banal it was possible for him to be.

VALLEY OF THE ARC (109) of 1888-1892.[93] The essential feature of this picture, which represents Cézanne's landscape-painting at its best, is a powerful rhythmic movement of color-volumes and -planes which carries the eye from the immediate foreground to the distant background, interpenetrates in all directions, and comes to rest in compositional equilibrium. The rhythm is slight in the foreground-bushes; it increases in size, power and degree of voluminousness in the pyramidal group of trees and houses immediately back of the bushes; it then diminishes in intensity as it passes through a relatively flat, directly receding plane in the middleground, which is patterned by color, light and line, and punctuated at irregular intervals by small upright color-masses; it rolls on backward and upward in the volumes of the foothills, gathers greater power and weight in the larger mountains, and reaches a climax in the mountain peak. The vaguely mottled area of sky behind this mountain peak acts as a foil to emphasize and set off the complex symphony of rhythms.

The composite series of these rhythms holds the attention by variety in color, illumination, linear definition, size, shape, position, degree of massiveness, and solidity of the constituent units, a variety which heightens their decorative, expressive and compositional effectiveness. All the plastic factors participate in this movement, and the interrelated and piled-up rhythms are comparable to those in a Bach fugue, but the components are even more complex and varied.

The space itself is variedly rhythmic because of differences in size of the intervals between the various masses and planes. The perspective is so merged with color that it cannot be separated from it; indeed, color gives to the perspective its compelling charm. With all the activity of space and perspective, there is no over-accentuation: the distance, the spaciousness, that attend the grandeur and majesty of nature are fittingly rendered.

The general mass-composition tends toward a bilaterally sym-

[93] Illustrations, p. 228 and p. 293.

metrical distribution around central units. The clump of trees and houses in the foreground, for instance, functions as a central mass, and the bilaterally balanced units on each side consist of a comparatively flat receding plane and a large expanse of space, which set off the group of trees and houses as a large central pyramidal organization of masses in space. From this pyramid, the eye is carried upward and backward to the peak of the mountain in the background. Between the foreground-pyramid and the mass of the mountain, are a number of focal points with elements to the right and to the left which achieve symmetrical balance. In no case is there an exact duplication of units: each is so varied from the other that a picturesque variety results.

The modeling, done by Cézanne's usual hatchings of color-modulations animated by light, imparts a convincing feeling of three-dimensional solidity to the individual color-patches which build up the masses and create within each a rhythmic series of compact planes.

This picture shows that Cézanne was an impressionist to the extent that he made light one of his chief motifs and an integrating factor in his composition. All parts of the canvas are bathed in light, and the pattern made by the light is complex, infinitely varied, harmoniously related to the other factors, and a powerful reënforcement of the rhythm of color-chords that unifies the whole organization. Wherever the eye rests, the canvas is of compelling interest because of the organic fusion of the plastic means.

POORHOUSE ON THE HILL (110) of 1888-1894. The drawing of the masses of foliage is of the type illustrated at its best in "Well" (174): a continuous pattern of patches establishes the location of the individual units and builds up the composite dense volumes of foliage. The alignment of the brushstrokes at the boundaries or junction of the individual patches has a crenelated effect which is accentuated by the presence of irregular small areas or spots of bare canvas, so that the junction of the color-patches appears more ragged and the color-pattern is less flowingly continuous than in "Well." This picture illustrates also Cézanne's characteristic use of a short slightly curvilinear line, superposed on the edge of the mass of foliage, accentuating, as it were, its last plane, and emphasizing its curvilinear mass by the scalloped character of this line. This scalloped edge is also to be noted in Cézanne's "Mount Ste. Victoire and Viaduct" (95) hanging in the same museum.

RED EARTH (111), of 1889-1890,[94] presents one of Cézanne's most successful uses of color decoratively, expressively and compositionally, and, as an individual synthesis of the plastic means, it ranks with his achievements of the first order. The familiar characteristics and devices are present—the blue, orange and green color-scheme; the three-banded framework with the central area the most compact and complex; the hub-and-spokes rhythms; the compositional triangles and pyramids; the linear perspective; the color-planes in step-formation; the functional bare canvas; the thrust and counterthrust of linear directions; and the usual varied organization of the technique in patches, strips, areas and planes of parallel brushstrokes which contribute so much to the constructive rhythms and contrasts of the main component areas, and to the dynamic character of the form as a whole. Subtlety in the relationship of these constituents, together with a particular ingenuity of variation and a pervasively successful use of color, gives a rare esthetic content to the essential feeling, the inherent quality, of the particular landscape. Its richly decorative form offers a degree of sensuous appeal uncommon in Cézanne.

The foreground is a large plane composed of ill-defined mottled areas of generally horizontal and parallel brushstrokes interspersed with spots of tinted bare canvas which sparkle between the painted units and give the effect of light. A line of brushstrokes divides the foreground into two roughly triangular areas, one prevailingly orange, the other green. This linear arrangement extends upward and leftward and, together with the sequence of patches of color and light in the orange and green areas, it gives perspective to the foreground-plane as a whole. A similar function is discharged by the unit of wall, bushes and green band, which recedes diagonally from left to right, meets the line of brushstrokes near the mound on the left of the center, and sweeps along in a slightly curving direction to the extreme right. The relationships between this composite wall-unit and the transverse line of brushstrokes above noted constitute the outstanding elements in a hub-and-spokes compositional pattern in the foreground, in which the mound corresponds to the hub. The alignment of the brushstrokes and patches also contributes to this pattern.

[94] Illustrations, p. 229 and p. 299.

In the middleground the brushstrokes are predominantly vertical, smaller and individually more accentuated than in the foreground. Individual accentuated light and dark patches form a succession of receding vertical planes which convey the vague impression of a riser between two steps. This rhythm is diversified by variations from volume to volume in size, color, tone, pattern, direction, and degree of solidity, with the variations so subtly adjusted to one another that the general effect of a mounting recession is carried on systematically.

The grouping of the brushwork in this middleground is appropriately adapted to bring out the distinctive direction of the pattern in each area—horizontal in some of the linear boundaries of planes and in portions of ground on the hill at the upper left; vertical in some of the houses and most of the trees; and diagonal in the roofs and some of the masses of foliage. The vertical strokes frequently overlap and are grouped to make a contrasting pattern of undulating horizontal color-strips; the diagonal elements are definitely lines of color in the roofs, individual brushstrokes and linear sequences of parallel brushstrokes in the foliage; and the varied sets of linear directions are placed at such angles to one another as to establish a balance in the linear pattern. Since these lines and brushstrokes are integral parts of the drawing and modeling of the volumes, the linear balance assumes also the character of compositional thrust and counterthrust. This dynamic movement is very active throughout the entire area of the middleground, and its effect remains rectilinear even when, as in the trees and bushes, some curvature of contour is unavoidable. This linear emphasis, as usual, contributes to the attainment of perspective.

The same purpose is served by the shape of some of the horizontal strips of vertical brushstrokes which taper off at one of their extremities and thus produce an in-and-out movement winding obliquely through the masses and compositional intervals. The perspective of the picture as a whole is outlined by the relation of the curved contour of the mountain at the upper left, the large tree at the upper right, and the foreground-lines of brushstrokes and wall mentioned above; these factors work together to delimit the landscape both right and left, and far and near, and carry the eye to the distant focus. The general compositional movement is further emphasized by the placing of the brushstrokes in the areas in question: those in the mountain are generally parallel to its horizontal curve, those in the counterbalancing tree slant from upper right to lower left, and corresponding adjustments of technique to direction of placing occur in the two foreground-units. Upon this foundation of pattern, Cézanne establishes a general balance of thrusts and counterthrusts, embracing lines, planes and masses, which brings the entire composition into stability.

The treatment of the sky works harmoniously with that in the rest of the picture. The planes and brushstrokes in its relatively uniform color-area echo with contrasts the very active movement just below, though naturally with less varied color, less solid volumes, less clearly defined spatial intervals, and less perceptible technique. The brushwork is oblique in the main, with a small number of vertical strokes, and the tonal modulations and boundaries of areas are sufficiently definite to establish a series of receding planes which define the clouds and their spatial setting. The color-contrasts arising from extensive admixture of light in the large expanse of blue heighten the movement given to the sky by the position of the planes and placing of the brushstrokes; and the effect of recession in the whole sky is also reënforced by a continuous increase in illumination as the eye passes backward toward the horizon. Much of the pattern and flow of light throughout the sky arises from the tone and color of the canvas left entirely bare of paint in certain areas and only thinly covered in others. The area of the sky in its entirety thus enters into rhythmic relationship with the area of the foreground, which it balances in a different color; and the two together constitute the sandwichlike enframing of the multicolored middleground. All three areas, the foreground, middleground and background, are brought into a single harmonious unity by rhythmic duplication, in varying degree of accentuation, of the lines, planes, spatial intervals, and the pattern of color, light and shadow.

The unusual fluidity of color characteristic of this landscape has its source not only in the translucency and relatively even distribution of the pigment itself, and the subtle relationships between individual colors, between color and light and between light and dark, but also in the technique. The brushstrokes, patches and undulating strips pass more gradually into one another than is usual in Cézanne, and through most of the middle area of the picture the individual brushstrokes show a tendency to subdivision into two parallel areas made up of different tones of the predominant color. The color-transitions, thus made more numerous and less sharp, together with the general softening of contour, make possible an unusual effect of fluid color-suffusion. The luscious translucent color, in conjunction with the unobtrusive pattern, imparts to the solid and real landscape the feeling of richness, mellowness and general decorative quality that one associates with fine old oriental rugs. The color-suffusion, while very appealing in itself and enhancing the color-organization, is not so varied in its plastic functions, in its decorative aspects, or in its technical and plastic constituents as are the corresponding effects in a typical late Renoir. For Cézanne, however, the degree of internal glow in the color and of decorative charm in the ensemble are unusually high in this picture. The painting reveals a finer control of medium, a firmer integration of the pattern in the total form and less reliance upon a quasi mechanical use of technique than are to be found in most of his work.

SELF-PORTRAIT ON BLUE BACKGROUND (108), of 1888-1892,[95] a very powerful portrait, one of Cézanne's best, compares with the most successful characterizations of Titian, Tintoretto, El Greco, and Rembrandt, and is realized by a legitimate use of the plastic means. The figure is alive, the volumes are solid and real, the drawing is neither stiff nor rigid, and the modeling is done without obvious recourse to sharp contrasts or to blocks and facets. The constructive planes and volumes, like the entire figure, are much less angular, more fluid than is usual in Cézanne; there are no sharp contour-lines, and scarcely any evidence of difficulty in the placing of volumes in space.

The very simple composition consists of two interlocking pyramids—the upright forward-projecting mass of the figure, and the inverted triangle of receding space in the background.

An outstanding characteristic of the technique is that the patches have no definite outline and the resulting color-modulations produce a marked, though subtle, mottling of the surface-pattern, much in the manner of "Woman with Shawl" (118). This color-and-light mottling varies in degree of accentuation; it is most pronounced in the painting of the coat, but extends to all areas of the picture and plays no little part in its unification. The painting is "smooth," in the figurative sense, but not "slick": nothing is confused, nothing is tricky; it represents the modern apotheosis of the form of Tintoretto as embodied in his best portraits.

[95] Illustration, p. 252.

WOMAN WITH SHAWL (118) of the late 1880's.[96] The figure is strong and clear-cut, and there is no fumbling or incoherent use of means to come between the observer and the design itself. This is due both to the intrinsic quality of the plastic elements, especially the color, and to their relationship. Not only is the color satisfying sensuously, but adequate illumination makes it rich and deep. The interaction of the color of the shawl, face and hair enhances both the individuality and the collective activity of these units. From the glowing deep-blue and the quivering pattern of light, the shawl acquires its actual quality of fabric as well as its general aliveness; the delicate, fluid set of colors, of somewhat pastel or water-color character, which make up the hands, form a bizarre green-blue-pink-lavender color-unit which communicates to the hands its own fluidity and grace. Similar pastel-like tones are arranged in the face in a pattern of small angular areas, mosaiclike, in which the accents of eyes and nose are important focal elements. The subtlety of color-relations in this pattern, especially on the left side, links it with the treatment of the hands, and also of the shawl, which has less of Cézanne's characteristic angularity and rigidity and more grace than is usual in his pictures. In spite of elements of contrast in color, tone and light-pattern, the hair is of the same fluid character. Each part of the figure, in short, while retaining its distinctive quality, is united in an integral whole with all the other parts, a whole made dramatic by striking contrasts between light and dark tones. Convincing color, decorative appeal and fulness of expression reënforce one another in an ensemble in which the drama of contrasts remains subtle and restrained.

The figure is compositionally a pyramid, within which the constituent units are thoroughly stabilized. In addition to the generally harmonious use of color, light and shadow already noted, the planes and volumes are coördinated in an active plastic movement, in which contrast is everywhere present but never strident. The oval shape of the head, slightly tilted from the vertical, reappears with modifications in the horizontal-oblique slope of the upper part of the chest, in each of the two converging ovoid areas between shoulders and waist, in each of the arms and hands, in several parts of the brown dress, and in the portions of the blue shawl below the waist. These areas, interrelated in color as well as shape and placing, form both a tridimensional pattern and a subtle unit of

[96] Illustration, p. 231.

volumes and planes in deep space; in their entirety they constitute a hub-and-spokes- or rosette-motif, which radiates from about the woman's left wrist.

The quality of the painting deteriorates in the background as a result of generally inferior coördination between the constituents of the color-pattern. Up to the horizontal-oblique line dividing the setting into two parts, the blurred color-areas are sensuously appealing but the means employed to establish continuity with the figure—color-pattern, the colors themselves, quivering units of light, and shapes of the color-planes—fail to establish a coherent totality. An example of this deficiency is to be found in the set of linear directions which are carried over from the figure into the background, and are executed partly by sequences of brushstrokes or quills, partly by the light-pattern, partly by changes of tone. Some of these factors in the lower portion of the picture form an inverted triangle, much like those common in Cézanne's still-lifes, which is united with the upright pyramid in a comprehensive organizing diamond-pattern. This inverted triangle has its apex in the lighted tan area below the woman's right hand; it parallels on a different plane the V-shaped area of the shawl from shoulders to waist, and forms a compositional counterpoise to the upright pyramid of the figure as a whole. Subsidiary triangles appear in the color-areas of the background adjacent to the elbows, and these repeat in general shape the right and left shoulders. The triangles and pyramids in the figure are clean-cut, well defined and an integral part of the volumes and textures; the paralleling and counterbalancing triangles just noted in the linking of figure and setting are so diffuse that close inspection is required for their discovery, and the parts which lie in the background proper are loosely organized. Because of their vagueness these units fail to supply the compositional balance that the general pyramidal organization requires.

The part of the background above the dividing line is subdivided into an almost uniformly painted screenlike area on the right, and an area broken up by variations in color, light, pattern, and degree of spatial recession, on the left. The first area is leaden and opaque in color, and some of this leaden quality appears also on the other side, especially in the gray-blue tones in the lower part. The large expanse of dull and monotonous color does make a contrast with the luminous hues and vigorous drawing of the figure, but the discordant quality converts contrast into conflict and gravely impairs plastic unity. The area on the left, though it too suffers from the infusion of leaden tone, preserves more of the effective organization characterizing the figure. The imperfectly integrated area of light above and immediately to the left of the head further compromises the quality of the background as a whole; and the linear extension of that light is no less inadequately fused in the total form, even though it is compositionally useful in the rhythmic repetition of the contour of the head, accentuating its tilt and contributing to the general movement of planes which extends through the figure and out into the setting. Notwithstanding the defects noted, the excellence of the figure proper is sufficient to establish the picture as a fine example of Cézanne's portraiture.

GERANIUM AND APPLES (121), of c. 1890, is another instance of the frequent failure of Cézanne's planes and color-contrasts to carry space backward toward infinity. The pervasive waxy surface of the paint is, in great part, responsible for the inferior quality of color.

MOUNT STE. VICTOIRE WITH PINE TREE (124) of c. 1890.[97] The upright pyramid of the mountain in the background, with its apex decentered toward the right, is counterbalanced by the V-shaped opening of the bushes in the foreground, the apex of which is decentered toward the left; the familiar diamond so formed merges with the screenlike foreground-planes of bushes and trees to emphasize both the recession of space and the vista of distant landscape. The entire composition is fluid. Spatial relationships are well handled throughout, especially in the sequence of small volumes which punctuate the large expanse of valley in the center, and in the very subtle space-composition of trees and bushes in the foreground, in the left of which the clumps of foliage seem to flow toward each other through unaccentuated but adequate space. The color-scheme, rather low in key and with very few bright accents, is pervaded with a delicate, very attractive lavender suffusion that does much to unify the picture and to establish continuity in color-quality. The brittle texture of the wall in the foreground and the unusually literal rendering of the sky slightly lower the generally high standard of the picture as a whole.

[97] Illustration, p. 273.

CARD PLAYERS (125), of 1890-1892,[98] illustrates the fact that one element—in this instance, color-glow—may be in itself of such high quality that it can give distinction and character to an entire picture and yet not make the picture a really important work of art. The reason is that the color-glow is not supported by the other essential plastic factors.

The all-pervasive merging of light and color imparts a wonderful sparkling glow to the ensemble, but does not conceal a drawing so flabby that the units of the painting fail to assume definite identity either as volumes in space or even as representative objects. These shortcomings far outweigh the value of such fine achievements as the space-organization of the objects on the table which is attained with no resort to thick impasto or accentuated contour; the compositional spacing below the table and under the chair; the very attractive tortoise-shell color-pattern on the coat of the man in the center; and the combination of lightness and solidity in the rendering of the table.

In the background, especially in the left half, the planes, instead of receding in rhythmic order, are unorganized, confused and spatially ill-defined. Further defects appear in the rendering of the shadow cast by the yellow drapery on the wall, and of the space between this drapery and the wall: the pigment is thick and grainy to the left of that shadow and the shadow itself sinks in, creating a hole. Other sinking color-notes, which fail to function organically because of lack of internal illumination, are the two patches in the wall at the left, the knee of the man at the left, and what looks like the right cuff and side of collar of the man at the right. Drawing and modeling in general are also poor in quality, the two most flagrant examples being the flabby drawing of the profiled head of the man at the right, and the modeling of the flattened platelike face of the central figure in which the planes fail to exercise their necessary constructive function. Moreover, there is more than a suggestion of speciousness in the use of accentuated light as a focal spot in the background and as an outer contour-band duplicated by a vague band of shadow around the standing figure. The sum total of these defects results in so serious a plastic disintegration that convincing individual expression is compromised or lost. Their incongruity with the admirably conceived and executed units earlier referred to attests once more Cézanne's constantly recurring uneven control of his medium.

[98] Illustration, p. 271.

CARD PLAYERS AND GIRL (141) of c. 1892.[99] As noted
in the text, the ubiquitous contrast-motif is an important factor
in the drama and power of the form of this picture as a whole.
The contrasts, however, are always kept within the bounds of unity
by pervasive essential similarities. The combination of pyramidal
and enframing motifs, which compose the framework of the picture, is supplemented by various other familiar means of inter-
linking masses and areas. A slanting linear effect, cutting across
the left shoulder of the hatless man, is continued downward on
the right by the linear junction of the areas of light and shadow
through the blouse of the girl; the outline of the same man's right
arm is similarly continued through the front of the shirt and coat
of the man seated on the left, and thence along the oblique line of
shadow just above the latter figure's right elbow; the vertical
left outline of the standing man is continued by the shadow
across the upper back of the seated man at the left, and thence,
through his elbow and points of angles on his coat, to the leg of
the chair. The line of the floor, seen at the extreme left, is continued by that of the table top; the directions of the outlines of
the oblique legs under the table extend through various parts of the
figures and through the folds at the upper right and the shadows
at the upper left to the extreme upper corners of the picture.

These last lines, which are part of the V-motif or inverted
pyramid referred to in the text, are rhythmically echoed and re-
enforced throughout the picture, as for example by the angles
formed by the chins, by the lapels, by the hands, and by the intersecting figures. Counterbalancing the V-motif is the movement of
the upright pyramid, of which the main participant is the angle
made by the slant of the two main figures right and left, as their directions converge on the small picture hanging on the wall at the
top. The union of the upright and inverted pyramids forms the diamond-motif, by which the particular masses of the composition are
linked together at different levels from side to side, and from foreground to background. The diamond-motif is repeated also in deep
space by the interrelated head, arms and hands in each figure at the
table, and also by the head, shoulders and legs of the central figure.
The distribution of the cards and pipe on the table constitute a
hub-and-spokes- or rosette-motif in terms of planes. This rosette-
movement radiates outward: it is first continued by the volumes
of the hands, and then repeated by the seated figure on each side,

[99] Illustration, p. 276.

the standing man and the figure of the girl, as these are related
to the hatless central figure.

Light and shadow as well as line are used to emphasize space
and the relation of volumes in space. Around the head of the
hatless man and the elbow of the standing man, the accentuated
light serves this purpose; around the shoulders and arms of the
central figure, the deepened line of shadow plays the same part.
Light is also used in conjunction with color to interrupt the continuity of volumes, as between the body of the girl and that of the
man at the right, and likewise between the hat of the man at
the left and the dark shadowed area under the right elbow of the
standing man. Areas of light and shadow in the setting assume
the character of quasi voluminous planes, which participate in the
general dynamic movement of the composition; at the same time,
as no more than quasi voluminous, they set off by contrast the
fully solid volumes of the figures themselves. The shadows on
the left background convert the planes there into a series of semivolumes, which echo the solidity of the standing figure and form a
rhythm with its shape and mass. The type of distortion described
in the text as sunken light, in which an area of light seems actually
to lie below the surface on which it falls and at the same time yields
the effect of solid modeling, occurs in a number of units. The
drawer of the table is given voluminousness by this means, as is
also the light-shadow pattern which models the back of the chair
and is repeated, with appropriate modifications, in the coat of the
seated man on the left.

Important as the volumes in "Card Players and Girl" are, the
force and bizarreness of the design really arise from the setting
of these volumes in their respective planes. Each of the volumes
is constructed of planes, which enclose its substance like the walls
of a container, build up its mass and define its position in space.
In this process, however, the chief part of the work is done by
the shape of the planes constituting the volumes rather than by the
color. The color is smoky and tends somewhat to the leaden,
comparatively inert character from which Cézanne's color constantly suffers when it is inadequately vitalized by light. This relatively inadequate color imposes upon the pattern of planes and
shapes a disproportionate part in modeling and spatial organization, and the painting thereby suffers correspondingly in both its
decorative and its expressive functions.

The widespread radiation of the lines of perspective gives

rise to a very active series of movements which extend, and also contrast with, the dynamic interaction of the masses themselves; at the same time, the areas by which the continuity of the lines is broken take the form of clearly defined planes, and these repeat in the background and elsewhere the very pronounced pattern which is fundamental to the whole design.

Most of the traditions which affected Cézanne in his mature work show their influence in this picture. The Florentine tradition appears as usual in the emphasis upon linear continuity as a means to perspective, a practice particularly effective because of Cézanne's versatility in singling out the linear aspects of areas of light and shadow, planes, volumes, and quasi volumes. These linear aspects are used, in spite of interruption, to carry the composition back into deep distance as do, for example, the unbrokenly continuous back of the chair and slanting lines of the man's arms on the table.

Tintoretto and El Greco are suggested by the dramatic contrasts of light and color, though the pattern formed by these contrasts has none of the fluidity of the older painters. Drawing and modeling, especially in the hands and in the coat of the hatless man, are, each, a fusion of elements from Tintoretto, Hals, Daumier, and Manet, but with modifications which heighten the massiveness of the volumes. In the area under the table, the legs of the seated man, the legs of the chair and table, and the rungs of the chair are distorted in an attractive space-composition reminiscent of Chardin in its general effect, but looser because of the less clearly defined contours and the smoky color which fills the spatial intervals. The relation of the general enframing-type of composition to Titian's "Entombment" (230) and to Giotto's "Pietà" (212) is perceptible, and becomes especially obvious as the enframing-motif established by the figures is seen to be duplicated by the relation of the curtain on the right and the shadows on the left to the group of figures.[100] The Le Nains are recalled by the alignment of the principal figures on the same horizontal level, and by the quiet intimacy of the subject-matter. In the latter respect there is also an affinity with Dutch genre-painting, but the plastic organization as a whole is totally different from those of both the Dutch and the Le Nains, and is enriched by transfer of values from architecture, from sculpture, especially Egyptian, and even from natural landscape. The pro-

[100] Cf. Cézanne's variation on a similar motif in his "Three Bathers" (82).

cessional effect of the static figures deployed across the canvas has the power and majesty of a range of mountain peaks.

TWO MEN PLAYING CARDS (143) of c. 1892.[101] The laboriousness of Cézanne's efforts to attain expression is conspicuous in this picture because of the use of specious devices. Contrast is accentuated to the point of melodrama in the detached vivid streak of highlight on the bottle, in the glaring white pipe placed against the almost black background, and in the yellow-orange face and neck of the man at the left which are sharply set off by the black of his hair. Color in general is unevenly enriched by light, so that its compositional continuity is broken again and again. The shadows in the men's coats, for instance, do not connect with the areas of light but sink back, as though into holes, below the level of the area to which they should give solidity and textural quality. Color fails also in structural value, as in the coat of the man at the right which has a feeling of cardboard, of a painted surface rather than of a garment around a solid figure; again, the attempt to model the faces by means of contrasting color-planes results in a series of facets which yield chiefly ineffective patterns and distortions, with scarcely any sense of solidity and three-dimensional quality. Technique, on the whole, is not integrated in the form: in the background, for example, the pattern of brush-strokes, patches and lines is scarcely more than an inharmonious succession of ill-defined areas of mahogany-red and blackish blue, deficient in internal illumination and painty in surface and texture. Even the color-scheme, the most attractive feature of the picture, is specious rather than a product of organic relationships: the too obvious contrasts between the orange-brown tablecover, the light greenish-gray coat of the man at the right, and the dark slate-blue lavender coat and hat of the man at the left have only a superficial effectiveness. In short, the picture abounds in evidence that the work of Cézanne's maturity often suffers from the tricky devices and technical incompetency that afflict the paintings of his early period.

MAN AND SKULL (142) of c. 1892.[102] As noted in the text, the decentered composition of this picture, consisting of two upright masses balancing one another and interconnected by a variety

[101] Illustration, p. 270.
[102] Illustration, p. 259.

of plastic devices, has many sources in the earlier traditions. The problem of compositional unification is here solved by a great diversity of methods. The angles at which the planes are set supply what is perhaps the most fundamental means of creating an impression of continuous movement to and fro: the figure as a whole slants inward from right to left; it forms an angle with the side of the table which moves forward toward the left and in turn forms a projecting angle with the other side-plane of the table which recedes to the extreme left of the canvas; and these planes together form an accordion-pleat motif of planes in space.

The accordion-pleat motif as here used is essentially the same as it is in "Five Nudes" (74) and "Men Bathing" (164), in spite of the fact that in these other pictures only the apexes of the folds, back and front, are formed by solid bodies, and the walls of the folds are empty space,[103] while here the walls are solidly continuous. Moreover, the transverse movement of pleats is repeated by an ascending staircase movement, or rather two movements, one of which goes from right to left, from the floor through the legs of the chair, the man's lap, the right side and the top of the table, the sides and top of the books, to the drapery; the other from lower left to upper right, terminating in the man's body. This step-riser alternation is again repeated or suggested, on a smaller scale, in the relations of the table top to each of the groups of books and to the drapery; in the relation of the skull to its pedestal of books; in the planes of the chin, mouth and nose; in the drawing of the ear and modeling of the side and front of the face; even in the undulating up-and-down decorative edge of the table and in the color-patches of the garments covering the leg, arm and torso.

This angular meeting of planes runs all through the composition, recurring in the folds of the drapery below and above the table, the back and seat of the chair, and the hand in relation to the leg, and everywhere it produces the effect of dynamic thrust and counterthrust. An angular motif appears also in the modeling of the head and hand, in which the familiar broad outline and small color-patches forming planes give to the volumes a faceted character akin to that in the flesh-modeling in "Card Players and Girl" (141) and "Provence Peasant" (151). In "Man and Skull" in both head and hand, the color-patches are organized in two large composite planes, the junction of which forms a sort of wedge, and these wedges repeat on a smaller scale the general

---

[103] See p. 335 and illustrations, p. 200 and p. 201.

advancing and receding movement of the main compositional planes and masses.

Another familiar compositional device in "Man and Skull" is the diamond-motif, the four corners of which are formed by the skull, the corner of the back of the chair, the head, and the hand resting on the lap. Linear sequences also connect different areas or units, and are as ubiquitous as are the intersecting planes just discussed. The slanting line of the right side of the table, for example, is continued upward across the figure by the line of the breast pocket and the boundary of the area of shadow on the upper part of the arm; a counterbalancing diagonal line ascends and recedes from just inside the left elbow through the coat, shirt, corner of the books, right elbow, and the drapery near the top of the skull; other lines roughly parallel to this pass through the left side of the table, through the color-modulations in the wall at the right, and through the back of the chair, shoulder, head, and drapery. Innumerable other similar continuities of line or direction, which the imagination can easily carry over gaps or physical interruptions, link every part of the picture with every other, strongly reënforce the general drama of thrust and counterthrust, and collectively make up the surface-pattern of angular areas.

Within this surface-pattern itself, an additional note of drama is provided by a less obvious but equally pervasive set of curvilinear motifs. These motifs vary in degree of accentuation and of curvature, though, as always with Cézanne, they are invariably rigid rather than fluid. As an illustration, the accolade-motif, not unlike a brace or cupid's bow, which is most pronounced as a decorative feature of the table skirt, is repeated with variations in the edge of the piece of paper at the foremost corner of the table, in the paper on which the skull rests, in the temple of the skull, in the pattern within the skull, in the contour of the left hip and the junction line between the hand-and-cuff and the leg, and in the color-modulations of the background. In the drapery it recurs constantly in many forms and degrees of accentuation, forming, indeed, the most characteristic motif in the folds and floral ornaments. It is not only an element of pattern; sometimes it functions as a plane superimposed upon the plane of the drapery, or as a hollow rhythmically echoing the eyes, nose and temple bone of the skull. Some of the floral units which it constitutes are planes and volumes, definitely shaped, detached in space, and forming a kind of subsidiary dynamic space-composition, to which the drapery itself stands in the relation of background, not unlike the wall in relation to the foliage and plants in "Potted Plants" (116). At the same time the folds of the drapery in their turn repeat on a smaller scale the general drama of balanced movement of planes.

The exceedingly elaborate purposiveness of Cézanne's form, the coördination of every aspect and every detail with every other, is further apparent in the illuminated area on the front of the shirt. This area with its slightly curving contour enters into a sub-pattern of light and line with the curvilinear edge of the table, the rectilinear lighted areas of the paper underneath the skull, the paper at the corner of the table, the side of the books, the man's collar, the area of light below the man's left knee, and the accentuated band of light in the background around the shoulder.

These devices for linking together the parts of the picture are effective in varying degree. Sometimes the linear aspects accentuated are so well coördinated with the space, volume, light, and color that plastic integrity is completely preserved. Such is the case with the band of light over the shoulder which not only plays its compositional part satisfactorily in the pattern described in the preceding paragraph, but also conveys an adequate sense of the space between figure and wall. Similarly, in the left background an irregular oblique patch of darker color slanting downward from the left is part of the general linear sequence that runs diagonally toward the lower right along accentuated shadings in the drapery and the man's coat; and this patch, though it has no specific representational function, is so well adjusted in color to areas surrounding it that its plastic status is that of a plane related in space to planes in the drapery and wall. The folds of the drapery just back of the skull, the pattern of which echoes that of the skull itself and of the drapery above, constitute a kind of two-cornered hat, a volume acting as an intermediary between the bulky massive skull and the drapery against the wall. This volume, by its relation to the skull and the parts of the books projecting in front of the skull, also establishes a continuous enclosure for the space between the skull and the extreme left of the picture. This unit of space is in turn one of a series of quasi niches, which includes that containing the man's right elbow, those underneath the table, between the table top and the man's lap, under the chair, between the left elbow and the back of the chair, and so on. All of these are interlinked by the continuity of the space which moves in and out between the advancing and receding planes, and all of them, by virtue of their angular shape, provide variations on the familiar theme of thrust and counterthrust.

Another unit of space, behind and to the left of the skull, is related very much in the manner of Chardin to the left side of the table, the projecting corner of the books, the folds of drapery and the floor under the table. While this unit may be provisionally isolated for purposes of analysis, its relationships inevitably lead the eye through every part of the canvas, and include them all in the continuous alternating space-and-volume composition. In the unit underneath the table on the extreme left, there is an accentuated pattern of shapes and superposed lines, but both are so sensitively adjusted in color to the remainder of the composition that the whole unit is an integral part of the design, and the drapery itself has the effect of a columnlike support for the pedestal, consisting of the table top and books, on which the skull rests. In the skull and books, volume and space are clean-cut and vigorously defined; in the unit under the table, though individual identities are preserved, volume and space are much less emphatic, and the contrast between the two units effectively reënforces the general drama of the picture.

These two units, like the others already described, show an adequate balance of the plastic means, but others are less successfully realized. For example, in the linear definition of the man's head, from the crown to the neck, a gross accentuation of line leaves both the volume itself and the space which surrounds it plastically unconvincing. As with most of Cézanne's lapses, the cause is his failure to relate colors harmoniously. On the whole, the color is solid and, especially in its lighted areas, has a pronounced metallic, though deep, quality. The picture represents Cézanne's work at a high level, particularly from the standpoint of varied and skilful adaptation of means in the execution of an especially complex and difficult compositional plan.

PROVENCE LANDSCAPE (138) of the early 1890's.[104] With its pale, almost monochrome, and water-color-like ensemble, the picture is both strong and delicate, and these qualities are organic and pervasive. Distinctive features of the drawing are the ill-defined islands of light reminiscent of Chinese landscape-painting, and the use of shadow and light outside and not within the area

[104] Illustration, p. 220.

of the tree and limbs on the right, to give them massiveness and set them in space.

FOUR PEACHES (129), of the early 1890's,[105] illustrates one of Cézanne's most effective uses of slanting brushwork to pattern the surface of the canvas and to draw and model the volumes. Highly successful color-relations diminish the perceptibility of the individual strokes, and eliminate any suggestion of speciousness, of mechanical execution or of obvious surface-decoration. A feeling of richness and delicacy, worthy of Renoir, blends organically with the typical Cézannesque three-dimensional solidity. The full realization of the feeling of actual peaches is attained by color-relationships and an integrated pattern of patches and brushstrokes, enhanced by the exquisite decorative quality of the structural color and of the pigment itself.

MADAME CEZANNE IN YELLOW ARMCHAIR (135) of the early 1890's.[106] It is a mark of the prevailing ineptitude in critical circles that this picture enjoys a high reputation. The sensuous appeal of its color does not compensate for the poor relationships of color-planes in the modeling, the Courbet-like waxy flesh, the blotterlike surface of the paint, and the flabby, fiberless drawing of the entire figure.

MADAME CEZANNE IN RED, HOLDING HANDKER-CHIEF (133) of the early 1890's.[107] The very striking character of the composition—an unusual variation upon the diamond-theme —is due chiefly to an interplay of contrasting directions centering in the vertical-oblique figure. The generally vertical areas at right and left of the figure are held together by the slanting horizontal band of wainscoting; the slant of the figure is matched by the lower part of the curtain at the right, and is counterbalanced by the curvilinear-oblique upper part of the same drapery. The arms of the figure and various objects of the setting are also rhythmic variations upon the diagonal motif. The composite effect of the picture seems unnatural, just as do many pieces of fruit in Cézanne's still-lifes which appear to be on the verge of toppling off the edge of a table; but in spite of the lack of naturalistic or representational balance, the plastic equilibrium is so secure that one

[105] Illustration, p. 215.   [107] Illustration, p. 217.
[106] Illustration, p. 262.

might say, paradoxically, that the idea or motif of instability has been embodied in a stable plastic ensemble. The interplay of directions involves, of course, not only the linear effects but the volumes, planes and spatial units, with their contrasting rhythms of color. The organization is thus a series of alternating thrusts and counterthrusts of color-masses and colorful spatial intervals, which move forward and backward, upward and downward, toward and away from each other, in vertical, horizontal and oblique directions, both rectilinear and curvilinear.

This picture is both very characteristic of, and very unusual for, Cézanne. It is rich in plastic content and very strong, though not so strong nor so skilfully executed as some of his best work.[108] The technique, however, is well merged with the color: there is scarcely any evidence of the familiar piling up of thick paint in ridges on contours, or of Cézanne's constant resort to dark or light outlining bands. The solid modeling of the face is done in Cézanne's typical manner with planes and hatchings of structural color, but their interplay is not so subtle as in "Woman with Green Hat" (103). The color-ensemble as a whole is a fine harmony of contrasts: the focal red of the dress works in unison with the subdued grays, blues and tans of the drapery, the brighter areas of the flesh and the tans in various parts of the setting.

COMPOTIER, PITCHER AND FRUIT (128), of the early 1890's,[109] represents, on a large scale, most of the principles of Cézanne's dynamic space-composition applied to still-life, and is an unusually striking example of his precise and thoroughgoing coördination of technique and pattern with all the plastic functions, and with plastic form as a whole. The familiar devices are employed in the execution of each unit and area, but differences in accentuation, in the basis of organization, produce a constant succession of novelties in effect and a rhythmic play of contrasts that extend to every part of the canvas.

The composition combines the usual pyramidal and steplike disposition of masses. The plane of the table top rises and recedes and forms an angle of approximately ninety degrees with the planes of the background and the hanging tablecover in the foreground. The same plane is also an intermediate between two other planes—the quite small patterned triangular unit at the extreme

[108] Cf., e.g., "Woman with Green Hat" (103); "Harlequin" (105).
[109] Illustration, p. 278.

lower right, and the upper left area of the background—in the formation of a counterbalancing upward, right-to-left sweep across the entire picture. This effect of contrasting positions and movements, producing as always the drama of thrust and counterthrust, furnishes the keynote of the design, and is repeated on a smaller scale in each of the individual masses, both in their direction of placing and in their technical execution.

The most prominent element of the pyramid-theme appears in the white folded table cloth, which rises as a mountainlike volume with an active oblique movement that counterbalances the slant of the table top. Within the cloth itself a subsidiary composition embraces a number of peaklike masses directly related to the upright volumes of the pitcher, the dish with fruit, and the patterned drapery back of the table at the right. This drapery, a rounded pyramid, the arc of which sweeps upward from right to left, forms with the white table cloth a sandwichlike frame in deep space for the pitcher and fruit dish. The sweep of this drapery is counterbalanced by that of the drapery suspended above, which makes an inverted pyramid. Another pyramid appears in the upright part of the tan drapery at the left, the three columnlike folds of which lean toward each other and converge at the top. Around the main part of the composition as a whole extends an enframing device, composed of the wall at the left, the mahogany-colored background-plane at the right, and the plane of the overhanging tablecover in the immediate foreground, all of them primarily vertical and relatively flat and monochromatic. The intersection of these large vertical planes with the oblique table top is an important element in the drama of the composition.

Within the framework thus established the individual pieces of fruit carry out the theme of movement and contrast in direction, and collectively they form an undulating rhythmic sequence that enframes the mountainlike volume of the table cloth. All these themes, and especially that of thrust and counterthrust, reappear in the pattern which forms the foundation of the picture.

There are a number of other pattern-motifs that contribute to the effect of omnipresent contrast. One is the shape of the pitcher handle, which recurs in the general shape of the overhanging part of the tan drapery, in its folds, in the general shape and in the internal pattern of the drapery at the back of the table, in the sides of the peak of the table cloth, and in various other places. In each repetition, this theme has functions not only decorative and compositional, but specifically expressive. In the outline of the dish at the left, for example, it helps render shape, solidity and space; in the patterned drapery at the back of the table, it functions in terms of planes; in the overhanging tan drapery, it enters into the building up of volumes; in the accentuated highlight to the left center of the table cloth, it becomes part of an angular frame for a spatial interval; in the volumes of the fruit, where it has the form of a crescentlike band, it is one of the chief instruments of drawing and modeling.

Another motif is that of the rosette which, because of its accentuated center, is especially noticeable on the decorative motif of the pitcher, and is repeated, in varying degrees of distinctness and solidity, in the individual pieces of fruit. Variation in the placing of the center of the rosette differentiates the slant of each particular volume from that of the others. This motif is also repeated in part of the drapery back of the pitcher as a triangular plane emphasizing a conelike unit of space, which accentuates the enveloping movement of the drapery; it occurs again in the opening of the pitcher which, by virtue of its conelike shape, is a repetition of the fruit dish. In the opening of the pitcher and in the dish, the rosette-motif has the basic plastic function of depicting space; in the fruit, that of drawing and modeling; in the drapery, it forms a compositional plane.

The accentuated oval shape of the pitcher as a whole has a similar set of recurrences. It is repeated horizontally in the mouth of the pitcher and the rim of the dish; in the patterned arrangement of several groups of the fruit; in the two main folds of the overhanging drapery at the top; and in several individual pieces of fruit. The same motif is used vertically, in the peak of the white table cloth together with the three pieces of fruit at the base of the peak, and, among other areas, in the pyramidal mass of the fruit in the dish, as this mass is related to the bottom of the dish. Still another motif is the scalloped formation to be seen in the outline of the rim of the pitcher, in the floral ornaments on the pitcher, in the pattern of the drapery back of the table, in the modeling of the fruit, and on a large scale in the outlines and folds of the overhanging drapery, as well as in the undulating sequence of the fruit across the composition. In the overhanging tablecover in the foreground, a slight in-and-out movement is also suggested, and is rendered by a subtle pattern of light resulting from judiciously used areas of bare or thinly covered canvas. Indeed, the same undulating movement may be discerned in more general form as the eye passes from object to object in many parts of the canvas: it is one aspect of the angular zigzag movement of planes, linear outlines and spatial units which extends throughout the entire composition. Thus this motif, which is in itself decorative, takes its place on an equal footing with others more definitely expressive in function: it contributes not only to the play of dynamic forces but to the establishment of equilibrium and compositional unity. In addition to these more or less incidental motifs, linear continuities, which are in essence lines of perspective, form a network throughout the picture, many of them radiating from the peak of the white table cloth.

Integration of space-composition is achieved in Cézanne's usual manner by continuity of rhythm from foreground to deep distance. Modulated color-areas in the background form a series of receding semivoluminous planes with a suggestion of space infinity. Collectively these planes and their intervals unite in a single solid upright plane which is brought into relation with the masses in the foreground by the continuity of technical execution; there is also an effect of sharp contrast in the abrupt transition between the well-defined volumes of the foreground and the much less well-defined series of quasi voluminous planes that begin immediately above and to the rear of them. The same union of continuity with dramatic contrast appears within the background itself, as the eye passes from the dark, mahogany-colored, receding space-composition, just noted, to the bulging columns of the tan drapery at the left, and thence to the large structural plane of the blue wall, in which are consolidated a whole set of minor planes.

The three contrasting areas of the background are unified by a pattern of light and shadow, as well as by their common construction out of planes. Many of the shadows form bands and stripes, some of them well defined, others vague, which are repeated all through the picture and are intertwined with the more clean-cut lines of perspective, at the same time exercising, like Cézanne's other devices, a wide variety of plastic functions. The pronounced upright band of shadow cast on the wall at the left, for example, is part of a more extended light-shadow motif composed of areas in the columnlike folds of the tan drapery and in the wall on the left, and it forms an ascending pyramidal volume that duplicates, or rather expands, the column made by the folds of the tan drapery. This pyramidal formation occurs in the main background-planes, both relating them with one another and providing a further link between the entire background and the group of still-life objects in the foreground.

The general forms of organization employed in the composition as a whole are repeated in the drawing and modeling of particular objects, though always with such shifts in emphasis and in arrangement of details as are required by the individuality of each plastic unit. As usual the units, the pieces of fruit, for example, are definitely outlined, and they are modeled with brushstrokes combined into patches. These patches form angular planes, together with the familiar pattern of two intersecting sets of curves which yields, with the structural color, an emphatic three-dimensional quality. For instance, the apple near the right corner of the table in front of the white cloth has all these characteristics; what singles it out as a particular identity is the presence in it of the enframing-motif. The red area in it enframes the yellow, and the apple as a whole is in turn enframed by the fold of the cloth against which it is set. Moreover, the shape of the yellow area in this same apple is repeated in the area of shadow to the right and rear of the apple, and again in other parts of the canvas, so that it is closely linked with the entire pattern of shapes extending throughout the composition.

The same integrative principle is illustrated by the apple immediately to the right of the one just discussed, though with a different set of relationships. This unit is constructed out of practically the same colors as the other, but the degree of distortion is greater. The colors function more as planes extending in different directions and embodying the general principle of thrust and counterthrust; the outline of the volume tends to be squarish, a shape roughly duplicated in the curvilinear area of space outlined and enclosed by the fold of white table cloth immediately in front of it, and in another area of space just to the left of the apple. A set of dovetailing triangles which make up the internal pattern of this apple are continued and repeated in various adjacent parts of the white cloth, as well as in the space intervening between apple and cloth; these triangles in their relation to one another echo the thrust and counterthrust perceptible in a number of small units near by, as well, of course, as the same motif in the design as a whole.

Just behind this apple, the area of the table between the pitcher, the white cloth and the drapery at the rear, has a pattern of small irregular triangles suggesting, by their relations of tone and color, a movement of slight planelike volumes, and these echo the movement of the more definitely solid volumes enclosed in the folds of the patterned drapery to the left of the fruit dish. A similar embodiment in the technique of a principle or motif running through the general composition appears in the lemon at the front of the table, lying against an orange and an apple. The patch of highlighted yellow in this is aligned with 'other similarly shaped and placed patches in the white cloth, such as the peaklike fold in front of the orange before the pitcher. The two curvilinear outlines of the yellow patch also duplicate the main peaklike fold of the white cloth and that immediately below it, and the area of shadow placed just to the left of the same yellow patch embodies the crescent-motif which recurs in a large number of other areas. One extremity of this crescent is continued by the orange-brown line in the decorative theme on the brown tablecover; this line in turn forms angular junctions with others on both planes of the tablecover, and provides a zigzag movement in deep space that extends from the lower edge of the brown cover up to the fold of the white cloth. In this way, what may seem at first appearance to be a mere fragment of ornamental pattern on the tablecover becomes part of the broken lines of continuity which render perspective and participate in drawing, modeling and compositional integration.

Behind another lemon, immediately to the left of that already discussed, is a green piece of fruit containing an internal pattern of light and dark, which is repeated in the radiating lines and folds of the surrounding white table cloth. This green fruit is further linked with the fold immediately to the left by a V-shaped pattern which intervenes also between several of the other pieces of fruit. In the green pears in the rear to the left of the fruit dish, the internal pattern and the degree of three-dimensional quality are diminished, so that as masses in the space-composition these pears are of approximately the same status as the distorted, semivoluminous units of the patterned drapery.

The columnlike tan drapery, like the fruit, is modeled by a longitudinal-latitudinal intersection of lines, and this modeling is again modified in the interests of compositional continuity. The lines are slanted differently in the folds, with the direction of the slants duplicating respectively the slant of the cast shadow at the left, and that of the overhanging fold at the right, while the interaction of all these elements gives to the columnlike unit as a whole a generally triangular or pyramidal form, and thus makes it an organic part of the entire pyramidal composition.

From the foregoing analysis, it is apparent that this still-life not only contains practically all the main types of compositional order that enter into the mature forms of Cézanne, but it also illustrates the scope of his imagination and technical resources in bringing to a successful solution an extraordinarily complex problem of plastic organization.

GARDENER (130) of the early 1890's.[110] As stated in the text, the chief compositional problem in Cézanne's figure-pieces is the unification of the figures, whether single or grouped, with the background. In the early portraits and narrative pictures the comparatively low level of plastic integration tends to leave the composition fragmentary; such links as exist are usually specious—for example, illustrative detail reënforced by obvious rhythms and broad sweeping movements of masses, in which the contrast of light and shadow plays a very important part.[111] In the intermediate period, represented by "Man Putting on Coat" (56), the representative movement of subject-matter is less obvious, the plastic movement relatively more important, while the action depicted is more poised, less turbulent or melodramatic. Correspondingly, the compositional use of technique to unite figure and background is much more thoroughgoing, with brushstrokes less active as individual touches, and more and more grouped into definite areas in an all-inclusive pattern. Linear effects, with or without interruptions, carried over from one area of the picture to another, have begun to anticipate the intricate and closely woven fabric characteristic of Cézanne's mature work.

In "Gardener," represented movement has disappeared and the figure initiates a plastic activity of planes and volumes which spreads outward and backward from the hingelike figure itself to embrace the subsidiary masses and details of the setting. This receding and laterally spreading rhythm, which involves the principal upright masses and planes of the landscape, is echoed in, and counterbalanced by, the fanlike organization of the color-patches in the horizontal-oblique plane of the ground. The organization of the latter, together with the small planes back and to the sides of the man's feet, creates a circular plastic movement in deep space like that of a wheel with spokes, in which the function of the hub is assumed by the figure.

[110] Illustrations, p. 233 and p. 298.
[111] E.g., "Idyl" (26).

Technique, instead of maintaining an approximately equal degree of perceptibility throughout the entire surface, has become a more specific means of differentiating figure and background: it is much less apparent in the figure, which is treated more like the units of still-life, that is, as a unitary solid color-volume. Homogeneity of the brushstrokes within areas, greater emphasis upon the boundaries of areas and upon linear effects in general, together with an increasing definiteness of shape, all of which represent a marked advance over Cézanne's early form, distinguish "Gardener" from "Man Putting on Coat" (56) ; and these features are inevitably accompanied by the characteristic transformation of pattern into dynamic space-composition. With this transformation, more organic bonds between the units of the picture as a whole add substance to what was previously mere continuity of pattern. For instance, the general outline of the figure is roughly paralleled at right and left by the lines, the strips and areas of color, and the pattern of light and shadow in the bushes and branches; the man's arms, likewise, are duplicated in the parts of the green bush immediately adjoining them, and also in more distant units such as the deep green shadow and the area of blue sky at the upper left; again, the quill-like brushwork just below and to the right of the man's left hand repeats in that part of the setting the linear pattern made by the fingers. In each case, however, the elements repeated in the various parts of the composition are subsidiary to those other features that endow each unit with its distinctive characteristics: its qualities of color, of light, of shape, of degree of solidity, its particular identity as a plastic rendering of arm, bush, sky, or quill-like plane of foliage. Above all, each detail is subordinate to, and receives its plastic meaning from, the composition as a whole.

MADAME CEZANNE IN RED, HOLDING ROSES (134), painted in the early 1890's,[112] is an unsuccessful plastic organization, interesting chiefly as showing the persistence of Manet's influence upon Cézanne's late work. Modeling is attained by rather specious emphasis upon contrast of areas that function more directly as patches of light and dark than as planes of color; the shadow between the nose and the lower lip lacks internal illumination and appears to sink in; the line of contour near the edge of the face seems detached and projects in front of the mass which it outlines; at the contour of the dress, a peculiar use of bare canvas and of

[112] Illustration, p. 251.

edges only slightly covered by color gives rise to a ragged line of light which disrupts the form; the background is soft and indeterminate; and the surface of the whole picture is waxy.

WOMAN AND COFFEE POT (140) of the early 1890's.[113] This is a superb picture and a rare achievement even for Cézanne. It is not only fine in color and in compositional arrangement but is well lighted, and the color and light are perfectly integrated. In spite of numerous plastic units and factors in complex interrelationship, the general effect is that of simplicity. A further noteworthy feature is the relative absence of Cézanne's usual difficulty in placing masses in space. Only around the upper contour of the head, especially around the woman's left side, is there a conspicuous ridge of lumpy pigment indicative of repeated attempts to attain the tonal values requisite for a proper setting of the volume in space. There are no particularly outstanding or subtle units of space-composition, but the spatial location of each object is well defined, and the rhythms and contrasts of linear directions, of size, color and degree of three-dimensional quality produce an elaborate series of remarkably well-balanced thrusts and counterthrusts, bizarre in their ensemble and very picturesque.

As usual, extensive use is made of a heavy dark-blue line of contour, sometimes solidly continuous for several inches, sometimes subdivided into smaller sections, and sometimes decidedly ragged as, for instance, at the woman's left wrist. This broad linear contour creates at times a semblance of definite depth of space in which the volumes are set; this is particularly noticeable in the hands, the coffee pot and the cup.

The all-embracing light-pattern is very effective; its units vary in size, in color and in degree of intensity from the focal areas on the face, cup and coffee pot, to the spots of diminished but still active illumination on the door, the floral ornaments on the wall, the patches on the tablecover, and the superposed dashes of light on the blouse. In the cup, the interaction of color, light and technique produces a Chardin-like surface. In the table cloth and in the panels of the door, the areas of sunken light transform these planes into a series of color-units receding into deep space, giving to some of them, notably the panel above the coffee pot, the plastic characteristics of a landscape. All of the areas of light are well defined in shape, and their interrelationships with the equally well-

[113] Illustration, p. 250.

shaped patches of shadow give a very patterned character to the picture—a pattern which merges with, and becomes an organic part of, the total form, not a disorganized pattern of patches as, for instance, in "Mount Ste. Victoire Seen from the Chemin des Lauves" (189).

The effectiveness of the color-ensemble results chiefly from its contrasts of blues, grays and tones of terra cotta, the pattern of which is, as always in Cézanne, as much one of light and dark as of color. With all the rare finesse of execution and the general high quality of this picture, it does not reach the same level as "Woman with Green Hat" (103). In comparison with the latter, the planes of color are not so successfully related, the shadows are in relatively heavy paint, and the means of compositional organization are more obvious, more conventional and academic. This is another instance of Cézanne's lack of complete freedom in the use of his medium, even in one of his best works.

PEASANT IN BLUE BLOUSE (149) of the middle 1890's.[114] The generally bright, sensuously pleasing color-scheme is enlivened by numerous small spots of bare canvas and a very eloquent, though specious, focus of red. Color is not very solid nor is it uniformly well lighted, but it is very skilfully used in the modeling and in the rendering of space. Irregular Hals-like facets model the face somewhat in the manner of "Provence Peasant" (151), of the same period, but in a less blocklike form. The multiple outlines, used in various parts of the picture, and the disjointed drawing of the figure in the setting are legitimate distortions in the realization of a successful space-composition of slight volumes and planes. The form as a whole is an instance of skilled painting and sensuously good color so handicapped by an overaccentuated pattern that the net result is rather mediocre for Cézanne.

PROVENCE PEASANT (151) of the middle 1890's.[115] The jutting, voluminous, many-faceted masses in this picture are rendered by a technique which shows a closer approach than usual to Hals's and Manet's, but with plastic effects entirely different. Cézanne's effects—boxlike volume, general rigidity, dramatic contrasts of hollows and projections, especially in the head and hands—recall characteristics of Negro sculpture, and are due mainly to a

[114] Illustration, p. 256.
[115] Illustration, p. 258.

pattern of short, broad, definitely placed brushstrokes that are not only more complex and more varied in color than Manet's but also serve to draw masses more solid and weighty. This pattern is quite as obvious as in Hals, but it is more colorful and luminous, and by its greater simplification it eliminates surface-detail and accentuates three-dimensional solidity more effectively: its primary purpose is expressive, rather than illustrative and decorative.

Compared to the majority of Cézanne's portraits, "Provence Peasant" shows an additional variation upon his method of modeling by brushstrokes merged in continuous patches that fulfill definite compositional purposes. In this picture the patches, instead of being arranged in superposed planes, are so related as to form wedges and grooves that produce an in-and-out movement of planes in deep space, a movement that gives to the masses their characteristic wedgelike or boxlike character, and differentiates the form of "Provence Peasant" from, for example, that of "Woman with Shawl" (118), with its continuous flow of planes into the volumes.

The many-faceted, boxlike units form a major theme of the composition, one which is played upon with a great variety of emphasis. It is most pronounced in the head, is extensively employed throughout the figure, is much in evidence in the objects back of the chair in the lower left corner, and it sinks to a minimum in the ill-defined details at the upper right. The constituent planes of these rhythmically repeated patterns differ in size and color, so that the contrast-motif is everywhere emphasized, and this contrast-motif and the in-and-out movement in conjunction form an extremely important instrument of compositional unification.

This movement of patterned units is continued on a more extensive scale by the positions and directions of the larger masses: the torso projects forward and slants from upper right to lower left, the head is set at an angle to it; the back of the chair and the poker on the right are also placed obliquely, but the exact position of each is varied to make a contrast in direction with that of adjoining objects. The vertical tongues and the vertical line on the wall just back of the head emphasize the slant of the figure and at the same time provide a stabilizing counterpoise; the horizontal lines defining the mantelpiece and the middle of the wall on the right perform the same function for the shoulders and waist, which, in turn, are slanted at an angle to the entire mass of the figure.

An important adjunct in the organization of the compositional movement as a whole is the familiar diamond-shaped arrangement of masses in deep space. The general outline of the diamond runs from the head downward to the left, along the contour of the hair and through a patch of green on the wall, to the bottle on the mantelpiece; then still downward, along the woman's right arm, to the right-angle motif in her skirt at about the center of the lower edge of the picture; the side of this motif leads the eye upward to the right, through the woman's wrist and thumbs, toward the top of the tongues, from which point the course of the diamond proceeds upward to the left, through the knob of the poker, the modulations in the quasi volumes of color on the wall and the patch of shadow just above the forehead.

Although the composition is strikingly bizarre in effect, it is based on principles constantly present in Cézanne's work. Line as usual is emphasized and functions actively in the drawing, modeling, rendering of perspective, formation of pattern, and establishment of compositional unity. As usual, too, differently shaped planes in the background form vaguely definite color-masses, which carry out the general space-volume design. The upper surface of the book, which makes an emphatic plane in deep space, has a function analogous to that of the table-top plane in the still-lifes. The sunken light, the bare canvas for highlights and the interrelated contrasting curved and rigid lines to produce the effect of conventional modeling are also typical Cézanne devices.

The defective color-relationships, noted in the text as the chief shortcoming of the picture, are not, as usually in Cézanne, due to poor internal illumination, but to lack of harmony between the bright red of the dress and the other hues in the color-ensemble. The red, failing to become an integral part of the texture of the volumes, stands out in what seems to be superficially applied patches and streaks, with the result that the drawing and modeling of the garment suffer an appreciable loss in expressive power.

GUSTAVE GEFFROY (144) of c. 1895.[116] The extraordinarily striking character of this portrait is due to its tightly-knit and well-balanced composition of masses, its pervasive high degree of illumination and its vivid color-ensemble with very bright focal notes, chiefly of orange-vermilion. These features, however, fail to establish the picture in the first rank of Cézanne's work. Compositions similar to it in picturesque arrangement and compact order-

[116] Illustration, p. 253.

ing of numerous masses can be found in the work of Botticelli,[117] Ghirlandaio,[118] Holbein,[119] van Reymerswael,[120] Manet,[121] Degas,[122] and in any exhibition of academic pictures. The spots of accentuated light are inadequate as reënforcements of color, and the bright colors themselves are vivid decorative punctuations rather than components in a total effect of expressive color-power. The general style or execution is, superficially, in the best Cézanne tradition, but its patterns of color-patches, of light and of technique almost sink to the level of a *tour de force*. Instead of being means to an end, they are used in accordance with a mechanized formula which is responsible for the pronounced feeling of calculation characteristic of the entire form. This calculated quality, from which the sense of spontaneity is absent, is especially apparent in the over-accentuated focal areas of light and color, and in the compositional rhythms attained by the directions and positions, thrusts and counterthrusts of the various units.

"Gustave Geffroy" illustrates also Cézanne's constantly recurring inability to establish organic relationships between light and color. The frequently uneven quality in his pictures, of the sort revealed by holes or breaks in the plastic continuity of the form, is usually due to this poor coördination of light and color, which makes some areas seem overlighted, others dull and leaden. In this portrait, the contrast between very definite areas of bright illumination and of pronounced shadow, together with the striking pattern of color-patches, happens to yield a spectacular effect, but its spectacular quality is not to be confused with the solid plastic reality of Cézanne's work at its best.

The painting has, however, a number of superb passages: the man's left hand, much distorted but well modeled and colorful, is a thoroughly convincing plastic unit, as is also his right hand with its loose generalized drawing; the shirt front and parts of the coat are likewise well painted, adequately modeled and convincing in color; the bunch of flowers at the left shows Cézanne's creative use of Manet's technique and drawing; other superb notes of painting are the objects on the table at the lower right, and the subtle space-composition of the wall, the back of the mantelpiece and

[117] E.g., Botticelli's "Saint Augustine in his Study" (223).
[118] E.g., Ghirlandaio's "Saint Jerome" (224).
[119] E.g., Holbein's "Ambassadors" (233); "Merchant Georg Gisze" (234).
[120] E.g., van Reymerswael's "Two Bankers or Usurers" (235).
[121] E.g., Manet's "Emile Zola" (277).
[122] E.g., Degas's "Duranty" (286).

the mantelpiece itself. Against this record of noteworthy achievement must be noted the facts that the deep garnet of the back of the chair has no adequate solidity and is hardly more than a colored area; that the color-patches which model the head and face are so loosely organized that their effect is factitious rather than constructive or creative; that one row of brightly colored books—the second from the top—is hardly more than a pattern of stripes and bands of flashily contrasting colors and shapes, a defect which stands out the more because in the fifth row from the top the essence of books and shelf is rendered in a harmonious color-ensemble. This incongruity between finely and badly executed units is one of the chief reasons why the picture must be excluded from the category of Cézanne's really fine work.

STANDING NUDE (145) of c. 1895. This is said to be the only nude that Cézanne, in his mature period, painted from a model. The composition consists of a large upright figure placed against three broad horizontal bands in the setting, of which the central band is much the broadest. Color is almost completely dead in the background and is only passably illuminated in the painting of the nude. The figure itself is notable for its color-ensemble, in which a variety of blues, reds and greens diversify but do not overbalance a dominant yellowish hue. Black contour, area-lines and dark parallel thin streaks—strongly accentuated in the legs—practically surround all the parts of the figure. The latter is modeled by parallel bands that tend to form a swirl on the abdomen. The area-lines, which give the effect of the lead strips in stained glass, and also the multiple thin streaks at contours and the bands which do the work of modeling—all anticipate some of the distinctive characteristics in Cézanne's large "Nudes in Landscape" (191) painted in the latest period of his career.

NORMANDY FARM (114) of the late 1880's, ROAD AT MARINES (153) of c. 1896, BIG TREES (160) of the late 1890's, and QUARRY AT LE THOLONET (168), also of the late 1890's, provide good examples for a comparative study of two of Cézanne's technical devices to establish perspective: the use of bands and stripes in the directly receding table-top type of foreground-plane, and the use of quill-motifs in the drawing and spacing of planes that build up masses.

In "Normandy Farm" (114) [123] the effect of parallel bands and stripes in the foreground-plane is attained by subtle relationships between areas of light and of shadow within an almost monochromatic surface, varied slightly with modulations of green and pinkish tan. The mottling of this plane by tonal color-variations and an ill-defined pattern of generalized brushstrokes produces a subtle effect of parallel bands, a characteristic device of Cézanne's to make the horizontal foreground of his compositions recede directly into deep space.

The quill-motif in this picture appears in two typical but different forms: at the upper right a number of parallel, dark and slightly curvilinear brushstrokes are so aligned that the relatively sharp definition of one side of the patch and the contrast with the color and tone of the adjacent areas produce a linear effect and plane that resemble the rib and barbs of a quill. Elsewhere in the picture, a crisp, thin line of dark color is placed across an area composed of several patches of parallel brushstrokes; the line, unlike the more typical quill-motif just noted, forms a wedgelike accent among a mass of interpenetrating patches or planes.

The quill-motif in "Quarry at Le Tholonet" (168) [124] is rendered by another technical method: a horizontal or oblique definite line indicates the upper limit of the patch—the rib of the quill—and from it starts each of the parallel vertical brushstrokes—the barbs of the quill.

Still another variation of the quill-motif appears in "Big Trees" (160) [125] in the left side of the vista between the two main trees. The outstanding feature of the quill, here, is the lightness and delicacy both of its colors and of its execution: the rib of the quill is hardly a line, but rather a clean-cut accentuation of the color and tone along one side of the individual patches; and the parallel brushstrokes within the patch, contrasting as usual with the direction of the rib, make up the featherlike plane.

The stripes and bands are particularly marked in this picture because of the great variation in the color, size, shape, and pattern of the principal components. The band-effect is produced by a sequence of horizontal individual patches across the foreground. The brushstrokes are horizontal within some of the patches, vertical in others, or placed in various directions, overlapping each other, and either curved or straight. The patches as a whole tend

[123] Illustration, p. 211.
[124] Illustration, p. 260.
[125] Illustration, p. 238.

to be horizontal ovals, and they contrast with each other not only as they recede but also as they move laterally along the individual bands. The composite effect is not unlike a pattern of color-islands, of a type that may have been the source of Gauguin's familiar patterns.[126] The transition from the receding horizontal foreground-plane to the receding vertical units in the background is effected in great part by changes in the direction of the patches and brush-strokes. Up to the level of the base of the small narrow tree in the center, the patches and the broad single strokes which indicate the boundary of the foreground-plane are horizontal; above that point, both the patches and the parallel brushstrokes which build up the distant color-units are vertical-oblique and vertical.

The receding foreground-plane in "Road at Marines" (153) [127] is also rendered by parallel horizontal bands and stripes broken up into a variety of contrasting color-patches, but their contrasts in color and in pattern of brushstrokes are less pronounced than in "Big Trees" (160). Within the individual horizontal bands, the changes in color are gradual, the generally broad horizontal strokes are more or less of the same color within each patch, overlapping from area to area and varied but slightly in tone, so that the shape of the individual patches is rather ill-defined. The entire ground-plane is thus mottled with a series of parallel, loosely defined horizontal color-bands of light and dark, the pattern of which contributes to the perspective of the landscape.

APPLES AND ORANGES (159) of the late 1890's.[128] The pitcher is a stunning piece of painting, but lack of organic unity between Cézanne's typical technique and the bright colors tends to disrupt the composition as a whole.

ONIONS AND BOTTLE (167), of the late 1890's,[129] is a conspicuous failure for Cézanne. The color, while bright and adequately varied, lies almost entirely on the surface: the well-rounded and colorful onions and fruit, for instance, lack the essential feeling of their substance; the multicolored, patterned bottle has no structural solidity; and the table has the texture of cardboard. The drawing of the glass fails to differentiate its upper part from the background, and also creates a gap between the glass proper and the stem, so that the broken continuity between parts of the ob-

---

[126] Cf., e.g., Gauguin's "Haere Pape" (316).
[127] Illustration, p. 272.
[128] Illustration, p. 247.
[129] Illustration, p. 246.

ject is felt to be a hole in the picture. The pigment throughout is dry, thin, smooth, and somewhat waxy, and the background is essentially a mass of relatively uniform color only slightly patterned by dark and light areas, the relations of which totally fail to convey the effect of receding distance.

EIGHT WOMEN BATHING (161) of the late 1890's.[130] Color is very bright and juicy, technique takes the form of bands in which the direction of the brushstrokes runs at an angle to that of the band, and the composition combines both the tent and the hub-and-spokes types of organization.

FRUIT (163), of the late 1890's,[131] is a very strong picture even though sketchy and incomplete: the color has a Venetian richness, depth and glow, and the ensemble sparkles like a mass of jewels. However, as so often in Cézanne, even in his best work, the painting is not of equally good quality throughout: the drawing of the glass, for instance, is flabby, and the space back of the compotier is not realized in a degree commensurate with that of the other units of the space-composition.

AMBROISE VOLLARD (158) of c. 1899.[132] This portrait—adventitiously famous because of the renown of the sitter—is one of Cézanne's least successful achievements. The color is dull, the execution labored, most of the black lines of contour are exaggeratedly loaded with pigment, and the textures are painty. The modeling of the leg by parallel bands of color exemplifies a method of which Cézanne makes frequent use in his late work;[133] and the familiar parallel, multiple, thin, broken contour-lines appear also in various parts of the picture.

OLD WOMAN WITH ROSARY (178) of c. 1900. When Cézanne attempted to follow the form of the old masters, he rarely painted a good picture. In this portrait, for example, which goes back to the traditions of Rembrandt and the Dutch in general, and to Daumier in particular, the color is dull and dead, the execution is clumsy, the drawing tricky and superficial, and the general quality of the form is that of a mediocre painting by Daumier.

---

[130] Illustration, p. 277.
[131] Illustration, p. 223.
[132] Illustration, p. 263.
[133] Cf., e.g., "Nudes in Landscape" (191).

CHATEAU NOIR (186) of c. 1904. The dramatic effect is speciously attained by vivid contrasts of color and movement between the tan-orange upright castle, the light-blue turbulent sky and the green swirling clumps of foliage. The color is rich and glowing, but its operation in modeling and spacing is disastrously handicapped by the thick, heavy and lumpy paint, and by the ridged contours which take the place of color-modeling and bring confusion into the spatial organization of the masses. Although the technique of color-patches is typically Cézanne's, the fundamental effect of the picture as a whole is not unlike that of Jacob van Ruisdael's dramatic form, with a heightening in color-pitch.

LARGE BATHERS (190) of 1898-1905.[134] This, the largest in size of Cézanne's paintings, is an unfinished work which shows how he laid out the framework of a monumental composition, and how its units, in various stages of incompletion, appear when not tied together in a unified whole. It represents not a characteristic fully-arrived Cézanne expression, but an example of an expressive form arrested at a relatively early stage of its development.

The compositional framework of figures and landscape follows one of Cézanne's familiar motifs: the grouping of main masses into a tentlike frame through which a vista of landscape is perceived as a series of planes and volumes that punctuate rhythmically the receding space. How far short of realizing this typical form the painting was when Cézanne abandoned work upon it, is revealed by an objective study of the features common to all pictures that purport to be works of art.

Color is scarcely more than laid on as a general foundation and is thin, dry and lusterless; and these inadequacies, together with the lack of variation of tone in the large areas of blue and tan, explain the monotony of the color-ensemble. Cézanne had yet to consider, here, the sensuous quality of his color, its adjustment to light and the establishment of his usually meaningful color-relationships; hence, dullness of color adds to the monotony of the ensemble. The end-result is a dead, drab, almost monochromatic effect, totally different from the animation and variety afforded by the rich, deep, juicy, sparkling colors in Cézanne's best work.

The planes, which are fundamental to Cézanne's expression, are, in this "Large Bathers," in the primitive stage, not yet ready

[134] Illustration, p. 284.

to function adequately in the drawing and modeling of masses and in the definition of space. Throughout the picture the planes are so little varied in shape, size and color that they impart the feeling of mechanical execution to the total composition; this, too, contrasts strikingly with the variety of lively color-patterns in a finished, even mediocre, Cézanne. An outstanding instance of this aborted function of planes is the large, triangular, blue area at the extreme right of the landscape, bounded by the tree trunk. This area is filled with a conglomeration of units that depict neither foliage nor space, but constitute a pattern of accentuated angular units, screenlike in effect and incongruous with the other compositional factors.

The drawing and modeling of the figures on the whole attest a similarly aborted functional use of planes. In only two of the figures—that sitting at the left, and that standing against the tree at the right—are the color-planes coördinated well enough to draw and model the figures sufficiently to make expressive units of them. The figure at the extreme right in the foreground is a series of haphazard lines, dabs of dull color and large areas of bare canvas, all so utterly unrelated to each other that the drawing and modeling have barely been started. The extensive portions of bare canvas in the right foreground are similarly meaningless in the compositional make-up; that is, neither their shapes nor their color are related to the few dabs of pigment and sketchy lines in the parts immediately adjacent to form a unit congruous with any other unit in the composition. These esthetically barren large areas of unpainted canvas not only testify to the unfinished state of the painting, but are chiefly reminders of the general lack of substance in the picture as a whole.

Equally positive evidence that Cézanne abandoned work on this picture before he had attained either to his usual tightly-knit organization or to his characteristic expression of power, is afforded by the failure of color to render figures and clean-cut space with anything like his average fulness. The worst failure in this respect is illustrated by the two central figures of the group at the left: the seated figure's head, the standing figure's hand and the back of the furthermost figure are so confused in their spacing that neither the volumes nor their spatial intervals are distinct from each other. In other words, Cézanne had not arrived at the stage of execution at which he needed to make color and color-relationships establish the identity of each of the volumes and each of the spatial intervals.

The almost literal bilateral symmetry of the tentlike compositional framework explains the feeling of repose evoked by the painting, a feeling identical to that called forth by any similarly balanced arrangement of objects in the most commonplace situations of everyday life. That idea was Cézanne's legitimate point of departure in "Large Bathers," and he increased its human appeal by adding another universally attractive idea, that of bigness and vastness. So, by the very nature of things, the framework of "Large Bathers" has its intrinsic expressive value; but this is a far cry from the basic fact that the things in nature which have a universal appeal attain to the status of artistic expression only when the artist has stamped upon them the marks of individual creation. As the foregoing analytical notes indicate, Cézanne had hardly more than started to transfer the intrinsic values of a compositional framework into the realm of individual creation, when the process was interrupted. In other words, the analogue of "Large Bathers" is the framework of a building laid out from cellar to roof, but not yet provided with the necessities that make it habitable.

The bilateral symmetry of the framework is over-obvious, and so too is the device of extended arms and pointing fingers—like arrows indicating the direction of a road—to link together the two main groups of figures. And this obviousness, like the bare canvas, the dead monotonous color, the inadequate drawing, modeling and spacing, merely means that, for some reason, Cézanne never got around to the removing of these deficiencies; and this removing constitutes the necessary bridge to be crossed in order to convert his sketch into a completed painting. In short, the incompleted units and their existence as disparate unorganized parts of a composition-to-be, make of "Large Bathers" an unfulfilled promise, not an expression of either Cézanne's mature form or his high status as an artist.

NUDES IN LANDSCAPE (191) painted during the years from 1890 to 1906.[135] According to reliable data, Cézanne began this picture in the early 1890's and worked on it intermittently until 1906, the year of his death.

He achieves here, on a monumental scale, an effect of power

135 Illustration, frontispiece.

more complete than in any other of his paintings. The thrust and counterthrust of volumes placed at an angle to one another, with color reënforcing the movement, is characteristic of all his best work, such, for example, as "Bibemus Quarry" (155) of his late period, and his "Bathers at Rest" (63) of 1877. But in "Nudes in Landscape" the volumes have become more massive and more clean-cut in their detachment from the surrounding space. Composition of dynamic movement in three-dimensional space is basic also in, for example, "Compotier, Pitcher and Fruit" (128) but with less force in the individual units, less drama, and in a more restricted range of effects. The feeling of power, exemplified in "Card Players and Girl" (141), arises more in that picture from the bulk of the units than from their internal solidity; the poised movement is less dynamic than in "Nudes in Landscape"; and the composition, simpler and less varied, attains no comparable degree of creative expressiveness. The importance of "Nudes in Landscape," indeed, arises not from the introduction of any new plastic feature, but from the fact that it epitomizes Cézanne's career as a whole. What singles it out as supreme among his paintings is the plastic scale on which it is conceived, its immense range of human values and the high level of the expressive use of the plastic means.

The integration of light and color, as a result of which the dramatic light-shadow contrasts of the early period are transformed into a rich color-drama and made an extraordinarily effective instrument of compositional synthesis, is effected here with a degree of perfection elsewhere attained by Cézanne only in "Woman with Green Hat" (103). The dark setting is active not only as a background to the lighted figures but as an active participant in their spatial organization, as, for example, in the small dark interstices between the arms, hands and legs. In this adaptation of the Venetian tradition, the interstices are no longer, as in Cézanne's work of the sixties and early seventies, continuous in tone with the volumes which they set off, but instead are sharply contrasted, so that the volumes do not seem to emerge from the surrounding atmosphere, as they do in Titian and Tintoretto, but to project themselves from it with a decidedly sculpturesque feeling. In the process, extreme distortion is inevitable: the sole of the foot of the fourth figure from the right, for instance, appears to lack all connection with the foot itself; this apparent incongruity, nevertheless, produces a strikingly dynamic and picturesque unit of space-composition.

The general form of the composition combines characteristics of organizations of the frieze and pyramid types. The general frieze-like distribution of the entire group of figures links together two distinct pyramidal groups, one to the right, the other to the left, of the center. The pyramid at the right is in itself a highly intricate group of sculpturesque masses, and includes, besides the figures, the tree and foliage in the adjacent landscape. All the elements of this group are intricately intertwined, and their compact, yet clean-cut, arrangement in space suggests that in Poussin's "Ecstasy of St. Paul" (254) or "Holy Family" (255).

The pyramid at the left is constructed of simpler components, and is linked with the pyramid at the right in several ways: by the common relationship of the two groups to the pyramidal tree in the middle of the background; by a hub-and-spokes space-pattern of arms and cloths in the center, recalling Poussin's type of space-composition in his "Arcadian Shepherds" (253); by the rhythmic sequence of the draperies across the picture, all of which have similarities in color, shape, textural quality, and general direction of placing, so that collectively they have the effect of a frozen waterfall, with their rhythmic movement of pyramidal shapes and solid planes and volumes echoing that in the figures. In addition, the figures of both groups, placed in deep space, at many different angles, and with an unusually vigorous effect of thrust and counterthrust, are unified by the familiar diamond-motif, here rendered in a form suggesting that of an elliptical basket, the handle of which is formed by the converging branches of the trees at the top, while the bottom is defined by the sweeping curvilinear sequence of objects and masses from side to side of the picture—knee of figure against tree on the right, feet of figure seated at base of the tree, orange caldronlike object, dog, fruit basket, blue circular mass, and drapery on the left.

A community of character between the entire set of figures and the background further extends the dynamic force of the organization: the component parts of the background are solid masses in rhythmic lateral sequence, with dynamic interaction the same in kind as that of the figures, though less in degree; and the arrangement of this part of the picture repeats, reënforces and completes both the pyramid-motif and the frieze-motif. Cézanne's customary triple division of compositional planes in the landscape, with the foreground-plane accentuating perspective, serves here to develop the frieze-motif by an emphasis upon the lateral extension of the broad foreground-plane and the lateral sequence of the masses in the part of the setting above the whole group of figures; thus as in a frieze the main sculptural masses are placed within a horizontal band and set off by other bands above and below.

The interplay of all the compositional factors lends to each figure, to each element in the design, an extraordinary multiplicity of plastic relationships. One instance out of many is furnished by the figure leaning against the tree at the right; this is a very active unit in the pyramid on the right, and it has a further set of definite relations to the other figures and masses in its immediate vicinity; it is also a counterbalancing element to the figure and tree at the other end of the total group of figures; as such, it is one of the terminal elements in the frieze; and in its relation to the tree trunk and branches, it is also an essential element in the all-inclusive pyramid of the entire composition. Detailed examination shows not only all the other figures but also their parts, their heads, arms, hands, legs, and draperies, to be similarly interlocked with other units throughout the canvas as well as with the composition in its entirety.

The coördination between compositional design and technical execution is strikingly precise and flexible even for Cézanne. Line is broader, darker, more lustrous in color than usual, and it so consistently encircles each mass as to resemble the lead strips in stained glass, conferring at the same time upon the enclosed masses an effect of heightened voluminousness. The actual construction of the line both enforces the contrast-motif and preserves unity: the line is broken up in cross-section into thin parallel multiple streaks that often assume the character of area-lines, while longitudinally it is often a series of dashes.[136] Changes of color in the streaks and dashes enhance variety and drama, and the lines of contour contribute greatly to the decorative pattern, to the picturesqueness of the form, to compositional spacing, and to the expressiveness of drawing and modeling.

Volumes are drawn and modeled in harmony with the character of the line. They are striated and largely built up of parallel ribbonlike stripes recalling the pattern of mosaics; these stripes, in turn, are in many instances built up of alignments of brushstrokes or long dashes, the pattern of which is in direct rhythmic relation-

[136] See detail illustrated, p. 304.

ship with the broad contour-lines or area-lines that help set off the masses in space.[137]

In addition to the contrasts of color, light, line, technique, and direction of placing, by which the general unity of the picture is diversified, there is also a play upon the degree of sculptural quality in the volumes, which are of varying weight and consistency. In the figure at the extreme right, in the right arm of the figure in profile near the center and, most notably, in the figure on the extreme left, there is an apparent reduction in density of material, so that the material seems translucent, as though made of stained glass or fused quartz, though there is no suggestion of brittleness. This resembles an effect frequently characteristic of Masaccio,[138] and is combined with certain Sienese effects, such as those in which an undercoat of green is perceptible in the surface of the picture.

The actual character of the painted surface, the ruggedness, even the crudeness of the way in which pigment is applied, together with the typical broad simplifications, all carry out the theme of intense power exerted on a large scale. While the tremendous power of the total effect is obviously heightened by the quality of the color, the pattern, the drama of light-and-dark contrasts, the forceful linear rhythms, all these are subsidiary to what their conjoined activity achieves—the dynamism of the contrast and architectural equilibrium of sculpturesque masses. The painting thus represents not only a more ambitious flight of its creator's imagination, but the embodiment of a wider range of human values than does any other work of Cézanne.

[137] See detail illustrated, p. 296.
[138] Cf., e.g., Masaccio's "Madonna and Child" (218).

CATALOGUE DATA

CATALOGUE DATA[1]

THE three following lists contain the titles of the pictures and other works of art, together with their corresponding numbers, as they appear in the text. The oil paintings by Cézanne (list A) are arranged in chronological order, and the works belonging to each year or period are listed alphabetically. The aquarelles, lithographs and drawings by Cézanne (list B), commencing with No. 192, are arranged alphabetically, not chronologically, because the dates ascribed to many of them are questionable and almost impossible to check.

To assist in identification, such descriptive details are given as the size of the paintings and the collections in which they are to be found. Dimensions are given in inches, the first enumerated being the height of the picture. When reference is made to the exhibition "Cézanne" held at the Musée de l'Orangerie, Paris, in 1936, it refers to data from the second edition of the catalogue.

Following the enumeration of Cézanne's work, a third list (list C), "Miscellaneous Works of Art," commencing with No. 210, includes data on paintings and sculpture referred to in the text as having a bearing on Cézanne's work. Painters and traditions in this list have been classified in a sequence roughly chronological and the individual works are arranged alphabetically under the tradition or artist to which they belong.

For the purpose of convenience, the titles in the three lists are given in English and also in the language in which the pictures are catalogued in their respective collections, or in the language of the country in which they are to be seen or have been shown in the exhibitions noted in the following catalogue data.

[1] The inclusion of page references converts this section into a supplementary index. The letter "n." after a page number indicates that the reference is contained in a footnote; and more than one "n." after a page number indicates a corresponding number of footnote references on that page.

LIST A

CEZANNE
OIL PAINTINGS

Early 1860's

NO.

1. **Hide and Seek.** 77½" x 86⅝". Collection Mr. le Dr. Frédéric Corsy, Jas de Bouffan, Aix-en-Provence—"Le Jeu de Cache-Cache." Page 105 n.
2. **Judgment of Paris.** 6" x 8¼". Collection Mr. Paul Cézanne, *fils*, Paris—"Le Jugement de Pâris." Page 9 n. Analysis, page 307. Illustration, page 147.

Circa 1864

3. **Artist's Sister.** 21¾" x 15". City Art Museum of St. Louis, No. 34.34, "La Tante Marie." Pages 10 n., 11 n. Illustration, page 148.

Circa 1864-1868

4. **Banquet.** 51⅛" x 31⅞". Collection Mr. René Lecomte et Mme., *née* Pellerin, Paris—"L'Orgie." Page 11 n.

Circa 1865-1866

5. **Uncle Dominique.** 18" x 15". Collection Mr. et Mme. Jean-Victor Pellerin, Paris. Exhibition "Cézanne," Musée de l'Orangerie, Paris, 1936, No. 1, "Portrait d'Homme dit l'Oncle Dominique." Pages 11 n., n., 74 n., 311 n.

1865-1867

6. **Head of Man.** 20" x 17¾". Collection Mr. René Lecomte et Mme., *née* Pellerin, Paris. Exhibition "Cézanne," Musée de l'Orangerie, Paris, 1936, No. 2, "Tête d'Homme." Pages 10 n., 11 n., n., n., 13 n., 74-75, 74 n. Illustration, page 149.

1866-1868

7. **Artist's Father.** 78" x 46½". Collection Mr. René Lecomte et Mme., *née* Pellerin, Paris. Exhibition "Cézanne," Musée de l'Orangerie, Paris, 1936, No. 3, "Portrait du Père de l'Artiste." Pages 11 n., 13-14, 74 n. Illustration, page 151.

1867

NO.
8. **Abduction.** 35½″ x 46″. Dated. Collection Mr. J. Maynard Keynes, London. Exhibition "Cézanne," Alex. Reid & Lefèvre, Ltd., London, 1935, No. 1, "L'Enlèvement." Pages 8 n., 10 n.

Circa 1868

9. **Achille Emperaire.** 78¾″ x 48″. Collection Mr. René Lecomte et Mme., *née* Pellerin, Paris. Pages 11 n., 74 n. Illustration, page 150.
10. **Antony Valabrègue.** 45⅝″ x 38⅝″. Collection Mr. et Mme. Jean-Victor Pellerin, Paris. Pages 11 n., 13 n., 75, 315. Analysis, pages 311-312. Illustration, page 152.
11. **Christ in Limbo.** 66¼″ x 39¾″. Collection Mr. René Lecomte et Mme., *née* Pellerin, Paris. Exhibition "Cézanne," Musée de l'Orangerie, Paris, 1936, No. 7, "Le Christ aux Limbes." Page 105 n. Analysis, page 311. Illustration, page 153.

1868-1870

12. **Alexis and Zola.** 51½″ x 63½″. Collection Messrs. Wildenstein & Co., New York City and Paris. Exhibition "Cézanne," Musée de l'Orangerie, Paris, 1936, No. 178, "Alexis et Zola." Pages 8 n., 14 n. Analysis, page 312. Illustration, page 155.

Circa 1869

13. **Herrings.** 12½″ x 15¾″. Collection Mr. Josse Bernheim-Jeune, Paris. Exhibition "Cézanne," Musée de l'Orangerie, Paris, 1936, No. 10, "Les Harengs." Page 12 n.

Circa 1869-1870

14. **Black Clock.** 21½″ x 29½″. Collection Mr. Edward G. Robinson, Beverly Hills, California. Exhibition "Cézanne," Musée de l'Orangerie, Paris, 1936, No. 11, "La Pendule de Marbre Noir." Pages 14 n., 66. Illustration, page 162.

Late 1860's

15. **Autopsy.** 19¼″ x 31½″. Collection Mr. René Lecomte et Mme., *née* Pellerin, Paris—"La Toilette Funéraire." Pages 9 n., 10 n., 11 n. Illustration, page 156.

NO.

16. **Autumn.** 21¼" x 25½". Collection Mr. Ambroise Vollard, Paris. Exhibition "Cézanne," Musée de l'Orangerie, Paris, 1936, No. 18, "Paysage d'Automne." Pages 16 n., 52.

17. **Boy Leaning on Elbow.** 23¼" x 20". Collection Mr. Joseph Müller, Soleure, Switzerland. Exhibition "Cézanne," Musée de l'Orangerie, Paris, 1936, No. 4, "Le Garçon Accoudé." Page 14 n., n.

18. **Donkey Thieves.** 16" x 21⅛". Collection Rothermundt, Dresden—"Der Esel und die Diebe." Pages 8 n., 10 n., n., 12 n., 13 n., n., 73 n., 309. Analysis, pages 307-308. Illustration, page 158.

19. **Girl at Piano.** 22½" x 36¼". Museum of Modern Western Art, Moscow, No. 554. Exhibition "Cézanne," Musée de l'Orangerie, Paris, 1936, No. 8, "La Jeune Fille au Piano." Pages 14 n., 15, 131 n. Analysis, pages 309-310. Illustration, page 157.

20. **Murder.** 25¼" x 32". Collection Frau J. Elias, Berlin—"Der Mord." Pages 8 n., 73 n. Illustration, page 161.

21. **Picnic.** 23⅝" x 31⅞". Collection Mr. René Lecomte et Mme., *née* Pellerin, Paris—"Déjeuner sur l'Herbe." Pages 14 n., 15, 19 n. Illustration, page 160.

22. **Railroad Cut.** 31½" x 50¾". Neue Staatsgalerie, Munich, No. 8646, "Der Bahndurchstich." Pages 12 n., 14, 14 n., 15 n., 16 n., 52, 53 n., 54 n. Illustration, page 172.

23. **Reading at Zola's.** 20½" x 22". Collection Mr. et Mme. Jean-Victor Pellerin, Paris—"La Lecture chez Zola." Pages 8 n., 19 n., 40 n., 308 n. Analysis, page 309. Illustration, page 154.

24. **Scipio.** 42⅛" x 32¾". Collection Mr. Michel Monet, Giverny, France—"Portrait du Nègre Scipion." Pages 10 n., 11 n.

25. **Two Men and Two Women.** 11" x 14¼". Collection Mr. René Lecomte et Mme., *née* Pellerin, Paris—"La Promenade." Page 13 n. Illustration, page 164.

1870

26. **Idyl.** 25½" x 32". Dated. Collection Mr. et Mme. Jean-Victor Pellerin, Paris. Exhibition "Cézanne," Musée de l'Orangerie, Paris, 1936, No. 12, "Idylle." Pages 9 n., 11 n., n., 12 n., 36 n., 73 n., 308 n., 380 n. Illustration, page 165.

Circa 1870

27. **Green Jar and Pewter Pitcher.** 24¾″ x 31½″. Collection Mr. Gaston Bernheim de Villers, Paris. Exhibition "Cézanne," Musée de l'Orangerie, Paris, 1936, No. 14, "Pot Vert et Bouilloire d'Etain." Pages 14 n., 66. Analysis, page 312. Illustration, page 163.

28. **Head of Emperaire.** 17¾″ x 16½″. Collection Mr. le Dr. Frédéric Corsy, Jas de Bouffan, Aix-en-Provence. Exhibition "Cézanne," Musée de l'Orangerie, Paris, 1936, No. 6, "Portrait d'Emperaire." Page 11 n. Illustration, page 166.

1870-1873

29. **Dante's Boat.** 10″ x 13″. Collection Galerie Gold et Blot, Paris—"La Barque de Dante." Page 105 n.

Early 1870's

30. **Boyer.** 21½″ x 15¼″. Metropolitan Museum, New York City, No. C333-2. Page 14 n., n. Analysis, pages 313-314. Illustration, page 168.

31. **Four Women.** 7″ x 7″. Barnes Foundation, Merion, Pa., No. 796. Illustration, page 167.

32. **House at Auvers.** 22″ x 26⅜″. Collection Mr. Rudolf Staechelin, Basel. Exhibition "Cézanne," Musée de l'Orangerie, Paris, 1936, No. 25, "Maison à Auvers." Pages 36 n., 54 n., n.

33. **Modern Olympia.** 22″ x 21½″. Collection Mr. René Lecomte et Mme., *née* Pellerin, Paris. Exhibition "Cézanne," Musée de l'Orangerie, Paris, 1936, No. 16, "Une Moderne Olympia." Page 47 n. Analysis, page 314. Illustration, page 178.

34. **New Olympia.** 18¹⁄₁₆″ x 21⅝″. Collection Mr. Paul Gachet, Auvers-sur-Oise. Exhibition "Cézanne," Musée de l'Orangerie, Paris, 1936, No. 28, "La Moderne Olympia." Pages 16, 18 n. Analysis, page 314. Illustration, page 179.

35. **Red Roofs.** 28¾″ x 36¼″. Collection Mr. et Mme. Jean-Victor Pellerin, Paris. Exhibition "Cézanne," Musée de l'Orangerie, Paris, 1936, No. 13, "La Neige Fondant à l'Estaque." Pages 12 n., 36 n., 51. Analysis, pages 312-313. Illustration, page 159.

NO.
36. **Road.** 22½" x 27½". Museum of Modern Art (Collection Lillie P. Bliss), New York City. Page 52.
37. **Two Strollers.** 22¾" x 17¾". Collection Mr. Paul Cézanne, *fils*, Paris. Exhibition "Cézanne," Musée de l'Orangerie, Paris, 1936, No. 21, "Les Deux Promeneuses." Page 12 n. Analysis, page 313. Illustration, page 170.
38. **Valley of Jas de Bouffan.** 15⅜" x 21¼". Collection Mr. Paul Cézanne, *fils*, Paris—"Le Bassin du Jas de Bouffan." Page 16 n.
39. **Water Mill.** 16⅛" x 21¼". Private Collection, Breslau—"Landschaft mit Wassermühle." Page 17 n.
40. **Well Driller.** 7¼" x 6". Barnes Foundation, Merion, Pa., No. 1169. Illustration, page 192.

Circa 1871
41. **Avenue of Jas de Bouffan.** 15" x 18". Collection Mrs. Edith Wharton, Saint-Brice-sous-Forêt, France. Exhibition "Cézanne," Musée de l'Orangerie, Paris, 1936, No. 24, "L'Allée du Jas de Bouffan." Pages 16 n., 52-53. Illustration, page 174.
42. **Presumed Portrait of Valabrègue.** 23½" x 19¾". Collection Mr. et Mme. Jean-Victor Pellerin, Paris. Exhibition "Cézanne," Musée de l'Orangerie, Paris, 1936, No. 17, "Portrait Présumé d'Antony Valabrègue." Page 14 n. Analysis, page 315. Illustration, page 169.

1872
43. **Louveciennes.** 28¾" x 36⅜₆". Collection Mr. René Lecomte et Mme., *née* Pellerin, Paris. Exhibition "Cézanne," Musée de l'Orangerie, Paris, 1936, No. 23. Pages 16 n., 36 n., 53 n., 105 n.

1873
44. **House of Père Lacroix.** 24⅛₆" x 23¼". Dated. Private Collection, New York City. Pages 17 n., 59 n.

Circa 1873
45. **Suicide's House.** 21¾" x 26¼". Louvre (Collection Camondo), Paris, No. 151, "La Maison du Pendu." Pages 17 n., 54 n. Illustration, page 173.

Circa 1873-1874

NO.

46. **Jug, Wineglass and Fruit.** 24" x 28¾". Collection Mme. Jacques Doucet, Paris. Exhibition "Cézanne," Musée de l'Orangerie, Paris, 1936, No. 30, "Nature Morte." Pages 18 n., 70 n., 310 n. Analysis, pages 315-316. Illustration, page 186.

1873-1875

47. **Auvers-sur-Oise: Village Panorama.** 25½" x 31½". Art Institute (Collection Mrs. L. L. Coburn), Chicago, No. 33. 422. Page 17 n.

Circa 1875

48. **River and Hills.** 17" x 31½". Barnes Foundation, Merion, Pa., No. 208. Pages 17 n., 28 n., 32 n., 40 n., 41 n., 54-58, 60, 67, 343 n. Illustration, page 176. Detail illustrated, page 294.

1875-1878

49. **Combat of Love.** 17¼" x 22". Collection Mr. René Lecomte et Mme., *née* Pellerin, Paris. Exhibition "Cézanne," Musée de l'Orangerie, Paris, 1936, No. 66, "La Lutte Amoureuse." Analysis, pages 328-329. Illustration, page 182.

Middle 1870's

50. **Banquet Table.** 10⅝" x 20¹⁄₁₆". Collection Mr. Maurice Denis, Saint-Germain-en-Laye, France. Exhibition "Cézanne," Musée de l'Orangerie, Paris, 1936, No. 32, "Table de Banquet." Pages 18 n., 94, 341 n. Illustration, page 187.

51. **Cakes and Fruit.** 20⅞" x 24¾". Collection MM. J. et G. Bernheim-Jeune, Paris. Exhibition "Cézanne," Musée de l'Orangerie, Paris, 1936, No. 34, "Nature Morte aux Biscuits." Page 37 n.

52. **Choquet in Armchair.** 18⅜" x 14¾". Museum of Modern Art (Collection Lillie P. Bliss), New York City. Pages 26 n., 63 n. Illustration, page 193.

53. **Cupid's Arrow.** 8¼" x 8¼". Collection Mr. Percy M. Turner, London. Exhibition "Cézanne," Musée de l'Orangerie, Paris, 1936, No. 29, "La Flèche de l'Amour." Page 18 n. Analysis, pages 316-317. Illustration, page 184.

54. **Don Quijote.** 13¾" x 9½". Collection Mr. René Lecomte et Mme., *née* Pellerin, Paris—"Don Quichotte." Page 19 n.

NO.
55. **Fruit and Tapestry.** 17½" x 21½". Barnes Foundation, Merion, Pa., No. 190. Pages 37 n., 38 n., n., 68-70, 310 n. Analysis, pages 318-323. Illustration, page 190. Detail illustrated, page 297.

56. **Man Putting on Coat.** 12½" x 9½". Barnes Foundation, Merion, Pa., No. 1134. Pages 34 n., 76-79, 331 n., 380, 381. Analysis, pages 317-318. Illustration, page 171.

57. **Mount Ste. Victoire and Valley.** 17¾" x 21". Barnes Foundation, Merion, Pa., No. 300. Pages 30 n., 33 n., 40 n., 46 n., 56-58, 331 n., 343, 343 n. Illustration, page 177. Detail illustrated, page 296.

58. **Plate with Grapes and Peach.** 6½" x 11½". Barnes Foundation, Merion, Pa., No. 241. Pages 31 n., 66-67, 68, 345 n. Illustration, page 188. Detail illustrated, page 292.

59. **Quay on the Seine.** 23¼" x 28⁵⁄₁₆". Kunsthalle, Hamburg, No. 2374, "Die Seine." Page 323. Illustration, page 175.

60. **Temptation of St. Anthony.** 18½" x 22". Collection Mr. et Mme. Jean-Victor Pellerin, Paris. Exhibition "Cézanne," Musée de l'Orangerie, Paris, 1936, No. 33, "La Tentation de Saint-Antoine." Pages 16, 36 n., 329 n. Illustration, page 181.

Circa 1876

61. **Head of Victor Choquet.** 18¼" x 14¼". Collection Mr. Victor Rothschild, London. Page 29 n. Analysis, pages 323-324. Illustration, page 194.

Circa 1876-1877

62. **Eternal Feminine.** 17" x 21". Collection Mr. et Mme. Jean-Victor Pellerin, Paris. Exhibition "Cézanne," Musée de l'Orangerie, Paris, 1936, No. 37, "L'Eternel Féminin." Analysis, page 324. Illustration, page 180.

1877

63. **Bathers at Rest.** 31½" x 39". Barnes Foundation, Merion, Pa., No. 906. Pages 6 n., 20 n., n., 32 n., n., 37 n., 38 n., 54 n., 59 n., 63, 89-91, 109, 394. Analysis, pages 324-328. Illustration, page 198. Detail illustrated, page 292.

Circa 1877

NO.
64. Compotier, Glass, Apples and Knife. 18⅛″ x 21⅝″. Collection Mr. René Lecomte et Mme., *née* Pellerin, Paris. Exhibition "Cézanne," Musée de l'Orangerie, Paris, 1936, No. 39, "Compotier, Verre et Pommes." Pages 26 n., 36 n., 70-71, 316, 329 n., 330 n. Analysis, page 329. Illustration, page 191.

65. Three Apples. 6½″ x 4″. Barnes Foundation, Merion, Pa., No. 57. Pages 329 n., 330 n. Analysis, page 329. Illustration, page 301.

1877-1882

66. Estaque. 20½″ x 25¼″. Collection Frau Margarethe Oppenheim, Berlin. Pages 26 n., 329 n.

67. Fruit Dish. 17″ x 21⅝″. Ny Carlsberg Glyptotek, Copenhagen, No. 867, "Frugt Stand." Page 330 n.

68. Leda and the Swan. 23″ x 29″. Barnes Foundation, Merion, Pa., No. 36. Pages 20 n., 26 n., 28 n., 41 n., 43 n., 329 n. Illustration, page 185. Detail illustrated, page 294.

69. Pears on Chair. 7¾″ x 14¼″. Barnes Foundation, Merion, Pa., No. 18. Pages 329 n., 330 n. Analysis, page 330. Illustration, page 203.

70. Val Harmé at Auvers. 21″ x 33¾″. Collection M. Knoedler & Co., New York City—"Auvers, le Quartier du Val Harmé." Pages 17 n., 26 n.

1878-1880

71. Head of Choquet. 13¾″ x 10¼″. Collection Mr. Rudolf Staechelin, Basel, Switzerland—"Bildnis Choquets." Exhibition "Cézanne," Musée de l'Orangerie, Paris, 1936, No. 40, "Portrait de Choquet." Analysis, page 338. Illustration, page 195.

72. Madame Cézanne with Striped Skirt. 28¼″ x 22″. Collection Mr. Robert Treat Paine, Boston. Exhibition "Cézanne," Musée de l'Orangerie, Paris, 1936, No. 46, "Madame Cézanne à la Jupe Rayée." Analysis, page 338. Illustration, page 209.

1879-1882

73. Poplar Trees. 24⅜″ x 30¾″. Louvre, Paris, No. 102, "Les Peupliers." Page 30 n.

Late 1870's

NO.

74. **Five Nudes.** 15½" x 16½". Barnes Foundation, Merion, Pa., No. 93. Pages 20 n., 26 n., n., 27 n., 30 n., n., 31 n., 37 n., 41 n., 43 n., 44 n., n., 47 n., 63, 74 n., 87 n., 121, 130 n., 329 n. Analysis, pages 330-332; in comparative study, pages 332-338. Illustration, page 200. Details illustrated, pages 302 and 303.

75. **Four Bathers.** 10½" x 13½". Barnes Foundation, Merion, Pa., No. 951. Page 44 n. Illustration, page 183.

76. **Hill of Le Galet at Pontoise.** 19⅝" x 28¾". Collection Mr. Carroll S. Tyson, Philadelphia. Exhibition "Cézanne," Musée de l'Orangerie, Paris, 1936, No. 51, "La Côte du Galet à Pontoise." Pages 25, 36 n. Analysis, pages 339-340.

77. **Ile-de-France.** 23⅝" x 28¾". Collection Mr. Georges Renand, Paris. Exhibition "Cézanne," Musée de l'Orangerie, Paris, 1936, No. 48, "Paysage d'Ile-de-France." Page 54 n. Illustration, page 196.

78. **Luncheon in the Open.** 13½" x 15¼". Collection Mr. et Mme. Jean-Victor Pellerin, Paris. Exhibition "Cézanne," Musée de l'Orangerie, Paris, 1936, No. 44, "Le Déjeuner sur l'Herbe." Page 308 n. Analysis, page 339. Illustration, page 202.

79. **Plums and Pears.** 7¾" x 14". Barnes Foundation, Merion, Pa., No. 50. Page 68. Illustration, page 189.

80. **Self-Portrait in Front of Window.** 24" x 20". Collection Lord Ivor Spencer Churchill, London. Exhibition "Cézanne," Musée de l'Orangerie, Paris, 1936, No. 41, "Cézanne au Chapeau." Analysis, pages 338-339. Illustration, page 205.

81. **Self-Portrait on Pink Background.** 26" x 21¾". Collection Mr. René Lecomte et Mme., *née* Pellerin, Paris. Exhibition "Cézanne," Musée de l'Orangerie, Paris, 1936, No. 47, "Portrait de Cézanne sur Fond Rose." Analysis, page 339. Illustration, page 204.

82. **Three Bathers.** 9½" x 12½". Barnes Foundation, Merion, Pa., No. 96. Pages 44 n., 367 n. Analysis, page 332; in comparative study, pages 332-338. Illustration, page 199.

Circa 1880

83. **Interior with Nude.** 12½" x 9½". Barnes Foundation, Merion, Pa., No. 12. Pages 28 n., 94, 341 n. Illustration, page 206.

1880-1882

NO.
84. **Red Apples.** 18″ x 21¾″. Collection Mr. Gabriel Cognacq, Paris. Exhibition "Cézanne," Musée de l'Orangerie, Paris, 1936, No. 54, "Pommes Rouges." Pages 71, 94, 330 n. Analysis, pages 340-341. Illustration, page 214.

Early 1880's

85. **Mountains in Provence.** 20¾″ x 28¼″. Collection Miss G.-E. Davies, Gregynog, Newtown, England. Exhibition "Cézanne," Musée de l'Orangerie, Paris, 1936, No. 42, "Montagnes en Provence." Page 27 n. Analysis, pages 341-342. Illustration, page 212.
86. **Nude Seated on Bank.** 9¼″ x 8¾″. Barnes Foundation, Merion, Pa., No. 1155. Illustration, page 232.
87. **Plaza, Auvers-sur-Oise.** 20″ x 24¾″. Barnes Foundation, Merion, Pa., No. 3. Pages 59, 343 n. Illustration, page 210.
88. **Self-Portrait with Palette.** 36″ x 28¾″. Collection Mr. Paul Cézanne, *fils,* Paris—"Cézanne à la Palette." Page 339. Illustration, page 216.

Circa 1882

89. **Spring House.** 23″ x 19¼″. Barnes Foundation, Merion, Pa., No. 129. Analysis, page 342. Illustration, page 218.

Circa 1885

90. **Bay of Marseilles Seen from Estaque.** 22¾″ x 28½″. Louvre, Paris, no No. (gift of G. Caillebotte), "L'Estaque." Pages 26 n., 36 n., 37 n., 342 n.
91. **Country Home.** 12¾″ x 17½″. Collection N. E. and M. Mullen, Merion, Pa. Illustration, page 213.
92. **Gardanne.** 25″ x 39″. Barnes Foundation, Merion, Pa., No. 917. Pages 41 n., 46 n., n., 59-60. Analysis, pages 343-345. Illustration, page 221.
93. **Near Gardanne.** 19⅜″ x 23¼″. Collection Mr. David Eccles, London. Exhibition "Paintings from the Ambroise Vollard Collection," Knoedler Galleries, New York City, 1933, No. 6, "Environs de Gardanne." Pages 41 n., 343 n.

1885-1887

94. **Blue Vase.** 24″ x 19¾″. Louvre (Collection Camondo), Paris, No. 154, "Le Vase Bleu." Analysis, page 346.

NO.
95. **Mount Ste. Victoire and Viaduct.** 25¾" x 32⅛". Metropolitan Museum, New York City, No. C333-4. Page 357.

Middle 1880's

96. **Farm of Jas de Bouffan.** 23" x 28¼". Barnes Foundation, Merion, Pa., No. 188. Exhibition "Cézanne," Musée de l'Orangerie, Paris, 1936, No. 59, "La Ferme du Jas de Bouffan." Illustration, page 225.
97. **Girl with Bird-Cage.** 17¾" x 14⅝". Barnes Foundation, Merion, Pa., No. 280. Page 37 n. Illustration, page 207.
98. **Madame Cézanne with Striped Blouse.** 24½" x 20". Collection Mr. Henry P. McIlhenny, Philadelphia. Exhibition "Cézanne," Musée de l'Orangerie, Paris, 1936, No. 58, "Mme. Cézanne au Corsage Rayé." Pages 14 n., 313 n. Analysis, page 343.
99. **Self-Portrait with Bowler Hat.** 16½" x 13¼". Collection Mr. Gaston Bernheim de Villers, Paris. Exhibition "Cézanne," Musée de l'Orangerie, Paris, 1936, No. 57, "Cézanne au Chapeau Melon." Analysis, page 343. Illustration, page 208.
100. **Six Bathers.** 15¾" x 20¹³⁄₁₆". Collection Lord Ivor Spencer Churchill, London. Exhibition "Cézanne," Musée de l'Orangerie, Paris, 1936, No. 81, "Baigneurs." Pages 12 n., 40 n.
101. **View of Estaque.** 28¾" x 39¼". Metropolitan Museum, New York City, No. C333-3. Analysis, pages 342-343.
102. **Yellow House.** 25" x 32". Barnes Foundation, Merion, Pa., No. 246. Illustration, page 224.

1888

103. **Woman with Green Hat.** 38½" x 31½". Barnes Foundation, Merion, Pa., No. 141. Pages 6 n., 11 n., 21 n., 29 n., 33 n., 79, 82-85, 87, 91, 338 n., 339 n., 374 n., 394. Analysis, pages 348-353. Illustration, page 230.

1888-1890

104. **Bridge at Créteil.** 28" x 35½". Museum of Modern Western Art, Moscow, No. 559, "Les Bords de la Marne." Exhibition "Cézanne," Musée de l'Orangerie, Paris, 1936, No. 74, "Le Pont de Créteil." Analysis, pages 354-355. Illustration, page 197.

NO.

105. **Harlequin.** 39¾″ x 25½″. Collection Mr. et Mme. Jean-Victor Pellerin, Paris. Exhibition "Cézanne," Musée de l'Orangerie, Paris, 1936, No. 73, "Arlequin." Pages 6 n., 374 n. Analysis, page 354. Illustration, page 236.

106. **Mardi-Gras.** 40″ x 32″. Museum of Modern Western Art, Moscow, No. 549. Exhibition "Cézanne," Musée de l'Orangerie, Paris, 1936, No. 72, "Mardi-Gras." Pages 32 n., 354. Analysis, pages 353-354. Illustration, page 239.

1888-1892

107. **Nine Bathers.** 23⅝″ x 32¼″. Collection Mr. le Baron Napoléon Gourgaud, Paris. Exhibition "Cézanne," Musée de l'Orangerie, Paris, 1936, No. 80, "Baigneurs." Pages 31 n., 40 n.

108. **Self-Portrait on Blue Background.** 21½″ x 18″. Collection Mr. et Mme. Jean-Victor Pellerin, Paris. Exhibition "Cézanne," Musée de l'Orangerie, Paris, 1936, No. 82, "Portrait de Cézanne sur Fond Bleu." Pages 6 n., 11 n. Analysis, page 360. Illustration, page 252.

109. **Valley of the Arc.** 28″ x 35½″. Barnes Foundation, Merion, Pa., No. 13. Pages 6 n., 30 n., n., 31 n., 36 n., 40 n., 41 n., 58 n., 61, 63, 94, 131 n. Analysis, pages 355-356. Illustration, page 228. Detail illustrated, page 293.

1888-1894

110. **Poorhouse on the Hill.** 25″ x 32″. Metropolitan Museum, New York City, No. C333-1. Analysis, pages 356-357.

1889-1890

111. **Red Earth.** 31¼″ x 39″. Barnes Foundation, Merion, Pa., No. 909. Pages 28 n., 39 n., 40 n., n., 41 n., 46 n., 48 n., n., 60-61, 62, 63, 63 n., 83 n., 94, 341 n., 343 n. Analysis, pages 357-360. Illustration, page 229. Detail illustrated, page 299.

Late 1880's

112. **Approach to Jas de Bouffan.** 31½″ x 25¼″. Barnes Foundation, Merion, Pa., No. 939. Illustration, page 234.

NO.

113. **Madame Cézanne with Drapery Background.** 39″ x 30¼″. Collection Mr. Robert H. Tannehill, Detroit. Exhibition "A Nineteenth Century Selection—French Paintings," Bignou Gallery, New York City, 1935, No. 2, "Portrait de Madame Cézanne." Pages 79, 79-80, 81.

114. **Normandy Farm.** 19¼″ x 25⅜″. Collection Mr. Marshall Field, New York City. Exhibition "Paintings from the Ambroise Vollard Collection," Knoedler Galleries, New York City, 1933, No. 8, "Ferme Normande: la Cour Plantée." Pages 41 n., 387. Analysis, page 388. Illustration, page 211.

115. **Pine Tree at Montbriant.** 31½″ x 39″. Collection Mr. René Lecomte et Mme., *née* Pellerin, Paris. Exhibition, "Cézanne," Musée de l'Orangerie, Paris, 1936, No. 71, "Le Grand Pin à Montbriant." Pages 94, 341 n. Analysis, pages 346-347. Illustration, page 240.

116. **Potted Plants.** 35¾″ x 28¼″. Barnes Foundation, Merion, Pa., No. 235. Page 371. Illustration, page 219.

117. **Sugar Bowl, Pitcher and Fruit.** 24″ x 35⅜″. Museum of Modern Western Art, Moscow, No. 562. Exhibition "Cézanne," Musée de l'Orangerie, Paris, 1936, No. 68, "Nature Morte." Analysis, page 346. Illustration, page 222.

118. **Woman with Shawl.** 35½″ x 28¼″. Barnes Foundation, Merion, Pa., No. 710. Pages 36 n., 76 n., 79, 80-81, 82, 84, 360, 384. Analysis, pages 361-363. Illustration, page 231.

Circa 1890

119. **Boy in Red Vest.** 25″ x 21″. Barnes Foundation, Merion, Pa., No. 20. Illustration, page 257.

120. **Fruit and Blue Drapery.** 9⅞″ x 14″. Barnes Foundation, Merion, Pa., No. 152. Illustration, page 242.

121. **Geranium and Apples.** 28¾″ x 36¼″. Collection Mr. Adolph Lewisohn, New York City. Exhibition "Cézanne," Musée de l'Orangerie, Paris, 1936, No. 70, "Pot de Géranium et Pommes." Pages 72, 313 n. Analysis, page 363.

122. **Gray Jug and Fruit.** 23¼″ x 28½″. Barnes Foundation, Merion, Pa., No. 94. Pages 41 n., 45. Illustration, page 274.

123. **Jug and Fruit.** 16⅛″ x 28⅜″. Collection Mrs. Chester Beatty, London. Exhibition "Paul Cézanne," Bignou Gallery, New York City, 1936, No. 18, "Nature Morte à la Draperie Bleue." Pages 29 n., 32 n., 131 n.

124. Mount Ste. Victoire with Pine Tree. 25½" x 37½". Collection Mr. René Lecomte et Mme., *née* Pellerin, Paris. Exhibition "Cézanne," Musée de l'Orangerie, Paris, 1936, No. 91, "La Montagne Sainte-Victoire au Pin Parasol." Pages 40 n., 47 n. Analysis, page 363. Illustration, page 273.

1890-1892

125. Card Players. 25½" x 32". Collection Mr. Stephen C. Clark, New York City. Exhibition "Cézanne," Musée de l'Orangerie, Paris, 1936, No. 83, "Les Joueurs de Cartes." Page 87 n. Analysis, page 364. Illustration, page 271.

126. House at Bellevue. 25½" x 32". Folkwang Museum, Essen, Germany. Exhibition "Cézanne," Musée de l'Orangerie, Paris, 1936, No. 85, "Maison de Bellevue." Pages 94, 346. Analysis, page 347. Illustration, page 280.

127. Two Card Players. 17¾" x 22½". Louvre, Paris, No. 153, "Les Joueurs de Cartes." Page 87 n.

Early 1890's

128. Compotier, Pitcher and Fruit. 28" x 35½". Barnes Foundation, Merion, Pa., No. 910. Exhibition "French Art," Burlington House, Piccadilly, London, 1932, No. 432, "Nature Morte." Pages 12 n., 28 n., 39 n., 73, 73 n., 119 n., 394. Analysis, pages 374-380. Illustration, page 278.

129. Four Peaches. 9½" x 14". Barnes Foundation, Merion, Pa., No. 21. Page 71. Analysis, page 373. Illustration, page 215.

130. Gardener. 25" x 21". Barnes Foundation, Merion, Pa., No. 534. Pages 32 n., 33 n., n., n., n., 78-79, 343 n. Analysis, pages 380-381. Illustration, page 233. Details illustrated, page 298.

131. House on Hillside. 25¼" x 31¼". Barnes Foundation, Merion, Pa., No. 41. Page 48 n. Illustration, page 249.

132. Large Oak. 28¼" x 23¼". Barnes Foundation, Merion, Pa., No. 940. Exhibition "Paul Cézanne," Bignou Gallery, New York City, 1936, No. 17, "Le Grand Chêne." Illustration, page 235.

133. Madame Cézanne in Red, Holding Handkerchief. 45¾" x 35". Collection Mr. et Mme. Jean-Victor Pellerin, Paris. Exhibition "Cézanne," Musée de l'Orangerie, Paris, 1936, No. 76, "Grand Portrait de Mme. Cézanne en Rouge." Page 6 n. Analysis, pages 373-374. Illustration, page 217.

Circa 1895

144. Gustave Geffroy. 45¾″ x 35″. Collection Mr. René Lecomte et Mme., *née* Pellerin, Paris. Exhibition "Cézanne," Musée de l'Orangerie, Paris, 1936, No. 93, "Portrait de Gustave Geffroy." Analysis, pages 385-387. Illustration, page 253.

145. Standing Nude. 36½″ x 28″. Collection Mr. et Mme. Jean-Victor Pellerin, Paris, "Nu Féminin." Analysis, page 387.

Middle 1890's

146. Girl with Doll. 36¼″ x 29⅛″. Collection Mr. Alphonse Kann, Saint-Germain-en-Laye, France. Exhibition "Cézanne," Musée de l'Orangerie, Paris, 1936, No. 92, "Jeune Fille à la Poupée." Pages 29 n., 31 n., 36 n.

147. House and Wall. 25″ x 31¼″. Barnes Foundation, Merion, Pa., No. 89. Pages 40 n., 94, 347 n. Illustration, page 248.

148. Oranges and Bottle. 18¾″ x 28″. Barnes Foundation, Merion, Pa., No. 7. Pages 6 n., 28 n., 31 n., n., 37 n., 47 n., 69 n., 72, 125 n., 131 n., 143 n., 310 n., 339 n. Illustration, page 226. Detail illustrated, page 293.

149. Peasant in Blue Blouse. 32″ x 25½″. Collection Mrs. A. Conger Goodyear, New York City. Exhibition "Cézanne," Musée de l'Orangerie, Paris, 1936, No. 88, "Le Paysan en Blouse Bleue." Page 31 n. Analysis, page 383. Illustration, page 256.

150. Plain, Trees and Hills. 24″ x 31¼″. Barnes Foundation, Merion, Pa., No. 911. Pages 41 n., 69. Illustration, page 244.

151. Provence Peasant. 35½″ x 28¼″. Barnes Foundation, Merion, Pa., No. 164. Pages 18 n., 37 n., 79, 82, 83-84, 85-86, 85 n., 122 n., 369, 383. Analysis, pages 383-385. Illustration, page 258. Detail illustrated, page 300.

152. Viaduct. 35¾″ x 28¼″. Museum of Modern Western Art, Moscow, No. 548, Exhibition "Cézanne," Musée de l'Orangerie, Paris, 1936, No. 103, "Le Viaduc." Pages 40 n., 346. Analysis, page 347. Illustration, page 261.

Circa 1896

153. Road at Marines. 25″ x 37¾″. Barnes Foundation, Merion, Pa., No. 941. Pages 41 n., 387. Analysis, page 389. Illustration, page 272.

Circa 1897

NO.
154. **Mount Ste. Victoire.** 28½" x 36". Collection Mr. Paul Cézanne, *fils,* Paris. Exhibition "Paul Cézanne," Bignou Gallery, New York City, 1936, No. 20, "La Montagne Sainte-Victoire." Page 28 n.

1898

155. **Bibemus Quarry.** 35½" x 28". Barnes Foundation, Merion, Pa., No. 34. Pages 6 n., 12 n., 26 n., 27 n., 33 n., 59 n., 61, 62-63, 94, 341, 394. Illustration, page 255. Detail illustrated, page 295.

1898-1905

156. **Study of Bathers.** 28¾" x 36¼". Collection Mr. Ambroise Vollard, Paris—"Ebauche de Baigneuses." Page 91 n.

Circa 1899

157. **Agar in the Desert.** 19¾" x 22". Collection Baron von Simolin, Berlin—"Hagar und Ismael." Page 105 n.
158. **Ambroise Vollard.** 39⅜" x 32". Collection Mr. Ambroise Vollard, Paris. Exhibition "Cézanne," Bignou Gallery, New York City, 1936, No. 22, "Portrait d'Ambroise Vollard." Pages 29 n., 31 n., 36 n. Analysis, page 390. Illustration, page 263.

Late 1890's

159. **Apples and Oranges.** 28¾" x 36¼". Louvre (Collection Camondo), Paris, No. 155, "Pommes et Oranges." Analysis, page 389. Illustration, page 247.
160. **Big Trees.** 31⅞" x 25⅝". Private Collection, London. Exhibition "Paintings from the Ambroise Vollard Collection," Knoedler Galleries, New York City, 1933, No. 9, "Les Grands Arbres." Pages 41 n., 387, 389. Analysis, page 388. Illustration, page 238.
161. **Eight Women Bathing.** 11" x 20". Collection Mr. Sidney W. Brown, Baden, Switzerland. Exhibition "Cézanne," Musée de l'Orangerie, Paris, 1936, No. 109, "Baigneuses." Pages 32 n., 91 n. Analysis, page 390. Illustration, page 277.
162. **Flowers.** 27¼" x 22½". Barnes Foundation, Merion, Pa., No. 44. Illustration, page 267.

NO.
163. **Fruit.** 25½" x 35½". Museum of Modern Art (Collection Lillie P. Bliss), New York City. "Still-Life with Apples." Analysis, page 390. Illustration, page 223.

164. **Men Bathing.** 11½" x 15½". Barnes Foundation, Merion, Pa., No. 101. Pages 19 n., 20 n., 34 n., 47 n., n., n., 48 n., 87 n., 332 n. Analysis, page 332; in comparative study, pages 332-338. Illustration, page 201.

165. **Millstone in Woods.** 30¹¹⁄₁₆" x 36¼". Collection Mr. et Mme. Jean-Victor Pellerin, Paris. Exhibition "Cézanne," Musée de l'Orangerie, Paris, 1936, No. 99, "La Meule." Page 36 n.

166. **Mount Ste. Victoire through Trees.** 21⅝" x 18⅛". Collection Mr. Robert H. Tannehill, Detroit. Exhibition "Paintings from the Ambroise Vollard Collection," Knoedler Galleries, New York City, 1933, No. 13, "La Montagne Sainte-Victoire." Page 94. Illustration, page 264.

167. **Onions and Bottle.** 26" x 32". Louvre, Paris, no No. (Gift of Mr. A. Pellerin). Exhibition "Cézanne," Musée de l'Orangerie, Paris, 1936, No. 98, "Oignons et Bouteille." Pages 72, 313 n. Analysis, pages 389-390. Illustration, page 246.

168. **Quarry at Le Tholonet.** 31⅛" x 25". Collection Mr. Ambroise Vollard, Paris. Exhibition "Paintings from the Ambroise Vollard Collection," Knoedler Galleries, New York City, 1933, No. 11, "La Carrière du Tholonet." Page 387. Analysis, page 388. Illustration, page 260.

169. **Red Rock.** 35¾" x 26". Collection Mr. Ambroise Vollard, Paris. Exhibition "Paintings from the Ambroise Vollard Collection," Knoedler Galleries, New York City, 1933, No. 12, "Le Rocher Rouge." Page 63 n.

170. **Rocks at Bibemus.** 25⅝" x 21¼". Collection Mr. Henri-Matisse, Nice and Paris—"Rochers de Bibémus." Page 43 n. Illustration, page 266.

171. **Rocks—Forest of Fontainebleau.** 28⅞" x 36⅜". Metropolitan Museum, New York City, No. C333-6. Page 43 n.

172. **Table, Napkin and Fruit.** 17½" x 21¼". Barnes Foundation, Merion, Pa., No. 711. Pages 30 n., 45. Illustration, page 227. Detail illustrated, page 297.

173. **Two Pitchers and Fruit.** 25" x 31¼". Barnes Foundation, Merion, Pa., No. 148. Illustration, page 279.

NO.
174. Well. 25¼" x 31½". Barnes Foundation, Merion, Pa., No. 165. Pages 27 n., 28 n., 30 n., 33 n., n., n., 40 n., 41 n., 43 n., 59 n., 61-62, 63, 63 n., 83 n., 94, 123 n., 341 n., 347. Illustration, page 241. Detail illustrated, page 299.

175. Woods. 20¹/₁₆" x 24". Kunsthaus, Zurich, No. 1392, "Waldinneres." Pages 36 n., 43 n.

Circa 1900

176. Corner of Quarry. 17¾" x 21½". Barnes Foundation, Merion, Pa., No. 218. Pages 43 n., 63 n., 83 n. Illustration, page 283.

177. Drinker. 18" x 14¾". Barnes Foundation, Merion, Pa., No. 189. Exhibition "Cézanne and the Impressionists," Bignou Gallery, New York City, 1935, No. 2, "Le Buveur." Pages 29 n., 314 n. Illustration, page 269.

178. Old Woman with Rosary. 33½" x 25⁹/₁₆". Collection Mme. Jacques Doucet, Paris. Exhibition "Cézanne," Musée de l'Orangerie, Paris, 1936, No. 105, "La Vieille au Chapelet." Pages 6 n., 32 n., 36 n. Analysis, page 390.

179. Rocks and Trees. 31½" x 25¼". Barnes Foundation, Merion, Pa., No. 286. Pages 28 n., 33 n., n., 63 n., 83 n., 94, 341 n. Illustration, page 254. Detail illustrated, page 295.

Early 1900's

180. Bathers. 51¼" x 76¾". Collection Mr. René Lecomte et Mme., *née* Pellerin, Paris—"Baigneuses." Page 91 n.

181. Ginger Jar and Fruit. 28½" x 23¼". Barnes Foundation, Merion, Pa., No. 23. Pages 28 n., 31 n., n., 37 n., 38 n., 39 n., 40 n., 41 n., n., 45, 46 n., 47 n., 69 n., 72, 94. Illustration, page 268. Details illustrated, pages 300 and 301.

182. Group of Bathers. 9" x 10½". Barnes Foundation, Merion, Pa., No. 1179. Exhibition "Paul Cézanne," Bignou Gallery, New York City, 1936, No. 28, "Baigneuses." Pages 18 n., 30 n., 31 n., 74 n. Illustration, page 285. Detail illustrated, page 302.

183. Mount Ste. Victoire with Two Houses. 31½" x 39¼". Museum of Modern Western Art, Moscow, No. 568. Exhibition "Cézanne," Musée de l'Orangerie, Paris, 1936, No. 108, "La Montagne Sainte-Victoire." Page 346. Analysis, pages 347-348. Illustration, page 282.

NO.

184. **Three Skulls.** 21¼″ x 25⅚₆″. Collection Frau Gertrude Dübi-Müller, Soleure, Switzerland. Exhibition "Cézanne," Musée de l'Orangerie, Paris, 1936, No. 110, "Trois Crânes." Pages 6 n., 32 n.

185. **Village Church.** 36¼″ x 28¾″. Barnes Foundation, Merion, Pa., No. 970. Exhibition "The Post-Impressionists," Bignou Gallery, New York City, 1937, No. 2, "L'Eglise de Village." Illustration, page 265.

Circa 1904

186. **Château Noir.** 28¾″ x 36¼″. Collection Mr. Paul Rosenberg, Paris. Exhibition "Cézanne," Musée de l'Orangerie, Paris, 1936, No. 111, "Le Château Noir." Pages 6 n., 32 n. Analysis, page 391.

187. **Skull and Fruit.** 24¼″ x 25½″. Barnes Foundation, Merion, Pa., No. 329. Pages 28 n., 32 n. Illustration, page 275.

Circa 1904-1905

188. **Vallier.** 42¼″ x 28¾″. Collection Mr. René Lecomte et Mme., *née* Pellerin, Paris. Exhibition "Cézanne," Musée de l'Orangerie, Paris, 1936, No. 112, "Portrait de Vallier." Pages 6 n., 32 n.

Circa 1905

189. **Mount Ste. Victoire Seen from the Chemin des Lauves.** 28¾″ x 36¼″. Philadelphia Museum of Art. Pages 28 n., 64 n., 383. Illustration, page 281.

Between 1898-1905

190. **Large Bathers.** 82¼″ x 98½″. Philadelphia Museum of Art. Exhibition "Cézanne," Musée de l'Orangerie, Paris, 1936, No. 107, "Les Grandes Baigneuses." Page 44 n. Analysis, pages 391-393. Illustration, page 284.

Between 1890-1906

191. **Nudes in Landscape.** 52⅜″ x 81½″. Barnes Foundation, Merion, Pa., No. 934. Exhibition "Paintings from the Ambroise Vollard Collection," Knoedler Galleries, New York City, 1933, No. 15, "Les Grandes Baigneuses." Pages 20 n., 21, 21 n., n., 28 n., 29 n., n., 30 n., 31 n., n., 37 n., 38 n., 74 n., 89-90, 91-93, 109, 387, 390 n. Analysis, pages 393-397. Frontispiece. Details illustrated, pages 296 and 304.

LIST B

CEZANNE
AQUARELLES, LITHOGRAPHS AND DRAWINGS

Aquarelles

NO.

192. **Garden at Les Lauves.** 16½" x 20⅝". Collection M. Knoedler & Co., New York City—"Jardin des Lauves." Page 94 n.

193. **General View of Aix from the Garden of Les Lauves.** 12¼" x 18½". Collection Mr. Paul Cézanne, *fils*, Paris—"La Cathédrale d'Aix, vue du Jardin des Lauves." Page 93 n.

194. **Group of Houses.** 12" x 18¾". Barnes Foundation, Merion, Pa., No. 651. Illustration, page 288.

195. **House Tops.** 16½" x 21¼". Louvre, Paris, No. 214, "Toits de Maisons dans un Paysage." Page 94 n., n., n., n.

196. **Medea.** 15" x 9¾". Kunsthaus, Zurich, No. 2371. Exhibition "Cézanne," Musée de l'Orangerie, Paris, 1936, No. 120, "La Médée de Delacroix." Page 105 n.

197. **Mountain Peak.** 12" x 18½". Barnes Foundation, Merion, Pa., No. 654. Page 94 n.

198. **Mountain Range.** 12" x 18¾". Barnes Foundation, Merion, Pa., No. 650. Pages 93 n., 94 n., n. Illustration, page 287.

199. **Mount Ste. Victoire with Tree.** 13½" x 21¼". Collection, Mr. Paul Cézanne, *fils*, Paris. Exhibition "Cézanne," Musée de l'Orangerie, Paris, 1936, No. 122, "Montagne Sainte-Victoire." Page 94 n.

200. **Nudes in Woods.** 8" x 11¾". Collection Mr. Paul Cézanne, *fils*, Paris. Exhibition "Cézanne," Musée de l'Orangerie, Paris, 1936, No. 137, "Baigneuses." Page 94 n.

201. **Park of Château Noir.** 18¼" x 12". Collection M. Knoedler & Co., New York City—"Parc au Château Noir." Pages 93 n., n., 94 n.

202. **Peak of Ste. Victoire.** 12" x 19". Barnes Foundation, Merion, Pa., No. 652. Page 94 n. Illustration, page 286.

203. **Smoker.** 18½" x 13¾". Barnes Foundation, Merion, Pa., No. 653. Page 94 n. Illustration, page 291.

NO.
204. **Trees.** 18⅛" x 12¼". Collection M. Knoedler & Co., New York City—"Paysage." Pages 93 n., 94 n., n. Illustration, page 290.

205. **Woodside.** 12" x 18½". Barnes Foundation, Merion, Pa., No. 655. Page 94 n.

Lithographs

206. **Bathers in Landscape.** 9" x 11". Barnes Foundation, Merion, Pa., No. 699. Illustration, page 289.

207. **Nudes.** 9" x 11". Barnes Foundation, Merion, Pa., No. 490. Page 328 n.

Drawings

208. **Three Nereids.** 12¼" x 17¾". Collection Mr. Paul Cézanne, *fils*, Paris. Exhibition "Cézanne," Musée de l'Orangerie, Paris, 1936, No. 164, "Copie d'Après Rubens." Page 105 n.

209. **Venus and Cupids.** 7½" x 4¾". Collection Mr. Adrien Chappuis, Paris. Exhibition "Cézanne," Musée de l'Orangerie, Paris, 1936, No. 146, "Vénus et les Amours." Page 12 n.

LIST C

MISCELLANEOUS WORKS OF ART

Greek Sculpture (fifth century B.C.)

210. **Frieze of the Parthenon,** East Side. British Museum, London. Pages 21, 92.

211. **Metopes of the Parthenon.** British Museum, London. Pages 21, 92.

Giotto (1266-1337)

212. **Pietà.** Fresco. Cappella degli Scrovegni all'Arena, Padua. Page 367.

213. **Saint Francis, Supporting the Lateran, Appears to Pope Innocent III.** Fresco. Chiesa Superiore di San Francesco, Assisi—"San Francesco veduto in sogno dal pontefice Innocenzo III." Page 86 n.

NO.
Carpaccio, Vittore (c. 1450-1522)

225. **Saint Ursula Leaving her Father.** National Gallery, London, No. 3085. Page 327 n.

Dürer, Albrecht (1471-1528)

226. **Four Saints.** Die Alte Pinakothek, Munich, Nos. 540 and 545, "Die vier Apostel"—"Paulus und Marcus" and "Johannes und Petrus." Page 75.

Michelangelo (1475-1564)

227. **Last Judgment.** Fresco. Cappella Sistina, Vaticano, Rome—"Il Giudizio Universale." Pages 20 n., 44, 327.

Giorgione (1477-1510)

228. **Sleeping Venus.** Staatliche Gemälde-Galerie, Dresden, No. 185, "Schlummernde Venus." Page 310 n.
229. **Two Saints.** Barnes Foundation, Merion, Pa., No. 816. Pages 86 n., 86 n.-87 n.

Titian (c. 1477-1576)

230. **Entombment.** Louvre, Paris, No. 1584, "La Mise au Tombeau." Page 367.
231. **Venus with Dog.** Uffizi, Florence, No. 1437, "Venere Giacente." Page 310 n.

Piombo, Sebastiano del (c. 1485-1547)
Attributed to

232. **Christ in Limbo.** Prado, Madrid, No. 346, "Bajada de Cristo al Limbo." Pages 105 n., 311.

Holbein, Hans, the Younger (1497-1543)

233. **Ambassadors.** National Gallery, London, No. 1314. Page 386 n.
234. **Merchant Georg Gisze.** Kaiser-Friedrich-Museum, Berlin, No. 586, "Bildnis des Kaufmanns Georg Gisze." Page 386 n.

Reymerswael, Marinus van (1497-1567)

235. **Two Bankers or Usurers.** National Gallery, London, No. 944. Page 386 n.

Tintoretto, Il, Jacopo Robusti, called (1518-1594)

NO.

236. **Paradise.** Louvre, Paris, No. 1465, "Le Paradis." Page 328 n.
237. **Susanna at the Bath.** Louvre, Paris, No. 1464, "Suzanne au Bain." Page 86 n.
238. **Two Prophets.** Barnes Foundation, Merion, Pa., No. 807. Pages 34 n., 86 n.
239. **Venetian Senator.** Barnes Foundation, Merion, Pa., No. 836. Pages 72 n., 131 n., 310 n.
240. **Woman of Samaria.** Barnes Foundation, Merion, Pa., No. 823. Page 37 n.

Veronese, Paolo (1528-1588)

241. **Baptism of Christ.** Barnes Foundation, Merion, Pa., No. 800. Page 39 n.

Greco, El, Domenico Theotocopuli, called (1541-1614)

242. **Annunciation.** Barnes Foundation, Merion, Pa., No. 117. Page 19 n.
243. **Laocoön.** Collection Prince Paul of Jugoslavia, Belgrade. Page 19 n.
244. **Mocked Christ.** Barnes Foundation, Merion, Pa., No. 90. Pages 19 n., 34 n., 326.
245. **Nativity.** Metropolitan Museum, New York City, No. G791-1. Page 19 n.
246. **Vision of St. Hyacinth.** Barnes Foundation, Merion, Pa., No. 876. Pages 19 n., 86 n., 328 n.

Rubens, Sir Peter Paul (1577-1640)

247. **Annunciation.** Barnes Foundation, Merion, Pa., No. 813. Page 12 n.
248. **Disembarkation of Marie de Médicis at Marseilles.** Louvre, Paris, No. 2090, "Débarquement de Marie de Médicis à Marseille." Page 105 n.

Hals, Frans (c. 1580-1666)

249. **Dutch Burgher.** Barnes Foundation, Merion, Pa., No. 262. Page 18 n.

Ribera, Jusepe (c. 1588-1652)

250. **Entombment.** Louvre, Paris, No. 1725A, "Le Christ au Tombeau." Page 9 n.
251. **Martyrdom of St. Bartholomew.** Prado, Madrid, No. 1101, "El Martirio de S. Bartolomé." Page 9 n.
252. **Dead Christ.** National Gallery, London, No. 235. Attributed to Ribera. Page 9 n.

Poussin, Nicolas (1594-1665)

253. **Arcadian Shepherds.** Louvre, Paris, No. 734, "Les Bergers d'Arcadie." Page 395.
254. **Ecstasy of St. Paul.** Louvre, Paris, No. 722, "Ravissement de Saint Paul." Page 395.
255. **Holy Family.** Louvre, Paris, No. 713, "Sainte Famille." Page 395.

Velásquez, Don Diego de Silva y (1599-1660)

256. **Meeting of Tipplers.** Prado, Madrid, No. 1170, "Los Borrachos." Page 312 n.

Rembrandt van Rijn (1606-1669)

257. **Head of St. Matthew.** Collection Mr. Joseph Widener, Elkins Park, Pa. Page 75 n.

Lancret, Nicolas (1690-1743)

258. **Hide and Seek.** Engraving. Collection not known. Original painting in collection of ex-Kaiser Wilhelm, Castle of Doorn, Holland. Page 105 n.

Chardin, Jean-Baptiste Siméon (1699-1779)

259. **Various Utensils.** Louvre, Paris, No. 101, "Ustensiles Variés." Page 18 n.

Delacroix, Eugène (1798-1863)

260. **Agar in the Desert.** Collection Mr. Paul Cézanne, *fils,* Paris —"Agar dans le Désert." Page 105 n.
261. **Dante's Boat.** Louvre, Paris, No. 207, "Dante et Virgile." Page 105 n.

NO.
276. **Dead Christ with Angels.** Metropolitan Museum, New York City, No. M311-4. Page 314 n.
277. **Emile Zola.** Louvre, Paris, no No. (gift of Mme. Zola). Page 386 n.
278. **Georges Clémenceau.** Louvre, Paris, no No. (gift of Mrs. H. O. Havemeyer). Page 312 n.
279. **In a Boat.** Metropolitan Museum, New York City, No. M311-8. Page 55 n.
280. **Luncheon on the Grass.** National Gallery, London (lent by Courtauld Institute of Art, London, through Home House Trustees)—"Déjeuner sur l'Herbe." Pages 97, 312 n.
281. **Soldier Examining his Rifle.** National Gallery, London, No. 3294B. Page 18 n.
282. **Tarring the Boat.** Barnes Foundation, Merion, Pa., No. 166. Page 77 n.
283. **White Peonies.** Louvre, Paris, No. 175, "Pivoines Blanches." Pages 66 n., 67 n., 312 n.
284. **Woman in Landscape.** Barnes Foundation, Merion, Pa., No. 820. Page 314 n.

Degas, Edgar (1834-1917)

285. **Dancers with Hair in Braids.** Barnes Foundation, Merion, Pa., No. 143. Page 55 n.
286. **Duranty.** Collection Sir William Burrell, Glasgow. Page 386 n.

Sisley, Alfred (1839-1899)

287. **River Scene with Ducks.** Dated 1881. Barnes Foundation, Merion, Pa., No. 224. Page 55.

Monet, Claude (1840-1926)

288. **House Boat.** Barnes Foundation, Merion, Pa., No. 730. Page 55.

Bazille, Frédéric (1841-1870)

289. **Family Party.** Louvre, Paris, No. 15, "Réunion de Famille." Page 17.

Renoir, Auguste (1841-1919)

290. **Apples in Dish.** Dated 1883. Fogg Art Museum, Harvard University, Cambridge, Mass., Accession No. 1934.29. Page 118.

NO.
291. **Bathers in Forest.** Barnes Foundation, Merion, Pa., No. 901. Page 59 n.
292. **Bathing Group.** Barnes Foundation, Merion, Pa., No. 709. Pages 21 n., 34 n., 36 n.
293. **Beautiful Season: Conversation.** Collection Mr. Ambroise Vollard, Paris. Exhibition "Paintings from the Ambroise Vollard Collection," Knoedler Galleries, New York City, 1933, No. 25, "La Belle Saison: la Conversation." Page 119 n.
294. **Beautiful Season: Promenade.** Collection Mr. Ambroise Vollard, Paris. Exhibition "Paintings from the Ambroise Vollard Collection," Knoedler Galleries, New York City, 1933, No. 24, "La Belle Saison: la Promenade." Page 119 n.
295. **Children at Wargemont.** Dated 1884. National-Galerie, Berlin, No. 1008, "Der Nachmittag der Kinder in Vargemont." Page 118 n.
296. **Dance in the Country.** Dated 1883. Collection Durand-Ruel, Paris and New York City. Exhibition "Renoir," Musée de l'Orangerie, Paris, 1933, No. 68, "La Danse à la Campagne." Page 119 n.
297. **Dovecote at Bellevue.** Barnes Foundation, Merion, Pa., No. 969. Page 118 n.
298. **Fruit of the Midi.** Dated 1881. Art Institute (Collection Ryerson), Chicago, No. 2155. Page 118.
299. **Girl in Field.** Dated 1884. Collection Jacques Seligmann and Co., New York City. Exhibition "Renoir," Musée de l'Orangerie, Paris, 1933, No. 73, "L'Eté." Pages 118 n., 119 n.
300. **Grape Gatherers Resting.** Barnes Foundation, Merion, Pa., No. 937. Page 118 n.
301. **Jeanne Samary.** Dated 1877. Collection Comédie Française, Paris. Exhibition "Renoir," Musée de l'Orangerie, Paris, 1933, No. 37. Page 119 n.
302. **Madame Renoir.** Philadelphia Museum of Art. Pages 118 n., 120-121.
303. **Madame Renoir at the Gate.** Dated 1884. Collection Mrs. Ralph Booth, Detroit. Page 118 n.
304. **Mother and Baby.** Collection Mrs. Chester Beatty, London. Exhibition "Renoir," Musée de l'Orangerie, Paris, 1933, No. 80, "La Mère et l'Enfant." Page 120.
305. **Mother and Child.** Barnes Foundation, Merion, Pa., No. 15. Page 47 n.

NO.

306. Near Pont-Aven. Private Collection, London. Exhibition "Paintings from the Ambroise Vollard Collection," Knoedler Galleries, New York City, 1933, No. 31, "Environs de Pont-Aven." Page 120.

307. Pasture along the Seine. Private Collection, near London. Exhibition "Paintings from the Ambroise Vollard Collection," Knoedler Galleries, New York City, 1933. No. 29, "Pâturage au Bord de la Seine." Pages 119-120.

308. Peninsula of St. Jean. Barnes Foundation, Merion, Pa., No. 240. Page 59 n.

309. Seated Nude. Barnes Foundation, Merion, Pa., No. 16. Page 47 n.

310. Summer. Barnes Foundation, Merion, Pa., No. 933. Pages 118 n., 119 n.

311. Three Pears. Barnes Foundation, Merion, Pa., No. 49. Pages 118 n., 119.

312. Two Figures in Landscape. Barnes Foundation, Merion, Pa., No. 587. Page 59 n.

313. Two Women in Park. Barnes Foundation, Merion, Pa., No. 289. Page 34 n.

314. Woman at Rest in Landscape. Barnes Foundation, Merion, Pa., No. 220. Pages 47, 47 n., n.

Gauguin, Paul (1848-1903)

315. Flowerpiece. National Gallery, Millbank, London, No. 3289. Page 316 n.

316. Haere Pape. Barnes Foundation, Merion, Pa., No. 109. Pages 121, 389 n.

Gogh, Vincent van (1853-1890)

317. Factories. Barnes Foundation, Merion, Pa., No. 303. Pages 55 n., 123 n.

318. Flowerpiece and Fruit. Barnes Foundation, Merion, Pa., No. 928. Page 123 n.

319. Houses and Figure. Barnes Foundation, Merion, Pa., No. 136. Page 55 n.

320. Man Smoking. Barnes Foundation, Merion, Pa., No. 119. Pages 122-123.

Matisse, Henri- (1869-   )

NO.
321. **Academy Figure.** Collection Mr. Frank Stoop, London. Exhibition "Henri-Matisse," Galeries Georges Petit, Paris, 1931, No. 5, "Académie Bleue." Page 132 n.

322. **Bathers at the Seashore.** Formerly in the collection of Mr. Georges Bernheim et Cie, Paris. Exhibition "Henri-Matisse," Galeries Georges Petit, Paris, 1931, No. 145 (not listed in catalogue). Page 131 n.

323. **Blue Still-Life.** Barnes Foundation, Merion, Pa., No. 185. Pages 129 n., 130 n., n., 131 n., 132 n., 316 n.

324. **Blue Villa.** Barnes Foundation, Merion, Pa., No. 196. Page 133.

325. **Boy with Butterfly Net.** Collection Bignou Gallery, Paris and New York City. Pages 131 n., 132 n.

326. **Collioure.** Barnes Foundation, Merion, Pa., No. 73. Pages 129 n., 131 n., n., 132-133, 132 n.

327. **Composition with Melon.** Barnes Foundation, Merion, Pa., No. 64. Pages 129 n., 130 n., 131 n.

328. **Country House.** Collection Mr. Georges Renand, Paris. Exhibition "Henri-Matisse," Galeries Georges Petit, Paris, 1931, No. 64, "La Maison de Campagne." Pages 129 n., 131 n.

329. **Flowers in Pitcher.** Barnes Foundation, Merion, Pa., No. 205. Page 133.

330. **Fontainebleau: Entrance to the Forest.** Collection Mr. Peter Krag, Paris. Exhibition "Henri-Matisse," Galeries Georges Petit, Paris, 1931, No. 19, "Fontainebleau: l'Entrée de la Forêt." Page 132 n.

331. **Girl on Balcony.** Collection Mr. Joseph Müller, Soleure, Switzerland. Exhibition "Henri-Matisse," Galeries Georges Petit, Paris, 1931, No. 58, "Jeune Fille au Balcon." Page 130 n.

332. **Girl Reading.** Musée, Grenoble, France. Exhibition "Henri-Matisse," Galeries Georges Petit, Paris, 1931, No. 12, "Fillette Lisant." Page 131 n.

333. **Goldfish.** Barnes Foundation, Merion, Pa., No. 569. Page 132 n.

334. **Houses at Fenouillet.** Barnes Foundation, Merion, Pa., No. 358. Page 131 n.

NO.
335. **Moroccan Tray.** Collection Marie Harriman Gallery, Inc., New York City. Exhibition "Henri-Matisse," Galeries Georges Petit, Paris, 1931, No. 115, "Le Plateau Marocain." Pages 130 n., 131 n., 133.

336. **Odalisque with Magnolias.** Collection Mr. Gaston Bernheim de Villers, Paris. Exhibition "Henri-Matisse," Galeries Georges Petit, Paris, 1931, No. 105, "Odalisque aux Magnolias." Page 131 n.

337. **Oranges.** Collection Frau Thea-Sternheim, Paris. Exhibition "Henri-Matisse," Galeries Georges Petit, Paris, 1931, No. 13, "Nature Morte." Pages 129 n., 132 n.

338. **Painter in his Studio.** Collection Mr. Henri-Matisse, Nice and Paris. Exhibition "Henri-Matisse," Galeries Georges Petit, Paris, 1931, No. 37, "Le Peintre dans son Atelier." Page 132 n.

339. **Peaches.** Collection Mr. Sacha Guitry, Paris. Exhibition "Henri-Matisse," Galeries Georges Petit, Paris, 1931, No. 41, "Nature Morte aux Pêches." Pages 129 n., 130 n., 132 n.

340. **Reclining Nude.** Barnes Foundation, Merion, Pa., No. 199. Page 133.

341. **Red Madras Headdress.** Barnes Foundation, Merion, Pa., No. 448. Pages 130 n., 131 n.

342. **Rocks of the Valley of the Loup.** Collection Mattei, Marseilles. Exhibition "Henri-Matisse," Galeries Georges Petit, Paris, 1931, No. 119, "Les Rochers de la Vallée du Loup." Page 132 n.

343. **Seated Nude.** Barnes Foundation, Merion, Pa., No. 212. Page 130 n.

344. **Sideboard.** Musée du Luxembourg, Paris. Exhibition "Henri-Matisse," Galeries Georges Petit, Paris, 1931, No. 138, "Le Buffet." Pages 129 n., 130 n.

345. **Two Figures Reclining in Landscape.** Barnes Foundation, Merion, Pa., No. 893. Page 133.

346. **Woman on High Stool.** Collection Mr. Henri-Matisse, Nice and Paris. Exhibition "Henri-Matisse," Galeries Georges Petit, Paris, 1931, No. 26, "Figure au Tabouret." Page 131 n.

347. **Woman with Hat.** Collection Mr. Michael Stein, Palo-Alto, California. Exhibition "Henri-Matisse," Galeries Georges Petit, Paris, 1931, No. 9, "La Femme au Chapeau." Pages 130 n., 131 n.

Picasso, Pablo (1881-   )

Demuth, Charles (1883-1935)

Utrillo, V., Maurice (1883-   )

Modigliani, Amedeo (1884-1920)

Pascin, Jules (1885-1930)

NO.
363. **Southern Scene.** Barnes Foundation, Merion, Pa., No. 194.
Page 136.

Lurçat, Jean (1891-   )

364. **Rocks and Water.** Barnes Foundation, Merion, Pa., No.
907. Page 316 n.

INDEX

The arrangement of the preceding section—Catalogue Data—makes it serve as an index for the paintings and works of art mentioned in the text. The small "n." after a page number indicates that the reference is contained in a footnote.